International and C

Editor
Anthony J. Marsella
Alpharetta, Georgia, USA

Explores problems and challenges to mental health, psychosocial wellbeing, human growth and development, and human welfare that are emerging from our contemporary global context. It advances in psychological knowledge regarding the nature and consequences of the many social, cultural, economic, political, and environmental events and forces that affect individuals and communities throughout the world.

The series covers areas like therapy, assessment, organizational psychology, community psychology, gender, child development, and specific disorders. In addition, it addresses major global challenges such as poverty, peace, urbanization, modernization, refugees, and migration. The series acknowledges the multidisciplinary, multisectoral, and multicultural nature of the global context of our lives, and publishes books that reflect this reality.

Publish your next book in this series! Send your manuscript to Series Editor: Anthony J. Marsella, marsella@hawaii.edu.

More information about this series at http://www.springer.com/series/6089

Rachael D. Goodman • Paul C. Gorski
Editors

Decolonizing "Multicultural" Counseling Through Social Justice

Springer

Editors
Rachael D. Goodman
George Mason University
Fairfax
VA
USA

Paul C. Gorski
New Century College
George Mason University
Fairfax
VA
USA

ISSN 1574-0455
ISSN 2197-7984 (electronic)
ISBN 978-1-4939-1282-7 (hardcover)
ISBN 978-1-4939-1283-4 (eBook)
ISBN 978-1-4939-3585-7 (softcover)
DOI 10.1007/978-1-4939-1283-4
Springer New York Heidelberg Dordrecht London

Library of Congress Control Number: 2014949398

Printed on acid-free paper

Springer is part of Springer Science+Business Media (www.springer.com)

For my mom, who taught me through her love and example to put everything I have into making this world a better place for the people in it.

Rachael D. Goodman

For Bob, who gifted me a social justice worldview and self-view that have been the core of my spiritual being ever since.

Paul C. Gorski

Foreword

Decolonization of Mind and Behavior: A Responsibility of Professional Counselors

By Anthony J. Marsella

This volume is about counseling. But is also about something so much more than what we usually think about when we refer to counseling. This volume is about "multicultural" counseling—that is the responsibility and obligation of counselors to understand and respond to the process and product of counseling in a multicultural society. We are all aware that the dominance of North American and European cultural traditions and values that have governed counseling methods and practices have exacted a harsh toll upon racial and ethnocultural minority groups by imposing biased solutions to a spectrum of personal problems. These solutions have too often invalidated the life experience of these groups, compelling them to sacrifice their identities and histories in favor of pseudo adjustments to the dominant cultural traditions.

The question must be asked, "How can successful counseling ignore or be indifferent to the cultural context of a person's life.?" How can the personal history of being a racial or ethnocultural minority be avoided or denied with all of its consequences for accumulated injustices, oppression, and abuses? When this occurs, it is no longer counseling as a healing art and science that is present, rather it is simply a re-socialization. Re-socialization according to a dominant culture or power occurs when governments of repressive regimes create camps to destroy lives by indoctrination and the removal of any resistance. And here, the issue of "decolonization," which is the essence of this volume, emerges as a critical concept.

"Decolonization" is not a political term as some expect, and thus shy away from its use and understanding; rather it is about liberating the mind and behavior of a counselee within the context of exploring (1) the process of who they are at this time, (2) how they have become the person they are, and (3) why there may be dissatisfaction and problems, pain, and suffering in their life. "Decolonization" constitutes an effort to free a counselee from the sources of their imposed socialization that ultimately deny them the opportunity to explore their roots and to build their character and person within the historical context of their native cultural traditions.

De-colonization recognizes that the distribution of "power" is part of every relationship, and that this distribution can be asymmetrical. If the counselor fails to consider her or his role and function as sources of power, she or he can harm a counselee by imposing certain ill-considered methods and content rooted with cultural and historical contexts that sustain the abuses of power. In this age of reductionism, when so much emphasis is being placed upon the neurological and psychological determinants of human behavior that are located within the individual, there is a massive failure to grasp the cultural determinants. It is as if each individual is solely responsible for his or her actions, including their problems through choice and preference. But this ignores the complex forces that modulate mind and behavior, especially the sociocultural contexts that too often are rooted in the injustices associated with race, class, and status. Trying to heal a Muslim college student by focusing on their infirmities and complaints apart from the tragic context off vilification and abuse present in American society today cannot have successful outcomes for counselor or counselee. What is needed is an awareness of cultural determinants of behavior by both parties and a willingness to explore the role cultural abuse, denial, and oppression may play in the counselee's problems. In the case of many Muslim students and adults, the extensive and unwarranted criticisms of Islam is forcing Muslims to develop emotional and mental health related problems as a result of the obvious conflicts between their traditional beliefs and identities and the harsh and brutal assaults on them.

This view does not deny the pressures and values to acculturate to the demands of the larger society in which one is located, but rather to do so with a grasp and comprehension that the forces of acculturation must not be permitted to destroy diversity, for it is diversity that enables any culture to respond to demands with varied alternatives rather than fixed and static solutions. This view recognizes that adjustment to a dominant and "disordered" society requires that a counselee be given the opportunity to explore the issue of power and its sources in socializing individuals and groups and the potential for destruction to occur. My answer to many of these questions has always been to advocate "selective detachment."

Consider for a moment the African–American population in the United States. For more than 250 years, African Americans have been subject to the consequences of a denial of their history and roots. Even today, amidst increased freedoms, most African Americans and dominant White populations have little awareness of the traumatic toll exacted not only by 200 years slavery, but also by the post-slavery years of "peonage" ("slavery by any other name"), physical assaults, segregation, and widespread institutional racism, condemnation to poverty, and denial of legitimate efforts to discover identity and self-sufficiency as articulated by James Baldwin, Malcom X, Martin Luther King, Jr., and Randall Robinson.

The same can be said of so many different racial and ethnocultural groups whose individual and collective problems can be traced to the denial of their heritages and the abuses imposed upon them by those in power. Native Hawaiians (*Kanaka Maoli*) are yet another example of a people who have excessive medical, physical, psychological, and social problems not because of some defiant gene as some colonial powers would say, but because they have been denied the comfort, solace, and strength of their historic cultural identity. The healing that is needed is not to adjust to the dominant society even as conflicts abound, but rather to recover and assert identity, and to find in it the roots of responses to indignities, humiliation, and oppression. This is the case for Native American Indians, Latinos, Asians, and Middle-Eastern populations. Homogeneity is the problem. Heterogeneity is the answer.

It is essential as counselors and as human beings that we recognize the socialization matrix of a dominant culture and its consequences for nonmembers. Consider the fact that the dominant ethos of North American popular culture is rooted in individualism, materialism, commodification, consumerism, competition, celebritization, violence, sexual preoccupation, constant change, and technological fascination and acceptance. Now, juxtapose this against indigenous cultures that emphasize collective, spiritual, cooperative, traditional, and subjective experience. Clearly, there is conflict, and while the cultural encounters can become sources of benefit for all parties, they can also become sources of abuse and denial by cultures in power seeking to advance their ways of life.

In this scenario, and it is the scenario that exists in the United States, victims are created, and uninformed counseling can become a tool of the majority. There is a seductive appeal to North American popular culture as it enters/penetrates/dominates another culture. Some might say, "Why resist, it is much better than what they have?" No it is not! I do not wish to romanticize traditional cultures of Third World nations and people. But the implications of accepting and using the "American" way as an arbiter of normality must be considered before it is blindly accepted.

The fact of the matter is that the dominant North American and Western European cultures are themselves a function of historical powers that resulted in colonization of indigenous populations, established via imperialistic impulses. Consider that at one point in time, the sun never set on the British empire (India/Pakistan, Australia, Afghanistan, Canada, New Zealand, Hong Kong, Malaysia, Singapore, Palestine, South Africa, Ireland, Caribbean Islands, Malta, and on and on). In all these instances, the native people were compelled to submit to British occupation and exploitation and to the colonization of mind. They were taught, directly and indirectly, to feel inferior and inadequate before British culture and might. They were denied identity and personhood. In what may now be considered a historic irony, the national dish of England is curry—a reverse colonization that helped both to improve the British palate and to serve as a reminder that, as William Gladstone, a past British prime minister, once said, "God does not value a person from one nation over the life of a person from another nation." These words began the decline of the British Empire as conscience emerged as more important than power.

This then is the challenge for counseling as a profession and science—to be a source of recovery and healing by decolonizing mind and behavior, and by restoring the roots of resolve in the fundamental foundations of personal and cultural identity, and conscious and intentional choices for "selective detachment." Here I believe that the dominant White culture of power and hegemony also needs to consider its position and to grasp the consequences of colonization for themselves and others. There can be no doubt that the demographic profile for the United States and for many other Western nations is changing as population growth occurs among minority populations and declines among White populations. But the real issue for all parties is the need to recognize that each is a function of colonization of mind. It is only an issue of who has the power to shape mind and behavior and what are the personal, societal, and national costs of doing so for all.

Contents

Contributors

Fred Bemak Counseling and Development Program, College of Education and Human Development, George Mason University, Fairfax, VA, USA

Carissa Chambers Department of Counseling and Clinical Psychology, Teachers College, Columbia University, New York, NY, USA

Rita Chi-Ying Chung Counseling and Development Program, College of Education and Human Development, George Mason University, Fairfax, VA, USA

William L. Conwill Harrison Conwill Associates, Chicago, IL, USA

Adrienne M. Douglass Counseling and Development Program, College of Education and Human Development, George Mason University, Fairfax, VA, USA

Eduardo Duran Seventh Direction, Bozeman, MT, USA

Lisa M. Edwards Counselor Education and Counseling Psychology, Marquette University, Milwaukee, WI, USA

Judith Firehammer Seventh Direction, Bozeman, MT, USA

Anne M. Geroski The University of Vermont, Burlington, VT, USA

Rachael D. Goodman Counseling and Development Program, College of Education and Human Development, George Mason University, Fairfax, VA, USA

Paul C. Gorski Integrative Studies & Center for the Advancement of Well-Being, George Mason University, Fairfax, VA, USA

H. George McMahon Department of Counseling and Human Development Services, College of Education, University of Georgia, Athens, GA

Mariolga Reyes Cruz Footscray, Australia

Edil Torres Rivera Department of Counseling, The Chicago School of Professional Psychology, Chicago, IL, USA

Richard Q. Shin Counseling Psychology, School Psychology, and Counselor Education, University of Maryland, College Park, MD, USA

Lance C. Smith Graduate Counseling Program School, Counseling Program Coordinator, The University of Vermont, Burlington, VT, USA

Laura Smith Department of Counseling and Clinical Psychology, Teachers College, Columbia University, New York, NY, USA

Christopher C. Sonn College of Arts, Psychology Discipline, Victoria University, Footscray, Victoria, Australia

Regine M. Talleyrand Counseling and Development Program, College of Education and Human Development, George Mason University, Fairfax, VA, USA

Kevin A. Tate Department of Counselor Education and Counseling Psychology, Marquette University, Milwaukee, WI, USA

Joseph M. Williams Counseling and Development Program, College of Education and Human Development, George Mason University, Fairfax, VA, USA

Chapter 1
Introduction: Toward a Decolonized Multicultural Counseling and Psychology

Paul C. Gorski and Rachael D. Goodman

In many ways, multiculturalism has become a central part of the theoretical and professional discourses of counseling and psychology. Notwithstanding our concerns about multiculturalism's limitations as a framework for social justice, we appreciate the growing acceptance of culturally competent counseling, cross-cultural psychology, and other multicultural modes of practice and scholarship. We also appreciate that, although some counselors and psychologists continue to voice dissent about the importance of multiculturalism, a growing majority agree that it is important. As a result, we find ourselves spending less and less energy trying to convince colleagues of the merits of approaches that acknowledge difference and challenge the imposition of Euro-, cis-male-, Christian-, or hetero-centric norms onto counseling and psychology. This is an important step forward for our professions. We celebrate the risks taken by scholars and practitioners who came before us and who worked tirelessly, sometimes at their own professional or scholarly peril, to move multiculturalism, cross-culturalism, cultural competence, and other diversity-acknowledging frameworks from the margins toward the center of our disciplines.

Today, as we see it, the fields of counseling and psychology are at a critical juncture when it comes to social justice. We do not lack frameworks and approaches for deconstructing problematic counseling and psychology paradigms and practices,

P. C. Gorski (✉)
Integrative Studies & Center for the Advancement of Well-Being, George Mason University, 4400 University Drive, MS 5D3, Fairfax, VA 22030
e-mail: gorski@edchange.org

Integrative Studies, George Mason University, 210 E Fairfax Street #217, Falls Church, VA 22046, USA

R. D. Goodman
Counseling and Development Program, College of Education and Human Development, George Mason University, Krug Hall 201C, MS 1H1, 4400 University Drive, Fairfax, VA 22030, USA
e-mail: rgoodma2@gmu.edu

R. D. Goodman, P. C. Gorski (eds.), *Decolonizing "Multicultural" Counseling through Social Justice,* International and Cultural Psychology, DOI 10.1007/978-1-4939-1283-4_1

nor do we lack counselors and psychologists who desire to adopt the paradigms and practices that will help them connect more effectively with the full diversity of humanity or create a more equitable and just world. The danger, however, is that too often "multicultural" counseling and psychology are practiced or theorized in ways that actually replicate the power arrangements they ought to be dismantling. We worry that these paradigms and practices have been nudged closer and closer to the center of counseling and psychology discourses only after they've been scrubbed of their transformative natures. Although developed, perhaps, in attempts to enact social justice, many of these practices are softened or reshaped to comply with the very sorts of marginalization they were imagined to counteract.

In other words, as advocates for social justice in and out of the counseling and psychology disciplines, we recognize the *potential* that multicultural, cross-cultural, intercultural, and culturally competent frameworks offer us; we even appreciate the fact that the language of multiculturalism has become part of lexicon of counseling and psychology practice and scholarship. But upon digging a little deeper, we know that each of these frameworks can be, and far too often have been, operationalized in ways that replicate existing systems of power and privilege (Vera and Speight 2003)—in ways that colonize rather than decolonize counseling and psychology practice and scholarship. In our view, this is dangerous because well-meaning scholars and practitioners might adopt practices or viewpoints that are harmful to the people or communities they wish to serve, all the while believing that they are acting with integrity because the framework they are using has been described as "multicultural." As Prilleltensky (1997) reminds us, "Discourse without action is dangerous because it creates the impression that progress is taking place when in fact only the words have changed" (p. 530). We contend that multiculturalism without a social justice framework is dangerous because it creates the illusion that our practices address the oppressions of marginalized people and the oppressiveness of hegemony, even if its attention to marginalized groups and hegemony is superficial.

This book is, in part, one attempt by a group of practitioners, scholars, and activists who share our concerns to uncover some of the ways this happens. By doing so, we hope to hold ourselves and our colleagues accountable to the unfulfilled decolonizing potential of "multicultural" approaches to counseling and psychology. It is our attempt, in the words of Akena (2012), "to generate influential counterdiscourses" (p. 616) against applications of multicultural counseling and psychology that, as the authors in this volume attest, might be doing more harm than good. To be clear, we are not arguing for the abandonment of multiculturalism and its social justice potentials, nor for disregarding progress made by multi-, inter-, and cross-culturalists in their efforts to assert their own counterdiscourses in spheres that were—and sometimes still are—hostile to the mere acknowledgement of diversity. Instead we imagine ourselves building upon their work, ensuring that the persistent creep of colonialism doesn't thwart our collective vision, not just for some minimal bar of multicultural competence, but for a transformative multiculturalism grounded in ideals of equity and social justice.

We are, in essence, asking ourselves this: Can we imagine and practice forms of "multicultural" counseling and psychology that do not insist first and foremost on principles of equity and social justice and decolonization without rendering ourselves, even as well-intentioned practitioners and scholars, complicit with the very inequities and injustices we ought to be dismantling?

Colonizing Multicultural Counseling and Psychology

Evidence of this tendency to colonize, despite believing that we're decolonizing, is apparent in the very language used to describe the most popular frameworks for acknowledging and responding to difference: *cultural* competence, cross-*cultural* psychology, multi*cultural* counseling. Most popular frameworks for acknowledging and responding, not just to diversity, but to a legacy of inequity and injustice in counseling and psychology practice, centralize *culture* as though racism and heterosexism and other oppressions are primarily cultural phenomena rather than power phenomena or purposeful societal arrangements. We, and several of the contributors to this volume, wonder whether, as in a variety of other service-oriented fields and disciplines from education (e.g., Ladson-Billings 2006) to nursing (e.g., Racine and Petrucka 2011), the adoption of multiculturalism as it is often operationalized in the counseling and psychology disciplines reflects more an illusion of movement than actual movement toward social justice. We wonder whether the most popular practices derived from these frameworks allow individuals to avoid questions of power and hegemony by honing in on vague and oftentimes stereotypical notions of "culture."

Consider a comparative example. Aikman (1997), who tracked the intercultural education movement's conceptualization and implementation throughout Latin America during the 1980s and 1990s, observes that this movement "developed out of concern and respect for indigenous knowledge and practices, but primarily in response to the exploitation, oppression, and discrimination of indigenous peoples" (p. 466). In other words, intercultural education initially was meant to upend colonial educational structures whose impacts ranged from "debasing" indigenous cultural beliefs to denying indigenous experience altogether (Wane 2008)—a form of cultural genocide. Indigenous communities in many parts of Latin America lobbied for their governments to embrace intercultural education. In many cases their governments responded, but when they did, they almost never operationalized intercultural education in ways that threatened the existence of exploitation and oppression. For example, the Peruvian government hired the NGO Foro Educativo to design the country's framework for intercultural education. Foro Educativo (as cited by Aikman 1997) proceeded to replace the decolonizing vision of intercultural education with one that nodded to diversity but demanded no real power shift at all, offering this as a framework:

> Interculturality…is a space for dialogue which recognizes and values the wealth of cultural, ethnic, and linguistic diversity in the country, promotes the affirmation and development of different cultures which co-exist in Peru and constitutes an open process toward cultural exchange with the global society. (p. 469)

Recognizing the bait-and-switch, many of the indigenous communities that once enthusiastically endorsed intercultural education grew to abhor it in practice. They resented the way it essentially reproduced existing power hierarchies. They resented the way, in Aikman's (1997) words, "interculturality remain[ed] embedded in relations of internal colonialism" (p. 469). Once conceived as a way to interrupt marginalization and colonialism, intercultural education had been reframed and recast in order to protect the interests of the powerful.

This, of course, is a problem that follows the popularization of any progressive movement or paradigm: if we aren't vigilant about protecting its integrity, it can grow to look more and more like the thing it was created to destroy. Imagine the school administrators who want to develop a program to address racial injustice and end up hosting *Taco Night* or the *International Dance Showcase*—events that often inaccurately highlight superficial aspects of a culture while ignoring the ways in which members of the groups being "celebrated" are marginalized. In a capitalist society, this risk is exacerbated as movements and paradigms are commodified. It's easy to market and sell multicultural counseling or psychology textbooks that simply describe "how to counsel African Americans" and "how to counsel Latinos" (as though these are monolithic groups). Such a paradigm expects virtually nothing of the colonizer; it is no threat to existing social conditions or to the colonizer's sense of power and privilege, asking only that we "understand" these groups' "differences" from a supposed "norm." It fails to interrogate the sociopolitical forces that create injustice and the kinds of systemic oppression trauma experienced by marginalized groups. Marketing and selling multicultural counseling or psychology textbooks that insist that, in order to be multiculturally competent, we must interrogate our own socializations, our complicities in systems of oppression, and our power and privilege are altogether more difficult projects. This is particularly true given that it would require the predominantly White counseling and psychology students to examine how they've been socialized, despite all their good intentions, to participate in and benefit from structural racism.

In *Decolonizing "Multicultural" Counseling and Psychology,* we apply Hernandez-Wolfe's (2011) conception of coloniality as "the systemic suppression of subordinated cultures and knowledges by the dominant Eurocentric paradigm of modernity, and the emergence of knowledges and practices resulting from this experience" (p. 294). Several scholars have connected this sort of coloniality to counseling and psychology paradigms and practices, including those that were originally conceived as counterhegemonic. We recognize the complexity of their task and the one we undertake in this book; it is not easy to take the critical view that birthed multiculturalism—and other transformative movements—and turn that view on multiculturalism itself. But if our goal is social justice, we find few alternatives. This is especially true when we see in some of the most popular "multicultural" practices and paradigms the most common components of a colonizing ideology.

The examples are plentiful. For instance, one hallmark of a colonial ideology is dichotomous thinking (Shirazi 2011): white/of color, straight/gay, civilized/uncivilized, Christian/non-Christian, able-bodied/disabled, and binary conceptions of gender (Leigh 2009). Rather than bolstering an analysis of complex systems of power and privilege, these dichotomies support the analysis of disenfranchised people against a hegemonic norm.

We see additional evidence of the creep of colonial ideology into supposedly multicultural counseling and psychology practice and scholarship in widespread essentialism (Racine and Petrucka 2011), particularly in how complex identity groups are homogenized in order to fit into simplistic identity development models. It doesn't help, of course, that some of the most prominent authors of multicultural, cross-cultural, and cultural competence scholarship continue to organize entire fields of study into a sort of essentializing tour: *Here's what you need to know about Latinos. Here's what you need to know about the lesbian, gay, bisexual community. Here's what you need to know about people in poverty.* In *Multicultural Counseling and Psychotherapy: A Lifespan Approach* (2012) by Leroy Baruth and M. Lee Manning, a popular textbook in its fifth edition, chapters include: "Understanding Asian American Clients" and "Counseling Asian American Clients;" "Understanding Lesbian, Gay, Bisexual, and Transgender Clients" and "Counseling Lesbian, Gay, Bisexual, and Transgender Clients;" and so on. The trouble is that there is as much diversity within Asian Americans or within the lesbian, gay, bisexual, and/or transgendered (LGBT) community than there is *between* any two groups. Also, people experience these identities within a sociopolitical context that has very real implications for their psychological well-being. Moreover, to which chapter should we turn if we want to know how to understand and counsel a lesbian Asian-American low-income Muslim client? Is the Hmong community more or less the same as the Chinese, or Pakistani, or Malaysian community as far as counseling practice goes? Is it enough, anyway, to know a little bit about this or that identity group, paying no attention whatsoever, to intersectionality, or to religious, regional, economic, or other differences to religious, or regional, or economic or other differences within these enormous groups? If our goal is social justice, do we wish only to understand the cultural beliefs of an undocumented Mexican immigrant mother, or should we also wonder, with equal curiosity, about who benefits from the policies that prompted her decision to migrate, her vulnerability to wage discrimination, and other structural matters that inform her experience? To our chagrin, this fundamentally colonizing approach to training "multicultural" counselors is widespread.

Leigh (2009) worries about the assumptions we make even when we dig a layer deeper into individual identity groups, particularly in relation to "multicultural" scholarship. She explains, "A final danger lies in the academic theorizing of gender within Indigenous communities, which risks othering and homogenizing the category of Indigenous women" (p. 82). Unfortunately, in our experience, the dominant view in multicultural counseling and psychology remains a colonial view. When we focus on *that* group and *that* group and *that* group and what we need to know about vague, often stereotypical notions of their "cultures," we actually replicate a colonizing ideology.

A third way in which some scholars and practitioners of "multicultural" counseling and psychology have strayed into colonizing territory is by alluding to marginalized groups only in reference to their marginalization. Brown (1995) worries that, as a result, disenfranchised individuals often are positioned purely as victims, as targets, and as the objects of oppression. Li (2010) shares this concern, particularly as it relates to the scholarship of marginalization: "Academic and political discourse on marginalized groups' 'struggle for recognition' tends to identify the marginalized groups as passive victims" (p. 30). In our experience, then, it's the counselor or psychologist who is positioned, even if implicitly, as the active agent—sometimes even as the savior of disenfranchised communities (Deepak 2011). This discourse is heaviest, perhaps, in scholarship that calls on the do-gooder active agent—the counselor or psychologist—to *empower* the individual or community of color, the individual or community in poverty, or some other passive, dispossessed target. As Freire (2000) pointed out, true liberatory practices reject humanitarianism and approaches that view someone experiencing oppression as a passive object; instead they embrace what he called *humanization*, which focuses on one's own power and agency in the personal and collective struggle for freedom.

There are other examples, many of which are expounded upon by this book's contributors. Suffice it to say, for now, that separately and together they illustrate the same concern: much of what passes for multicultural counseling and psychology practice and scholarship more or less reproduces the unjust distributions of power and privilege that counterhegemonic frameworks and movements should upend (Vera and Speight 2003). As we mentioned earlier, this phenomenon is not unique to multicultural counseling and psychology. Critical scholars, community activists, and concerned practitioners have pointed to the same trends in a variety of other areas, including peace education (Brantmeier 2010), intercultural and multicultural education (Gorski 2008), migration studies (Fechter and Walsh 2010), and cross-cultural nursing (Racine and Petrucka 2011).

As multicultural counseling and psychology frameworks become more accepted and, as a result, grow into profitable industries, we believe it is time to ask some difficult questions. Whose cultures or knowledges are subordinated through popular applications of multicultural counseling and psychology? How have dominant paradigms—heteronormative, Eurocentric, patriarchal, corporate–consumerist–capitalist paradigms, among others—influenced multicultural counseling and psychology? In other words, what are the knowledges and practices that emerge when multicultural counseling and psychology are filtered through the hierarchical values that still dominate counseling and psychology theory and practice? How do some paradigms, frameworks, and practices commonly associated with "multicultural" counseling and psychology reflect the illusion of structural transformation (Shirazi 2011), or what González (2003) calls the "illusion of a free exchange of ideas" (p. 184), even as they, too, subordinate disenfranchised people and their knowledges?

Decolonizing Multicultural Counseling and Psychology

Certainly any colonizing theory or practice is harmful. But what could be more devastating than colonizing theories or practices embedded in frameworks made to appear liberatory? We struggle to think of anything.

How, then, would a *decolonizing* or social justice approach look? Scholars from a variety of fields and disciplines challenge us, first of all, to discard colonial frameworks wholly rather than, in Lorde's (1984) words, attempting to use the master's tools to tear down the master's house. In other words, it is not enough to try to build a social justice view onto or around a larger marginalizing structure (Hall 1996), especially if we're stuck using the sorts of essentializing, hegemonic thinking that comprise that structure's philosophical base (Shrazi 2011).

Nor can we continue to make vague, stereotypical notions of *culture* the centerpieces of multicultural counseling and psychology. A decolonial or postcolonial stance, after all, is concerned not merely with cultural differences or group identities but instead with differences of power and access and opportunity (Hernandez-Wolfe 2011). A *decolonizing* multicultural counseling and psychology recognizes that this focus on culture directs our attention down the power hierarchy to focus almost entirely on the experiences and identities of disenfranchised people. This phenomenon is, in many ways, a distraction rooted in Western epistemologies. A decolonizing view, instead, pushes us to gaze *up* the power hierarchy, where inequalities are embedded in systems and structures that privilege the few at the expense of the many.

Shome and Hedge (2002), nudging us past a decolonizing view and toward a postcolonial view, insist that "the postcolonial project's commitment and goals are interventionist and highly political. In its best work, it theorizes not just colonial conditions but also theorizes *why* those conditions are what they are, and how they can be undone and redone (although more work is needed on this latter aspect)" (p. 250). They ask us to reflect, once again, on *whose* multiculturalism we're practicing, to what end, and to whose benefit? When we choose to adopt a colonizing multiculturalism rather than a critical, transformative multiculturalism, who or what are we protecting?

These are the sorts of questions with which this book's contributors—practitioners, activists, and scholars of multiculturalism and social justice in the counseling and psychology disciplines—grapple. Each contributor or team of contributors has applied a critical lens to a particular paradigm or practice commonly associated with multicultural counseling and psychology in an effort to uncover the ways in which it reproduces colonial systems and knowledges. In the postcolonial spirit, they follow these analyses with new ways forward, new frameworks that are grounded in principles of equity, social justice, and the structural reconstruction of the counseling and psychology disciplines and, in fact, the larger society. It is our hope that this volume will guide us and our colleagues toward a new vigilance and a new commitment for equity and justice in counseling and psychology by generating a dialogue that is both critical and respectful and that is born out of our love and commitment for our professions, our colleagues, and the individuals and communities with whom we work. As Freire wrote (2000), "Dialogue cannot exist … in the absence of a profound love for the world and its people" (p. 77).

A Summary of the Remaining Chapters

We begin with "The Application of Critical Consciousness and Intersectionality as Tools for De-Colonizing Racial/Ethnic Identity Development Models in the Fields of Counseling and Psychology" (Chap. 2), in which Richard Q. Shin uses intersectionality and critical consciousness theories to identify limitations of the racial/ethnic identity stage models used in counseling and psychology. He particularly points out the need to examine how they contribute to—instead of disrupting—existing power relationships.

Next, in "Queering Multicultural Competence in Counseling" (Chap. 3), Lance C. Smith critiques the heteronormativity in "multicultural" counseling paradigms. He recommends a decolonizing framework that challenges heterosexual privilege and "affirming" counseling practices with lesbian, gay, bisexual, and queer clients.

Kevin A. Tate, Edil Torres Rivera, and Lisa M. Edwards collaborate on "Colonialism and Multicultural Counseling Competence Research: A Liberatory Analysis" (Chap. 4), in which they examine the colonial underpinnings of the counseling profession in general and the multicultural counseling competencies in particular. They then use liberation psychology as a lens through which to decolonize research within multicultural counseling.

Rachael D. Goodman proposes a decolonized perspective for trauma-informed practices and suggests key ways in which practitioners can enact liberatory trauma counseling by addressing sociopolitical context, indigenous ways of healing, and forms of resilience and resistance. Her contribution is titled "A Liberatory Approach to Trauma Counseling: Decolonizing Our Trauma-Informed Practices" (Chap. 5).

In "Decolonizing Psychological Practice in the Context of Poverty" (Chap. 6), Laura Smith and Carissa Chambers discuss the ways in which "help" offered to people living in poverty by counselors and psychologists often perpetuates marginalization. They call upon practitioners to address the sources of systemic oppression and to decolonize psychological practices in the context of poverty.

Eduardo Duran and Judith Firehammer share a methodology called *story sciencing* that draws on Aboriginal/Native perspectives and privileges indigenous ways of knowing instead of Western empiricism in "Story Sciencing and Analyzing the Silent Narrative Between Words: Counseling Research from an Indigenous Perspective" (Chap. 7).

Lance C. Smith and Anne M. Geroski collaborate on "Decolonizing Alterity Models Within School Counseling Practice" (Chap. 8). They describe the failure of the American School Counseling Association (ASCA) National Model to address injustice within school settings and offer a social justice model of alterity for school counselors.

In "Decolonizing Multicultural Counseling and Psychology: Addressing Race through Intersectionality" (Chap. 9), William Conwill challenges essentialist notions of race common in counseling and psychology. He then explicates the use of intersectionality as a framework for decolonizing practice.

Mariolga Reyes Cruz and Christopher C. Sonn propose a *decolonizing standpoint* for the examination of culture that takes into account the ways in which culture is shaped by sociohistorical and political processes and must be understood within, and not apart from, this context. Their contribution is titled "(De)colonizing Culture in Community Psychology: Reflections from Critical Social Science" (Chap. 10).

Finally, in "Decolonizing Traditional Pedagogies and Practices in Counseling and Psychology Education: A Move Towards Social Justice and Action" (Chap. 11), colleagues Rachael D. Goodman, Joseph M. Williams, Rita Chi-Ying Chung, Regine M. Talleyrand, Adrienne M. Douglass, H. George McMahon, and Frederic Bemak describe five key ways in which counseling and psychology educators and programs perpetuate coloniality and how they can move toward decolonizing practices, such as by positioning social justice education at the center of their teaching and program administration.

References

Aikman, S. (1997). Interculturality and intercultural education: A challenge or democracy. *International Review of Education, 43,* 463–479.

Akena, F. A. (2012). Critical analysis of the production of Western knowledge and its implications for Indigenous knowledge and decolonization. *Journal of Black Studies, 43,* 599–619.

Brantmeier, E. (2010). Toward mainstreaming critical peace education in U.S. teacher education. In C. S. Mallott & B. Porfilio (Eds.), *Critical pedagogy in the 21st century: A new generation of scholars* (pp. 3–38). Greenwich: Information Age Publishing.

Brown, W. (1995). Wounded attachments: Late-modern oppositional political formations. In J. Rajchman (Ed.), *The identity in question* (pp. 199–228). New York: Routledge.

Deepak, A. C. (2011). Globalization, power, and resistance: Postcolonial and transnational feminist perspectives for social work practice. *International Social Work, 55,* 779–793.

Fechter, A., & Walsh, K. (2010). Examining 'expatriate' communities: Postcolonial approaches to mobile professionals. *Journal of Ethnic and Migration Studies, 36,* 1197–1210.

Freire, P. (2000). *Pedagogy of the oppressed* (trans: M. B. Ramos). New York: Continuum International Publishing Group. (Original work published in 1970).

González, M. C. (2003). An ethics for postcolonial ethnography. In R. P. Claire (Ed.), *Expression of ethnography* (pp. 77–86). Albany: State University of New York Press.

Gorski, P. C. (2008). Good intentions are not enough: A decolonizing intercultural education. *Intercultural Education, 19,* 515–525.

Hall, S. (1996). When was the 'post-colonial'? Thinking at the limit. In I. Chambers & L. Curti (Eds.), *The post-colonial question: Common skies, divided horizons* (pp. 242–260). London: Routledge.

Hernandez-Wolfe, P. (2011). Decolonization and "mental" health: A Mestiza's journey to the borderlands. *Women & Therapy, 34,* 293–306.

Ladson-Billings, G. (2006). It's not the culture of poverty, it's the poverty of culture. *Anthropology and Education Quarterly, 37*(2), 104–109.

Leigh, D. (2009). Colonialism, gender, and the family in North America: For a gendered analysis of Indigenous struggles. *Studies in Ethnicity and Nationalism, 9*(1), 70–88.

Li, H. (2010). From decolonization of alterity to democratic listening. *Social Alternatives, 29*(1), 29–33.

Lorde, A. (1984). *Sister outsider: Essays and speeches.* Berkeley: Crossing Press.

Prilleltensky, I. (1997). Values, assumptions, and practices: Assessing the moral implications of psychological discourse action. *American Psychologist, 52,* 517–535.

Racine, L., & Petrucka, P. (2011). Enhancing decolonization and knowledge transfer in nursing research with non-western populations: Examining the congruence between primary healthcare and postcolonial feminist approaches. *Nursing Inquiry, 18*(1), 12–20.

Shirazi, R. (2011). When projects of "empowerment" don't liberate: Locating agency in a "postcolonial" peace education. *Journal of Peace Education, 8,* 277–294.

Shome, R., & Hedge, R. S. (2002). Postcolonial approaches to communication: Charting the terrain, engaging the intersections. *Communication Theory, 12,* 249–270.

Vera, E. M., & Speight, S. L. (2003). Multicultural competence, social justice, and counseling psychology: Expanding our roles. *The Counseling Psychologist, 31,* 253–272.

Wane, N. N. (2008). Mapping the field of Indigenous knowledges in anti-colonial discourse: A transformative journey in education. *Race Ethnicity and Education, 11*(2), 183–197.

Chapter 2
The Application of Critical Consciousness and Intersectionality as Tools for Decolonizing Racial/Ethnic Identity Development Models in the Fields of Counseling and Psychology

Richard Q. Shin

It is clear that racial and ethnic identity development models have made significant contributions to the fields of counseling and psychology over the past 30 years. The sheer size and span of the literature on these constructs demonstrate how impactful they have been on the fields (e.g., Atkinson et al. 1998; Cross 1971; Ong et al. 2006; Phinney 1989). These models have provided useful foundations for understanding the identity development processes and experiences that some people of color face.

The initial intention underlying these models was to help mental health professionals understand that people of color experience unique identity development processes as a result of oppression and marginalization. They were meant to push the mental health fields away from operating solely from a Euro-centric perspective. However, as the editors of the current book note, ideologies that initially are intended to disrupt the status quo always are susceptible to being co-opted or appropriated by dominant, hegemonic forces.

My primary motivation for writing this chapter is to create an honest and robust dialogue about negative, unintended consequences of the proliferation of racial/ethnic identity development models. I also am concerned with the question of whether we can transform this paradigm so that it can stay relevant in counseling and psychology theory and practice. I have no interest in denigrating the authors of these theories or in minimizing the positive impact that racial/ethnic identity models have had on countless folks of color. And for the purposes of transparency, I am a person of color who feels very grateful for being exposed to the concept of racial/ethnic identity development. I am a second generation Korean American, who lived and went to school in predominantly white contexts until college. Before I came into contact with racial/ethnic identity theories, I was extremely confused about my own racial/ethnic identity development. It is not hyperbole to say that I felt like a light bulb went on in my head the moment I was introduced to Phinney's (1989) ethnic

R. Q. Shin (✉)
Counseling Psychology, School Psychology, and Counselor Education,
University of Maryland, 3234 Benjamin Building, College Park, MD 20742, USA
e-mail: rqshin@umd.edu

R. D. Goodman, P. C. Gorski (eds.), *Decolonizing "Multicultural" Counseling through Social Justice,* International and Cultural Psychology, DOI 10.1007/978-1-4939-1283-4_2

identity formation model. I was astonished to see how my own ethnic identity development process fit neatly into the model, and I felt a significant sense of relief realizing that my experiences were not abnormal. It is astonishing to me now to realize that I traveled through the stages in a relatively linear fashion.

However, over the years, my affinity for racial/ethnic identity development models has been tempered by my growing levels of critical consciousness regarding issues of racism and white supremacy in the USA. White supremacy has been defined as the securing of white racial hegemony through "a process of domination, or those acts, decisions, and policies that white subjects perpetrate on people of color" (Leonardo 2004, p. 137). I prefer to use the term white supremacy, rather than white privilege, because the former creates the conditions in which the latter can exist. My increased consciousness regarding white racial domination represents an evolution in my thinking, so that I can no longer view theories and models within the mental health fields in isolation from the various forms of systemic, institutionalized discrimination that continue to plague our society. Even though one of these models spoke so profoundly to my own personal life experiences as an Asian American, I am now fully aware that there are many folks of color in the USA who simply do not fit into any of these identity development frameworks. Promoting narrow, oversimplified depictions of people of color is just one example of how the counseling and psychology fields have colluded with the existing social, political, and cultural status quo. A combination of these factors led me to agree to contribute a critical examination of the racial/ethnic identity development paradigm for this book.

Racial/Ethnic Identity Development Theories

It is beyond the scope of this chapter to provide a comprehensive review of all the prominent racial/ethnic identity development models. It also is not my objective to describe all of the most current iterations of these theories because my assumption is that most counseling and psychology educators and practitioners who are not experts on racial/ethnic identity development operate from their knowledge of the early forms of these theories. Having said that, in broad terms, racial and ethnic identity has been defined as the significance and meaning of race and/or ethnicity in people's lives (Sellers et al. 1998). Though there is much debate about the level of overlap and/or distinctiveness between the constructs of racial and ethnic identity (Cokley 2007; Phinney and Ong 2007), in this chapter, the terms will be used interchangeably (racial/ethnic identity) because my analysis is directed at the common threads that bind many, if not all, of these models together. For instance, most racial/ethnic identity stage models describe a transformational process of the attitudes of persons of color from racial or ethnic self-denigration to pride and self-acceptance (Yi and Shorter-Gooden 1999).

The idea of racial/ethnic identity development unfolding through linear stages has been applied by a variety of scholars to African Americans (Cross 1971), Asian Americans, and Latina/Latino Americans (Kim 1981; Ruiz 1990), and across all ethnic groups (Phinney and Ong 2007). Many of these models either explicitly or implicitly invoke a stage-like process whereby an individual begins with an uncritically accepted negative self-image or, at minimum, an unexamined or neutral racial/ethnic sense of self (Yi and Shorter-Gooden 1999). This beginning stage is then disrupted by a phase of active exploration and gradual rejection of the previously accepted idealized image of white culture and hegemony. The individual eventually arrives at a final stage of healthy integration, which includes the acceptance of one's racial/ethnic background as well as a respect for the cultural norms of other groups.

A number of theorists have revised their models to expand the meaning of the term *stage*. Helms (1995) replaced the term *stage* for *status* suggesting that the identity stages are permeable and not mutually exclusive categories. Other theorists acknowledged "blends of racial identity statuses" (Carter 1995, p. 125), as well as the notion that individuals cycle through some of the stages more than once as a result of contextual events that challenge their ethnic identities (Parham 1989).

Overgeneralization and Essentializing

A common criticism of racial/ethnic identity stage theories, offered previously by several scholars, is the fact that the models fail to capture the vast intra-group differences in identity development within all racial and ethnic groups (Constantine et al. 1998; Yi and Shorter-Gooden 1999). This, of course, has been a constant tension created by traditional mainstream psychology, which has been so focused on developing universal, linear models to describe the experiences of large demographic groups. For example, Sue and Sue (2003) have asserted that the ethical guidelines and standards of practice among fields like counseling and psychology are significantly skewed toward universality so that approaches to treatment can appear to be appropriate for all groups. The propagation of categorical stage models is not surprising considering that the field of psychology, like other social sciences, is built on the Cartesian–Newtonian paradigm (Capra 1982), which demands a mechanistic, reductionistic approach to studying complex human processes (Prilleltensky 1994).

When we consider the complexity of constructs meant to reflect how individuals view themselves in terms of race and/or ethnicity, it seems almost nonsensical to rigidly promote theoretical models that are based on the assumption that all members of a particular racial group perceive and experience racial issues similarly. For instance, Constantine et al. (1998) have critiqued Black identity theories for not addressing the impact of the African Diaspora (i.e., the dispersion of West and Central Africans to the Americas through the slave trade) on the racial identity development of various subgroups of Black Americans. These models also are inadequate in their lack of consideration for immigrants who have developed a positive sense of ethnic identity in their native countries (Uba 1994) or children who have a strong positive ethnic identity (Cross 1995). It is also unclear how well racial/ethnic identity models can capture the potential nuances of identity development that occur in tight-knit ethnic enclaves that exist all throughout the USA.

On the one hand, the problem of overgeneralization associated with racial/ethnic identity models can be viewed neutrally and as a necessary byproduct or challenge of applying any psychological theory to the real world. Therefore, one might argue, "This has always been an issue with identity development models, so it is not any more of a problem with racial/ethnic identity theories as with other identity theories." However, this argument ignores the socio-historical–political context in which psychological theories are promoted and practiced. Oversimplified, incomplete stories about people of color represent one of the ways in which the social sciences have helped to reify white supremacy in the USA. The many narrow and typically deficit-oriented theories regarding people of color have been termed "master narratives" (Montecinos 1995) and "majoritarian stories" (Solórzano and Yosso 2002) because they often are bound by the constraints of racism and white privilege. Hence, these stories "provide a very narrow depiction of what it means to be Mexican American, African American, White, and so on…. A master narrative essentializes and wipes out the complexities and richness of a group's cultural life" (Montecinos 1995, p. 293).

One of the pillars that upholds white supremacy, patriarchy, heteronormativity, class oppression, ableism, and other forms of systemic, institutionalized discrimination is the widely held belief that there are genuine realities or *essences* that underlie socially constructed categories like race, class, gender, sexual orientation, and (dis)ability. It is upon this foundational ideology that dominant, hegemonic forces can provide the rationale or justification for hierarchical social arrangements (e.g., Latina/Latino Americans experience higher levels of poverty because they generally do not like to work hard). Recent research has shown that essentialist beliefs about social groups defined by gender, race, and sexual orientation are prevalent (e.g., Jayaratne et al. 2006), associated with the justification of social inequalities (Verkuyten 2003), and the endorsement of stereotypes, prejudice, and discrimination directed toward racial minority groups (Jayaratne et al. 2006; Keller 2005).

At its heart, essentialism is "unavoidably a philosophical concept, one whose definition and critique quickly gets us into arguments which are as old as philosophy itself" (Sayer 2008, p. 454). An in-depth exploration of this debate is beyond the scope of this chapter, but it is important for me to make clear that my critique about racial/ethnic identity reinforcing essentialist notions of race is not an all-or-nothing proposition. By this I mean that the literature on racial/ethnic identity development has in fact documented an important process experienced by some individuals of color, but it has also simultaneously reinforced essentialist ideologies about race. The racial/ethnic identity development paradigm in the fields of counseling and psychology simply represents a tradition known by political theorists as "the politics of recognition" (Snyder 2012, p. 249). The defining feature of the politics of recognition is the demand that a devalued collective identity be included, affirmed, and valued, in other words "recognized." As stated at the beginning of the chapter, it is clear that the motivation underlying the racial/ethnic identity development paradigm was to problematize the ethnocentric, universalistic theories of human development. However, the exercise of engaging in the politics of recognition comes with inherent dangers. The endorsement of distinct racial/ethnic identity theories for African Americans, Asian Americans, and Latino/Latina Americans contribute to fixed visions of collective identities that serve to reify hierarchical relationships both within and between groups (Markell 2003; Oliver 2001; Phillips 2007). Let me emphasize again that there is no clear answer to the question of whether racial/ethnic identity development theories do or do not contribute to dominant essentialist discourses about race, however, I am very troubled by the fact that there has been no serious dialogue about this consequential tension within the counseling and psychology literatures.

Pathologizing and Assimilationism

One consequence of conceptualizing racial/ethnic identity development as a linear, staged unfolding is the crystallization of a supposed "ideal" or "normal" sequence, which naturally leads to implicit pathologizing of those who fall outside this pattern. Although clearly not the intent of the authors of racial/ethnic identity models, these theories have provided yet another tool in the hands of mental health professionals to diagnose members of marginalized groups with some form of deficiency. This is consistent with the long-standing tradition in the fields of counseling and psychology to transform oppressive, colonizing contexts into mental health disorders. Further, if a person of color dares to speak out in the face of a racially discriminatory situation, they can easily be "diagnosed" as having a primitive racial/ethnic identity. Take for instance the following conversation that the author experienced with a white colleague:

> **Colleague**: I need to speak with you about my advisee, Derek.
> **Author**: What's the problem?
> **Colleague**: He's claiming that the reason he received a poor grade on an exam was the result of our colleague being racially biased.
> **Author**: So how would you like to proceed?
> **Colleague**: Well I think you should talk to him to let him know he's wrong.
> **Author**: How do you know he's wrong?
> **Colleague**: Well obviously our colleague isn't racist and haven't you noticed that Derek is in the immersion–emersion stage of Black identity development?
> **Author**: No, I haven't come to this conclusion about Derek's racial identity. What makes you say he's at that stage?
> **Colleague**: Well, in addition to the fact that he's making this false claim about our colleague being racist, I've heard he's been very resistant to opening up in his experiential group. And it doesn't appear to be a group issue because all of the other members have been very open and vulnerable.
> **Author**: Isn't he the only person of color in that experiential group?
> **Colleague**: Yes and that's just my point. Derek is untrusting and suspicious of his white group members even though none of them have done anything racist. In fact, I've heard they've been bending over backwards to make him feel safe and comfortable, but he still won't open up. Unfounded feelings of anger and mistrust are hallmarks of people of color who have stunted racial identities.

This interaction made it clear to me how white counseling professionals could easily interpret people of color as unable to accurately identify racist situations if it is perceived that they have not reached the "highest" stages of racial/ethnic identity reflecting a "healthy acceptance of both dominant and minority cultural group components" (Sneed et al. 2006, p. 73).

It should not be surprising at all to social justice counselors and psychologists that racial/ethnic identity models could be so easily manipulated to support and reify white supremacy. All of these models are susceptible to the fundamental limitations of developmental stage theories in general. With identity stage models, development is seen as a process of "maturational unfolding…in which immature stages of lesser organization and differentiation are succeeded by more mature, complex, adaptive equilibria" (Steenbarger 1991, p. 288). These models inherently promote the notion that there is an "ideal" or "normal" developmental process, which leads to implicit pathologizing of the diverse range of life trajectories experienced by individuals. It is both insidious and convenient how racial/ethnic models can be used to "assess" people of color. Let us put this dynamic into context by considering some very important socio-cultural–historical factors.

Assimilationism or cultural hegemony is "the systemic tendency of one culture to negate another" (Berbrier 2004, p. 484). From the earliest days of the USA, "humanity" was defined as male, white, and propertied. In the case of African slaves in the USA, they were literally reduced to a fraction of a human being when the government classified slave representation to three fifths of a person. The colonization and attempted genocide of Native peoples in the USA were grounded in the belief that Native people were inherently inferior to European whites. And certainly, the long history of exclusion, violence, and discrimination aimed at Asians and Latinos/Latinas in the USA was justified through the dehumanization of these racial/ethnic groups. Articulated succinctly by Leonardo (2004), "It is easy to see that the white supremacist…subject represents the standard for human, or the figure of a whole person, and everyone else is a fragment" (p. 139).

The source of the problems associated with racial/ethnic identity models do not necessarily lie in the frameworks themselves. As opposed to acculturation models, which have been criticized for being apolitical and decontextualized (Bhatia and Ram 2009), almost all racial/ethnic identity models reference the damaging effects of racism on the psyche of people of color. The challenges stem from the fact that these models are embedded in the fields of counseling and psychology, which have been dominated by white privilege and mainstream values like extreme individualism, and the concomitant strong bias toward framing human problems in "apolitical, intrapsychic, and deficit-oriented diagnoses" (Prilleltensky 1997, p. 526). It is this context that has allowed racial/ethnic models to be used as tools for colonization. Like in the example described above, practitioners or educators with lower levels of critical awareness around issues of race and racism may be more inclined to conceptualize difficult cross-racial situations as a deficit within the person of color instead of as the result of a potentially oppressive context.

Another problem apparent in the case example above is the way that racial/ethnic identity development models can be used to support the assimilationist narrative directed at people of color. Examples of the subtle assimilationist messages embedded in some racial/ethnic identity models include phrases like, "have developed an inner sense of security and now can own and appreciate unique aspects of their culture as well as those in US culture" (Sue and Sue 2003, p. 225), "Identification for or against white culture is no longer an important issue" (Sue and Sue, p. 213; describing Kim's (1981) model of Asian American identity development), "Individuals at this stage have abandoned anger toward the majority group" (Phinney 1996). All of these descriptors are associated with the highest or most advanced stages in each of the models. Clearly, this is extremely problematic because it reinforces the dominant societal narrative that people of color "just need to get over" their exaggerated feelings of anger and resentment about racism because we are now supposedly living in a post-racial society. Pathologizing the legitimate anger experienced by people of color is also a byproduct of the individualistic bias in the fields of counseling and psychology, which sets the stage for victim blaming or holding "individuals responsible for the causes of and solutions to their problems" (Nelson and Prilleltensky 2005, p. 5). Now again, examining the descriptions of the stages described above without considering the systems of white hegemony and domination that exist in the contemporary US society does not necessarily illuminate the problem. However, if we do consider the pervasive forces of white supremacy in our society, then we can see how mental health professionals who are just as susceptible to internalizing prejudiced and stereotypical depictions of people of color as anyone else can use racial/ethnic identity models to: (1) conclude that a person of color is not a fully developed human being, and (2) challenge the accuracy of a person of color's perceptions of whites and racially discriminatory situations.

Intersectionality

One of the most common critiques of the racial/ethnic identity development paradigm is that the models fail to consider all of the other critical social identity categories that affect individuals' lives (Constantine et al. 1998; Yi and Shorter-Gooden 1999). Some of these identities provide access to unearned privileges while others result in exploitation and marginalization. In the contemporary US society, dominant social identities include being white, male, middle class, heterosexual, and physically/mentally abled. Devalued and marginalized groups include people of color; women; poor and working class people; lesbian, gay, bisexual, and transgendered individuals; and those with (dis)abilities (Johnson 2006). Most persons occupy both privileged and oppressed social locations. Take for instance a heterosexual identifying, Asian American woman. Due to her status as a woman of color, she is subjected to patriarchy and white supremacy, whereas her heterosexual identity affords her privileges associated with being a member of the dominant sexual orientation group.

Simply put, people of color in the USA are incredibly diverse in terms of age, class, gender, sexual orientation, immigration status, historical and contemporary experiences with oppression, generational level, and many other important sociodemographic variables. Ignoring some of these critical social identity categories and/or continuing to privilege race in discussions focused on oppression silences the pervasive damages caused by patriarchy, heteronormativity, class oppression, ableism, and other forms of systemic, institutionalized discrimination. This process is contradictory to Audre Lorde's insistence that we must not support a "hierarchy of oppressions" (1983). Privileging the suffering of one marginalized group over others significantly interferes with the development of coalitions aimed at liberating all those who are negatively impacted by systems of power and privilege.

It is sadly apparent that the racial/ethnic identity paradigm in the fields of counseling and psychology is painfully outdated when juxtaposed with the growing demands by feminist, critical, social justice counselors and psychologists to critically and simultaneously analyze the many intersecting social identities that affect everyone's lives. Unfortunately, this limitation is inherent in the broader "multicultural" and "diversity" education movements (Andersen and Collins 2007; Manning 2009), which foster a comparative instead of relational understanding of oppressive systems in society. This is why contemporary multicultural-social justice counselors and psychologists are adopting frameworks like the *matrix of domination,* which focus on the oppressive structural patterns that bind systems of discrimination like racism and heteronormativity together (Andersen and Collins). This analytic frame is consistent with the growing emphasis on social justice in the counseling and psychology fields (Toporek et al. 2009; Vera and Speight 2003) because it positions professionals to think critically about transforming structures instead of continuing to simply document the effects of various forms of discrimination on marginalized peoples. At minimum, moving toward a framework like the matrix of domination in the fields of counseling and psychology will require educators, researchers, and practitioners to supplement the use of racial/ethnic identity development models with theories that focus on other systemic, institutionalized forms of discrimination like patriarchy, heteronormativity, class oppression, ableism, and religious discrimination. Ideally, I would like to see the development of more comprehensive theoretical models and assessment measures that shift the current emphasis on marginalized individuals' identities toward their awareness of the interrelationships of the forms of oppression listed above.

Critical Consciousness

We may not have to search far for a useful tool for decolonizing the racial/ethnic identity development paradigm. Let us call back the spirit of an early psychologist and priest, Ignacio Martin-Baro, who served as the architect for the psychology of liberation (Comas-Diaz 2007). The psychology of liberation places at the forefront the goal of increasing people's awareness of oppression and of the ideologies and inequitable structures that keep them marginalized and oppressed. Because Paulo Freire's (1973) concept of *conscientization* or *critical consciousness* lies at the heart of the psychology of liberation, increased awareness must be coupled with enhancing a sense of agency and empowerment among members of marginalized groups. Feminist, critical, and liberation psychologists have long been in the process of transforming traditional psychological theories to place a greater emphasis on oppressive sociopolitical conditions (Evans et al. 2005; Prilleltensky 1997). There is a clear need for this process to take place with the racial/ethnic identity development paradigm.

The first step in decolonizing racial/ethnic identity models is to move the focus of these theories away from individual, intra-psychic interpretations. Unfortunately, the counseling and psychology fields continue to privilege individual level conceptualizations and interventions, which is inconsistent with the increasing awareness of how systemic, institutionalized barriers are the root cause for many of the psychological and social difficulties experienced by members of marginalized groups (Fouad et al. 2006; Prilleltensky 1997; Vera and Speight 2003). Conversations about the racial/ethnic identity of a client or student of color should always include a consideration of critical consciousness. Critical consciousness is an ideal tool for understanding the deleterious effects of white supremacy on the hearts and minds of individuals of color because the construct itself places a spotlight on oppression in all its forms and demands action against social and economic inequities. (For examples on how to incorporate critical consciousness into psychotherapy and research, see Comas-Diaz 2007; Watts et al. 2003.) This stands in stark contrast to racial/ethnic identity theories that afford acritical, unaware educators and practitioners another tool for assessing people of color as deficient.

Racial/ethnic identity models may also be decolonized by drawing from the concept of intersectionality. In practice, this would mean that whenever an educator or practitioner is considering a person of color's racial/ethnic identity, they would also attend to their other intersecting social identities. When working with persons of color, to increase their critical consciousness of the ways in which white supremacy has impacted their lives, there may also be a need to increase their awareness of how other forms of cultural hegemony (i.e., patriarchy, heteronormativity) have affected them. An excellent example of how to target issues associated with oppression *and* privilege in a clinical context is a framework called the cultural context model (CCM; Almeida et al. 2007), which has emerged out of the family therapy field. What makes this approach exceptional is the fact that therapists are given the charge never to privilege one discourse of oppression over others. For instance, when working with a Mexican American family, patriarchy, white supremacy, and homophobia may all need to be addressed simultaneously to achieve the highest level of safety and well-being for each family member. Following the principles of intersectionality, CCM therapists provide opportunities for their clients to gain awareness of how they can use their privileged social identities to participate in the liberation of other devalued and marginalized groups. Allies, or those who use their dominant status in a particular social identity category to advocate for the marginalized group, are crucial to the work of social justice (Munin and Speight 2010). As Audre Lorde (1984) states so eloquently while describing Paulo Freire's message in *The Pedagogy of the Oppressed* (1970), "the true focus of revolutionary change is never merely the oppressive situations which we seek to escape, but that piece of the oppressor which is planted deep within each of us…" (p. 123).

Conclusion

This chapter provided a critical analysis of the unintended negative consequences that the racial/ethnic identity paradigm has had in the counseling and psychology fields. The constructs of critical consciousness and intersectionality were offered as essential tools for the process of decolonizing racial/ethnic identity development models. As stated at the beginning of this chapter, my primary goal is to stimulate an honest and critical dialogue in the counseling and psychology fields because there simply has been no robust counter-narrative regarding the proliferation of this paradigm. Initiating such a professional exchange will be a necessary first step in assuring that these important theories in the multicultural counseling movement are not unintentionally reifying white racial hegemony and other forms of systemic, institutionalized discrimination.

References

Almeida, R., Vecchio, K. D., & Parker, L. (2007). Foundation concepts for social justice-based therapy: Critical consciousness, accountability, and empowerment. In E. Aldarondo (Ed.), *Advancing social justice through clinical practice* (pp. 175–206). Mahwah: Lawrence Erlbaum.

Andersen, M. L., & Collins, P. H. (2007). Why race, class, and gender still matter. In M. L. Andersen & P. H. Collins (Eds.), *Race, class and gender: An anthology* (pp. 1–16). Belmont: Wadsworth.

Atkinson, D. R., Morten, G., & Sue, D. W. (1998). *Counseling American minorities*. Boston: McGraw-Hill.

Berbrier, M. (2004). Assimilationsim and pluralism as cultural tools. *Sociological Forum, 19,* 29–61.

Bhatia, S., & Ram, A. (2009). Theorizing identity in transnational and diaspora cultures: A critical approach to acculturation. *International Journal of Intercultural Relations, 33,* 140–149.

Capra, F. (1982). *The turning point: Science, society, and the rising culture*. New York: Bantam.

Carter, R. T. (1995). *The influence of race and racial identity in psychotherapy-toward a racially inclusive model*. New York: Wiley.

Cokley, K. (2007). Critical issues in the measurement of ethnic and racial identity: A referendum on the state of the field. *Journal of Counseling Psychology, 54,* 224–234.

Comas-Diaz, L. (2007). Ethnopolitical psychology: Healing and transformation. In E. Aldarondo (Ed.), *Advancing social justice through clinical practice* (pp. 91–118). Mahwah: Lawrence Erlbaum.

Constantine, M. G., Richardson, T. Q., Benjamin, E. M., & Wilson, J. W. (1998). An overview of Black racial identity theories: Limitations and considerations for future theoretical conceptualizations. *Applied & Preventive Psychology, 7,* 95–99.

Cross, W. E. Jr. (1971). Negro-to-Black conversion experience: Toward a psychology of black liberation. *Black World, 20,* 13–27.

Cross, W. (1995). The psychology of nigrescence: Revisiting the cross model. In J. G. Ponterotto, J. M. Casas, L. A. Suzuki, & D. M. Alexander (Eds.), *Handbook of multicultural counseling* (pp. 93–122). Thousand Oaks: Sage.

Evans, K. M., Kincade, E. A., Marbley, A. F., & Seem, S. R. (2005). Feminism and feminist therapy: Lessons from the past and hopes for the future. *Journal of Counseling & Development, 83,* 269–277.

Fouad, N. A., Gerstein, L. H., & Toporek, R. L. (2006). Social justice and counseling psychology in context. In R. L. Toporek, L. Gerstein, N. Fouad, G. Roysircar, & T. Israel (Eds.), *Handbook for social justice in counseling psychology: Leadership, vision, and action* (pp. 1–16). Thousand Oaks: Sage.

Freire, P. (1970). *The pedagogy of the oppressed.* New York: Seabury.

Freire, P. (1973). *Education for critical consciousness.* New York: Continuum.

Helms, I. E. (1995). An update of Helms's White and people of color racial identity models. In I. G. Ponterotto, I. M. Casas, L. A. Suzuki, & D. M. Alexander (Eds.), *Handbook of multicultural counseling* (pp. 181–198). Thousand Oaks: Sage.

Jayaratne, T. E., Ybarra, O., Sheldon, J. P., Brown, T. N., Feldbaum, M., Pfeffer, C. A., & Petty, E. M. (2006). White Americans' genetic lay theories of race differences and sexual orientation: Their relationship with prejudice toward Blacks, and gay men and lesbians. *Group Processes and Intergroup Relations, 9,* 77–94.

Johnson, A. G. (2006). *Privilege, power, and difference* (2nd ed.). Boston: McGraw

Keller, J. (2005). In genes we trust: The biological component of psychological essentialism and its relationship to mechanisms of motivated social cognition. *Journal of Personality and Social Psychology, 88,* 686–702.

Kim, J. (1981). The process of Asian American identity development: A study of Japanese American women's perceptions of their struggles to achieve personal identities as Americans of Asian ancestry. *Dissertation Abstracts International, 42,* 155 1A (University Microfilms no. 81-18080).

Leonardo, Z. (2004). The color of supremacy: Beyond the discourse of 'white privilege'. *Educational Philosophy and Theory, 36,* 137–152.

Lorde, A. (1983). There is no hierarchy of oppressions. Bulletin: *Homophobia and Education, 14*(3/4), 9.

Manning, K. (2009). Philosophical underpinnings of student affairs work on difference. *About Campus, 14*(2), 11–17.

Markell, P. (2003). *Bound by recognition.* Princeton: Princeton University Press.

Montecinos, C. (1995). Culture as an ongoing dialogue: Implications for multicultural teacher education. In C. Sleeter & P. McLaren (Eds.), *Multicultural education, critical pedagogy, and the politics of difference* (pp. 269–308). Albany: State University of New York Press.

Munin, A., & Speight, S. L. (2010). Factors influencing the ally development of college students. *Equity & Excellence in Education, 43,* 249–264.

Nelson, G., & Prilleltensky, I. (2005). *Community psychology: In pursuit of liberation and well-being.* New York: Palgrave Macmillan.

Oliver, K. (2001). *Witnessing: Beyond recognition.* Minneapolis: University of Minnesota Press.

Ong, A. D., Phinney, J. S., & Dennis, J. (2006). Competence under challenge: Exploring the protective influence of parental support and ethnic identity in Latino college students. *Journal of Adolescence, 29,* 961–979.

Parham, T. A. (1989). Cycles of psychological nigrescence. *Counseling Psychologist, 17,* 187–226.

Phillips, A. (2007). *Multiculturalism without culture.* Princeton: Princeton University Press.

Phinney, J. S. (1989). Stages of ethnic identity development in minority group adolescents. *Journal of Early Adolescence, 9,* 34–49. doi:10.1177/0272431689091004.

Phinney, J. S. (1996). Understanding ethnic diversity: The role of ethnic identity. *American Behavioral Scientist, 40,* 143–152.

Phinney, J. S., & Ong, A. (2007). Conceptualization and measurement of ethnic identity: Current status and future directions. *Journal of Counseling Psychology, 54,* 271–281. doi:10.1037/0022-0167.54.3.271.

Prilleltensky, I. (1994). *The morals and politics of psychology: Psychological discourse and the status quo*. Albany: State University of New York Press.

Prilleltensky, I. (1997). Values, assumptions, and practices: Assessing the moral implications of psychological discourse and action. *American Psychologist, 52,* 517–535.

Ruiz, A. S. (1990). Ethnic identity: Crisis and resolution. *Journal of Multicultural Counseling and Development, 18,* 29–40.

Sayer, A. (2008). Essentialism, social constructionism, and beyond. *The Sociological Review, 45,* 453–487.

Sellers, R. M., Smith, M. A., Shelton, J. N., Rowley, S. A. J., & Chavous, T. M. (1998). Multidimensional model of racial identity: A reconceptualization of African American racial identity. *Personality and Social Psychology Review, 2,* 18–39.

Solórzano, D. G., & Yosso, T. J. (2002). Critical race methodology: Counter-storytelling as an analytical framework for education research. *Qualitative Inquiry, 8,* 23–44.

Sneed, J. R., Schwartz, S. J., & Cross, W. E. Jr. (2006). A multicultural critique of identity status theory and research: A call for integration. *Identity: An International Journal of Theory and Research, 6,* 61–84.

Snyder, G. F. (2012). Multivalent recognition: Between fixity and fluidity in identity politics. *The Journal of Politics, 74,* 249–261. doi:10.1017/S0022381611001563.

Steenbarger, B. N. (1991). All the world is not a stage: Emerging contextualist themes in counseling and development. *Journal of Counseling & Development, 70,* 288–296.

Sue, D. W., & Sue, D. (2003). *Counseling the culturally diverse* (4th ed.). New York: Wiley.

Toporek, R. L., Lewis, J. A., & Crethar, H. C. (2009). Promoting systemic change through the ACA advocacy competencies. *Journal of Counseling & Development*, *87*, 260–268.

Uba, L. (1994). *Asian Americans: Personality patterns, identity, and mental health.* New York: Guilford.

Vera, E. M., & Speight, S. L. (2003). Multicultural competence, social justice, and counseling psychology: Expanding our roles. *The Counseling Psychologist, 31,* 253–272.

Verkuyten, M. (2003). Discourses about ethnic group (de-)essentialism: Oppressive and progressive aspects. *British Journal of Social Psychology, 42,* 371–391.

Watts, R. J., Williams, N. C., & Jagers, R. J. (2003). Sociopolitical development. *American Journal of Community Psychology, 31,* 185–194.

Yi, K., & Shorter-Gooden, K. (1999). Ethnic identity formation: From stage theory to a constructivist narrative model. *Psychotherapy: Theory, Research, Practice, Training*, *36*, 16–26.

Chapter 3
Queering Multicultural Competence in Counseling

Lance C. Smith

Introducing Nichole: Trained in the Multicultural Counseling Competence Model

A few years ago, I began conducting research with heterosexual counselors who claim to hold positive dispositions towards persons with lesbian, gay, or bisexual (LGB) identities (Smith 2009a; Smith & Shin 2014). Nichole (pseudonym), a counselor within a community counseling agency, participated in one of the studies. She and I sat together for multiple interviews. Prior to the study, I was one of Nichole's graduate school instructors and clinical supervisors. Nichole graduated from a program that places a strong emphasis on training counselors to develop the awareness, knowledge, and skills (Sue, Arredondo, & McDavis, 1992) necessary for multicultural counseling competence (MCC).

By the time Nichole graduated, she had demonstrated herself to be a solid therapist with the potential to be a great therapist. I consistently observed her extending warmth, empathy, genuineness, and unconditional positive regard to her clients. She conceptualized clients' issues well, knew how to set accurate counseling goals, and skillfully developed and implemented effective interventions. Nichole was very engaged during supervision: open to feedback and willing to take risks. As a clinical mental health counselor, Nichole worked with a variety of clients whose presenting issues ranged from normative life stressors to more profound and pervasive mental and emotional disorders. Some of Nichole's clients identified as *queer*.

The term *queer* captures those who have been defined or have chosen to define themselves as sexual and/or gender outsiders. In the words of James T. Sears, queer individuals are "human beings who love, or make love to, the same or both genders; individuals who choose to change gender identities by dress, hormones, demeanor or surgery; persons who elect to behave in gender-discordant manners" (1999, p. 4).

L. C. Smith (✉)
Graduate Counseling Program School, Counseling Program Coordinator,
The University of Vermont, 102 Mann Hall, 208 Colchester Ave, The University of Vermont, Burlington, VT 05405, USA
e-mail: lance.smith@uvm.edu

R. D. Goodman, P. C. Gorski (eds.), *Decolonizing "Multicultural" Counseling through Social Justice,* International and Cultural Psychology, DOI 10.1007/978-1-4939-1283-4_3

To be an "outsider" means outside of what heterosexual/cisgender culture considers normal, e.g., lesbian, gay, bisexual, transgender, intersex, queer, and gender-nonconforming persons; transsexuals; cross-dressers; and others who identify outside the gender binary. Cisgender, by the way, is the term that describes individuals who are comfortable with the gender they were assigned at birth. Simply put, the dominant culture positions heterosexual and cisgender identities as normal and queer identities as abnormal.

For Nichole, there was no hesitancy to practice counseling with queer clients. Why should there be? Nichole described herself as "affirming" of persons who identify as LGB. In keeping with the MCC emphasis on developing knowledge of the cultural norms of diverse and nondominant groups, she utilized her course assignments during graduate school—research papers, literature reviews, and class presentations—to advance her knowledge about issues such as queer identity development and factors that contribute to substance abuse among the population. Indeed, she may have more knowledge of the literature related to the LGB community than the other clinicians within the agency. Having been trained in the MCC model, Nichole has an idea of the need to examine one's own attitudes and beliefs regarding diverse groups. During our interviews, Nichole points to her close friendship with a man who identifies as a gay as evidence of her "affirming street cred." In her mind, having a dear friend who is gay is a clear indication that she is incapable of holding deeply rooted bias or prejudice towards queer persons.

Nichole is also conscious of the systemic oppression of the LGB community. She is condemning of the queer stereotypes that she observes in the media. She becomes agitated and raises her voice as she tells me about feeling "really angry" when she encounters "homophobic" persons or rhetoric, how legislation denying same-sex couples the right to marry or adopt children is "a bunch of crap" and "very upsetting." She is supportive of the gay rights movement and votes for pro-gay candidates. In short, Nichole is an egalitarian, politically progressive, beneficent, socially conscious, heterosexual woman who is sensitive to issues of diversity, passionately opposes the oppression of LGB persons, is a good friend of a gay man, and has completed the necessary multicultural education and training that qualify her as competent to counsel persons who identify as queer.

At this point I invite you, the reader, to pause and reflect upon possible connections that you might have with Nichole. Whether you identify as queer or straight, were you trained in the MCCs? Do you consider yourself to be affirmative of queer identities? Do you have friends who identify as queer? Do you consider yourself to be a beneficent, egalitarian, and pluralistic person? Do you support gay rights? Do you have a rainbow sticker on your office door? Do you become activated when you hear "homophobic" slurs and rants?

Now let me tell you something else about Nichole; she perpetuates heterosexual hegemony. That is to say, it will be demonstrated later in this chapter how Nichole's actions, attitudes, and beliefs also promote heterosexual supremacy and privilege (McDowell & Hernandez 2010). Which leaves me with another question for you the reader: Have you ever considered the ways in which someone like yourself—with all of your beneficent attitudes and multicultural sensibilities—perpetuate a heteronormative world view? In other words, have you interrogated the ways in which you as a counselor or psychologist inadvertently contribute to the age-old heterosexual colonization of persons who identify as queer?

The Point of this Chapter

The purpose of this chapter is to "queer" the multicultural counseling paradigm within the field of counseling. Queering multicultural counseling is about honestly, fairly, and respectfully examining taken-for-granted assumptions within the paradigm, challenging the status quo of multicultural competence, deconstructing hegemonic practices, and promoting critical consciousness (Sears 1999). To do this, I am going to draw heavily from the narrative of Nichole. This is because one of the taken-for-granted assumptions of counselors who consider themselves to be multiculturally competent is that they are too open, too aware, too beneficent, too sensitive, and too knowledgeable to participate in hegemonic practices. Nichole's narrative will serve as a gateway toward understanding how well-intended counselors who have been trained within the MCC paradigm perpetuate heterosexual hegemony.

My hope is that well-meaning readers who see themselves as multiculturally competent and "affirmative" of persons who identify as LGB might recognize how they reproduce colonization in ways that are both overt and subversive, within both individual and systemic domains. Moreover, I intend to make the case that the MCC paradigm is inadequate to the task of interrupting heterosexual hegemony as it conforms to the heterosexual hierarchy. What is necessary for decolonizing the fields of counseling and psychology is a social justice (SJ) paradigm of counseling: a model that is nonconforming, that incessantly challenges hierarchy and the status quo.

Let me add that this type of critical self-reflection of our field and of ourselves is not easy. For those of us who consider ourselves to be multiculturally competent, it can be difficult if not painful to consider how we inadvertently oppress and marginalize others. As you are reading, I invite you to open yourself up to feeling uncomfortable. Observe possible intrapsychic dissonance and defense mechanisms such as denial, rationalization, or intellectualization. In order to decolonize the deeply rooted social and institutional forms of heterosexual hegemony within the MCC paradigm, it is imperative that we engage in challenging self-examination.

What Participation in Colonization Looks Like

I began this chapter by highlighting pieces of Nichole's narrative that position her as beneficent and affirming of LGB identities. Later in this chapter, I will highlight her overt expressions of heterosexual supremacy. Moreover, in order for us to thoroughly understand how a counselor like Nichole participates in colonization, we will begin by examining *what is absent* from her narrative. In other words, as a counselor who adheres to the MCC model and identifies as affirming of LGB identities, what is missing from Nichole's narrative is fundamental to understanding the deficits of her MCC training. Absent within her narrative is acknowledgement or understanding of SJ oriented constructs like the *discourse of heteronormativity, modern heterosexism, heterosexual privilege,* and *microaggressions.*

Unpacking these important constructs will bring the narrative landscape of heterosexual hegemony into focus. While these constructs are being mapped, we will immediately begin to see how heterosexual supremacy is perpetuated by individual counselors like Nichole *and* within the larger fields of counseling and psychology despite an emphasis on multicultural competence. Finally, upon having exposed the MCC model's inadequacy in addressing heterosexual colonization, this chapter will conclude by calling for a SJ model that seeks to decolonize the fields of counseling.

Heteronormativity

As I sit in dialogue with Nichole, it is immediately evident that she has yet to grasp how we all live in, move through, and constantly reproduce the dominant discourse of *heteronormativity*. Discourses are the patterns of meaning that human beings inhabit in order for us to make sense of phenomena in our world. In the words of Greenleaf and Bryant (2012, p. 20), "pre-existing in any individual's perceptions, thoughts and actions toward an object or phenomenon, is a discourse that explains the perceived reality of the object of phenomenon." It is the discourse of heteronormativity that positions queer identities as abnormal, outside, or disdained and heterosexual/cisgender identities as normal and preferred.

I like to use the following example to unpack the discourse of heteronormativity with my students. I enjoy attending college basketball games. At many universities, during halftime the crowd is entertained by the "Kiss Cam." During the Kiss Cam, television cameras roam the crowd looking for two folks who appear to be a couple, and project the unsuspecting couple's image up on the jumbotron screen for all to see. When the couple views themselves on the screen they are supposed to kiss. The couples that kiss with the most flare receive greater fanfare from the crowd. It is a fun, lighthearted moment that produces smiles and chuckles throughout the arena. Let me restate that it is lighthearted *for the heterosexuals* in the arena because every time (and I have observed hundreds of couples flashed up on the jumbotron) the crowd views what they expect, what is perceived as "normal" in our society. Pre-existing in everyone's minds prior to the camera actually landing on a couple is the expectation that a heterosexual couple will kiss for all to see.

According to Robinson (1999, p. 73), discourses write "[t]he ways in which people act on the world and the ways in which the world acts on individuals." For my young son, the Kiss Cam "writes" his world as one where only heterosexual looking couples kiss in public. He then "rewrites" this discourse when he draws pictures of people kissing—one male and one female. Dominant discourses serve to position individuals and groups in power relations with each other (Winslade et al. 1997), reinforcing systems of power and privilege by providing justifications for cultural and institutionalized forms of discrimination like racism, classism, sexism, heterosexism, and ableism. Very few people would label the Kiss Cam or my son's drawings as heterosexist or overtly prejudice, yet both phenomena deny the existence of queer identities or relegate them to the margins, while reifying the powerful notion that heterosexual/cisgender identities are the standard.

Once one develops an awareness of the role of dominant discourses in our world, one's experience of the Kiss Cam changes. It becomes impossible not to wonder, What it is like for those attending the game who identify as gay or lesbian. Do they feel marginalized? Do they feel like second-class citizens? Do they secretly wish for the camera to choose them? Do they feel fear, "What if the camera inadvertently falls on us?"

As another example, the discourse of heteronormativity brings into stark view the subtle, yet colonizing forces I observed at the dentist's office this morning: Adorning the walls of the waiting area were large prints of heterosexual couples and families. There were no pictures of anyone that could be assumed to be a same-sex couple—no matter how sparkling and beautiful their smiles. Also, awareness of the discourse of heteronormativity makes it possible to understand the colonizing effect of romantic comedies: That walking into a cinema we participate in heteronormativity by automatically anticipating that we will view and laugh about a heterosexual couple.

Heteronormativity explains why, even within the current paradigm of multicultural counseling, when counselors read a book chapter or scholarly article on the topic of couples and family counseling, the opening case study will almost certainly be about a man and a woman. Heteronormativity accounts for counseling literature referring to heterosexual couples as just "couples" but same-sex couples are distinguished as "gay couples" or "lesbian couples."

Given that Nichole was trained in the MCC paradigm, it is not surprising that Nichole's narrative is absent of the mention of dominant discourses like heteronormativity. You see the MCC model calls upon counselors to understand "socio-political influences" that negatively affect persons from traditionally underrepresented groups (Sue et al. 1992, p. 481). For many folks like Nichole, "socio-political influences" are defined as the visible, overt forces that oppress. Nichole can only see, and therefore only articulates, an awareness of conspicuous "homophobic" phenomena: legal sanctions against same-sex marriage, the Defense of Marriage Act (DOMA), and religious institutions that overtly discriminate against sexual minorities.

The MCC model falls short in helping counselors to recognize, understand, and map the invisible, incessant cultural messages and institutional policies that perpetuate heterosexual colonization. Indeed counselor's operating within the MCC paradigm—whose vision is limited to overt socio-political forces of queer oppression—will miss the colonization at play in Kiss Cams, office waiting rooms, romantic comedies, and couples-counseling literature.

Heterosexism

It is the discourse of heteronormativity that serves as the fertile soil and water for the intractable, weedy presence of *heterosexism* in the fields of counseling and psychology. The term heterosexism encompasses the discriminatory processes, acts, and attitudes that marginalize and oppress queer individuals, in both overt and covert ways. Traditional forms of heterosexism are conspicuous acts or expressions that position any form of gender identity or sexual orientation other than cisgender and heterosexual as morally deviant and socially abominable. Traditional heterosexism is probably better known by the term *homophobia*.

Expressed on the individual level, traditional heterosexism takes the form of cruel slurs, gay jokes, school bullying of suspected queer kids, as well as acts of heinous brutality and hate crimes. Expressed at the socio-political level, it takes the form of anti-sodomy laws, legislation that illegitimates same-sex marriage, and legal sanctions that deny same-sex partners the right to adopt children. Specifically within the counseling fields, counselors who refuse to work with LGB identified clients for religious reasons display traditional heterosexism. As we saw earlier in Nichole's narrative, she is very aware of traditional heterosexism, or in her language "homophobic acts." In fact, if Nichole's or anyone's understanding of heterosexism is restricted to the construct of homophobia, one may be unknowingly buttressing the discourse of heteronormativity.

Homophobia: A Problematic Term

Until the dominant discourse of heteronormativity is made visible, heterosexual hegemony will prevail. Here is what I meant when I suggested that referring to traditional heterosexism as *homophobia* results in tacitly buttressing heteronormativity. The power of dominant discourses like heteronormativity lie in their invisibility—if no one can see or name the social force that privileges some while oppressing others, then the force remains protected from dismantlement. The problem with the term homophobia is that it aids in keeping heteronormativity invisible. It does this because homophobia positions *all acts* of heterosexism as (a) located within "bad" individuals; (b) conspicuous and flagrantly discriminatory; and possibly even (c) equivalent to an amoral psychological condition such as a fear of heights (acrophobia).

The etiology of the term homophobia makes this clear. Within psychology, an individual is diagnosed with a *phobia* when an "established clinical condition with specific diagnostic criteria" is attributed to the person's behavior (Schiffman et al. 2006, p. 2). When considering the nature of societal oppression towards queer persons, the term *phobia* is grossly inadequate, if not strategically misleading. Phobias account for the behaviors of individuals, not institutions or societies. Phobias identify disabling fears that tend to be outliers within human experience, not ubiquitous behaviors that are commonplace within the majority of people. Phobias are medical conditions that are considered amoral, not acts of agency that carry a degree of culpability.

Let us unpack the misleading influence of *homophobia* a bit further. Nichole is passionate about interrupting "homophobic acts." But by writing the story of prejudice towards queer identities with the language of homophobia—and its connotations of overt discriminatory acts of individuals—Nichole has positioned herself, and her profession, as immune to complicity in heterosexual hegemony.

To her credit, it is not surprising that she continues to make use of the term *homophobia.* It is a term that remains prevalent in the counseling field's lexicon to represent negativity towards queer identities (Basow & Johnson 2000; Bieschke et al. 2008; Dermer, Smith & Barto 2010; Herek 2004; Russell 2007). The continued widespread use of the term *homophobia* is unfortunate, if not "potentially dangerous" (Schiffman et al. 2006, p. 77).

Modern Heterosexism

While much work needs to be done to end traditional heterosexism in our society, I have observed how the conspicuous and heinous qualities of traditional heterosexism serve to obscure the more insidious, and perhaps more damaging, effects of *modern heterosexism*. Modern heterosexism, similar to modern racism and modern sexism (Swim et al. 1995), is understood as subversive and covert form of discrimination. One example of modern heterosexism would be the attitude or expression that queer persons now experience a level playing field—if not preferential treatment—in society (Cowan et al. 2005). Modern heterosexism is at work when persons who express sadness at the latest story of a brutal hate crime also abstain from supporting gay rights organizations such as The Human Rights Campaign (HRC) or Parents, Families and Friends of Lesbians and Gays (PFLAG) in order to avoid promoting the "Gay Agenda." Those who state, "I don't have a problem" with queer identities but feel discomfort if someone mistakenly identifies them as gay are expressing modern heterosexism.

I have witnessed expressions of modern heterosexism by counselors that identify as multiculturally competent—who welcome working with a client who identifies as queer—but resist placing prints and photos of same-sex couples or gender-nonconforming individuals in their agency's waiting area because it "gives preferential treatment to a minority group" or such photos might "threaten the other clients." Modern heterosexism has a close relationship with a third concept that is important for us to map, *microaggressions.*

Microaggressions

The term microaggressions captures the everyday insults, indignities, and unconscious demeaning messages conveyed by members of dominant groups toward members of nondominant groups. Let me underscore that microaggressions are often the vehicle by which the most sensitive and pluralistic of counselors and psychologists unknowingly and unintentionally marginalize and oppress persons with nondominant social identities.

Microaggressions have been identified as occurring in three forms (Sue 2010): (1) microassaults, (2) microinsults, and (3) microinvalidations. To help us get a hold on how beneficent counselors perpetuate heterosexual and cisgender hegemony, I will highlight the form of microaggressions that is usually committed by egalitarian counselors who identify as multiculturally competent: *microinvalidations*.

Microinvalidations are communications that subtly exclude or nullify the feelings, thoughts, or experiential reality of a person with a nondominant social identity. For instance, during an intake session, when a therapist asks a client who identifies as lesbian if she has a husband or boyfriend, the counselor has subtly (and probably unintentionally) nullified the client's identity and relationship. When school counselors ask their students about their "mom and dad" they unintentionally marginalize students who have same-sex parents (or a single parent for that matter). When professors of counseling and psychology engage in role plays during couples and family counseling courses—and *only ever* ask students to take on heterosexual roles—they are abating the experiences of the queer students in the classroom as well as queer clients. When supervisees who identify as LGB approach their clinical supervisors to discuss perceived heterosexism at their internship site, and the supervisors communicate that the supervisees are probably misreading things, or that they need to work on their own reactivity, the supervisors are invalidating the supervisees' ubiquitous experiences of heterosexual oppression and tacitly supporting the heterosexist system.

I have witnessed all of these microaggressions expressed by counselors who view themselves as multiculturally competent: indeed, some of the behavior was mine. And all of the examples above can subtly nullify a queer client or student's reality and result in negative emotional effects. A growing body of literature has demonstrated the damaging impact of microaggressions on persons with nondominant social identities (Brondolo et al. 2008; Hwang & Goto 2009; Purdie-Vaughns et al. 2008; Sinclair 2006; Sue et al. 2009). With regard to queer persons specifically, Nadal et al. (2010) have identified chronic stress, depression, anxiety, lower self-esteem, and an increased number of sick days as psychological impacts of sexual orientation and transgender microaggressions. Whenever I teach on the topic of microaggressions, I find that my heterosexual and cisgender counseling students struggle to accept the idea that microaggressions can be many times more harmful to members of nondominant groups than overt hate crimes (Sue 2010).

Without a decolonizing model of counseling that names and integrates modern heterosexism and microaggressions, well-intended counselors like Nichole are unaware of the frequency with which they subtly invalidate the lived reality of their clients who identify as queer. In just a few more pages, I will argue that Nichole's identity of an "affirming" counselor is a microaggression in that it subtly invalidates the equitableness of queer identities—inconspicuously positioning them as inferior to heterosexual identities.

Heterosexual Privilege

Finally, absent from Nichole's narrative is any articulation of the final construct that needs unpacking: *heterosexual privilege.* Heterosexual privilege captures the unearned, unmerited societal and institutional benefits that one receives simply by identifying as heterosexual. McIntosh (1992, p. 10) defines privilege as "an invisible package of unearned assets that I can count on cashing in each day, but about which I was 'meant' to remain oblivious." Given that our society places a premium on meritocracy, it is critical to make the point that social privilege is never earned or achieved: It is awarded by being born into a dominant identity (or passing as a dominant identity). Moreover, heterosexual counselors accept their privilege as *prima facie*, being rather clueless about its existence and often failing to question their unmerited benefits.

Kim and Pukilla (2005) and Allen Johnson (2006) adapted McIntosh's (1992) groundbreaking knapsack of white privilege in order to convey the privileges that come with heterosexual status. Just a few of the many heterosexual privileges that have been identified follow. Because I am a heterosexual:

- My colleagues do not get defensive and uncomfortable when I talk about my partner.
- I can hold hands with my significant other in public without worrying about the possibility of being harassed or beaten.
- No one questions my right to raise children.
- My sexual orientation is never considered to be the single most important characteristic that defines who I am.
- I can be rest assured that whether I'm hired, promoted, or fired from a job, it will have nothing to do with my sexual orientation.
- I can turn on the television or go to the movies and be assured of seeing characters, news reports, and stories that reflect the reality of my life.

Given the focus of this book I would like to add a few others. As a heterosexual:

- If a counselor chooses not to work with me or refers me to another counselor, I know it will have nothing to do with my sexual orientation.
- I can feel confident that my child's school counselor will have picture books, coloring books, games, and toy figures that are representative of my parental unit and family structure.
- When applying to graduate school, I need not worry about choosing a program that will reject my application if they learn of my sexual orientation.
- Within my graduate school training, I can be assured that I will read case studies, watch video clips, role play, and hear anecdotes about couples and families like mine.
- No one paternalistically "affirms" my identity.

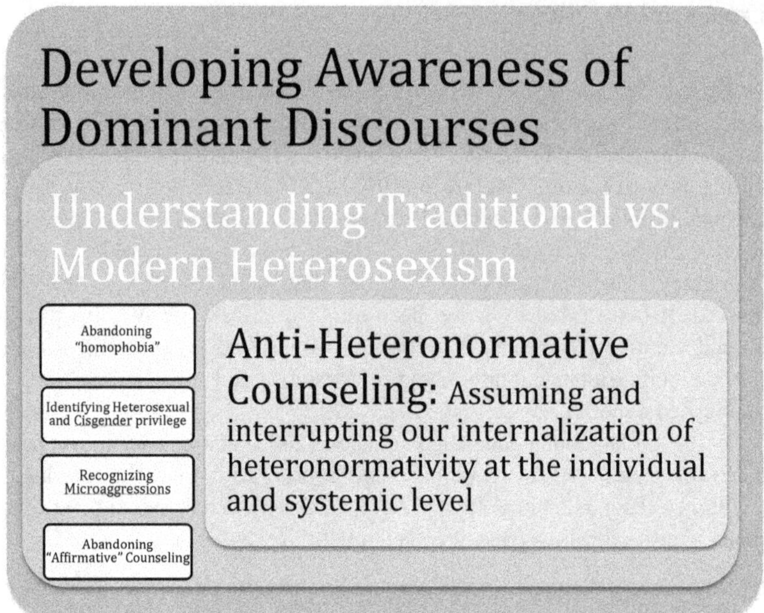

Fig. 3.1 A social justice model

The Work of Decolonizing

Having unpacked and mapped the constructs that are critical to this discussion, we can now move forward with examining how the fields of counseling and psychology might work towards decolonizing heterosexual dominance at both the individual and systemic level. In short, the fields of counseling and psychology need to move beyond the MCC paradigm to a SJ paradigm (see Fig. 3.1): A decolonizing paradigm that recognizes the complexity, power, and elusiveness of dominant discourses that influence all of us, individually and systemically, to oppress non-dominant groups. Such a paradigm will result in the axiomatic assumption that all counselors and psychologists have internalized heteronormativity; that privilege, modern heterosexism, and microggressions are a given in the lives and work of counselors; and that doing the hard work of interrupting our own participation in colonization is not an option.

Decolonizing at the Individual Level

Decolonizing at the individual level begins when counselors and psychologists integrate a deep awareness of heteronormativity, heterosexism, microaggressions, and heterosexual privilege into their lives. Within Nichole's graduate program, the

MCC model was championed and taught. But Nichole was not presented with a decolonizing SJ model, therefore she was not called upon to *assume*—no matter how beneficent and well-intentioned she conceives herself to be—that she has internalized heteronormativity. She was not invited to consider that interrupting oppressive discourses within ourselves requires a lifelong commitment to confronting internalized stereotypes and biases (Boysen 2010). Nichole was certainly not invited to consider how the fields of counseling and psychology often reproduce heterosexual and cisgender hegemony at the systemic level.

By reading this chapter, you have already taken such a step towards raising your consciousness. However, this process is challenging because it requires self-examination that can be painful. The MCC model also inadequately communicates the difficulty and pain involved in interrupting our internalization of dominant discourses like heteronormativity. For an example of how painful and challenging this process can be, let's return to the interview with Nichole.

In spite of her MCC training and "affirming" identity, Nichole reproduces colonization in part by failing to recognize that she has internalized the discourse of heteronormativity. As we move deeper into the interviews, Nichole hesitantly reveals that when she is in the presence of two women kissing, she hides her discomfort. She hesitantly tells the story of "being fake by just acting normal" and presenting "[herself] as open and non-judgmental" when observing or thinking about two women engaged in physical displays of affection. As we explore this response together, she struggles to find thoughts and language to aid her, and then ultimately lands on the term of being "confused" by lesbian sexual performativity. When I inquire about what exactly is confusing about two people desiring to express sexual affection to each other, she struggles, stammers, lowers her head, and then offers a statement that exemplifies modern heterosexism: "I just don't get it." As I sit with Nichole, her anxiety is palpable. With all of her good intentions, MCC training and self-positioning as affirming of persons who identify as lesbian, Nichole has internalized heteronormativity to the degree that physical affection or sexual activity between two women provokes dissonance and a negative emotional reaction.

While the role of heteronormativity within Nichole's attitude and feelings towards lesbian identity is hidden, connections between systemic influences and her attitude towards gay identity begin to emerge. As she continues with her self-interrogation, she also shares her struggle against the flamboyant, campy, dramatic, stereotypes she holds towards gay men: "[I]t's uncomfortable that I still have those stereotypes ingrained in my automatic reactions." But unlike her dissonance regarding women kissing, she is able to recognize a macro-level force at play. Nichole closely observes that she feels defeated, that she is "giving into the man" and "playing into the media and what I've heard from other people […] and I hate that!" And unlike her response to women kissing, when she observes herself sizing up gay men in a demeaning and superficial manner, she "stops [her]self" and reflects, "[W]hy am I going through these stereotypes automatically?"

As Nichole shares her experience with regard to stereotyping gay men, her emotions switch from anxiety and shame to frustration. She is more reflective and more aware. She is also able to offer a clear evaluation of herself—she does not like how she automatically stereotypes gay men and she attributes her behavior to the wider society—"the man" and "the media." Although not stated explicitly, heteronormativity is identified as the force informing her negative attitudes and beliefs regarding gay men. While her response to lesbian identities was internalized, her response to gay identities was externalized.

However, by the end of our interviews, Nichole appears physically weighed down with guilt and shame. In a final self-analysis, Nichole states with exasperation; "God, I'm so ashamed to admit [that] my honest reaction is 'I don't get it' [...] because you know I should treat [lesbian orientation] like, 'Oh it's this normal thing' [...] but of course we both know now what goes on in my head [...] I'm supposed to be this liberal person, but at the same time...."

What is unfortunate is that Nichole need not be surprised or confused when feelings of dissonance towards lesbian sexuality break into conscious awareness. While the MCC model calls on counselors to be aware of negative emotional reactions to clients, the model fails to assist counselors in identifying the etiology of such ugly emotional responses. Throughout our interviews, Nichole is unable to position her "confusion" and dissonance with lesbian sexuality within heteronormativity. She has yet to understand how the power of heteronormativity situates her own heterosexual sexuality as "normal," which is why she "gets" opposite-sex displays of affection, but not same-sex displays. For all of her knowledge of queer identities and issues, she never speaks about the privilege she has of being able to kiss in public without having to worry about the reactions of others. While she clearly feels shame regarding her negative attitudes, she does not map her attitude as a manifestation of modern heterosexism. Concomitant with Nichole's good intentions, her MCC training and self-identity of affirming construct a self-narrative that obscures the depths to which she has internalized the discourse of heteronormativity.

Decolonizing Counseling at the Systemic Level

Moving Away from "Affirming" Counseling

Finally, a critical component of heterosexual and cisgender hegemony is the maintenance of the heteronormative hierarchy. The MCC model is inadequate in that it fails to address such hierarchies. At this time, the fields of counseling and psychology are reinforcing the heteronormative hierarchy in the very language used to express a *positive disposition* towards sexual minorities and gender-nonconforming persons. Let me state this another way: As we express our very best intentions within an MCC paradigm, we are colonizing.

In Nichole's attempt to communicate her positive disposition to clients, she uses the language of "affirming LGB persons." *LGB-affirming* has replaced *LGB-accepting* as the predominant way to communicate a positive disposition (Bieschke et al. 2008; Chen-Hayes 2005; Israel & Hackett 2004; Rostosky et al. 2007). On the surface, *affirming* may not appear to be problematic. Indeed, I myself have frequently used this language in my own work (Smith 2009a, b). However, upon a critical analysis against the backdrop of heteronormativity, it becomes clear that such language inconspicuously reproduces the heteronormative hierarchy.

Consider this: Affirmation of one group by another group is only meaningful when there is sufficient social power held by the ones *doing* the affirming. In other words, because members of a nondominant group lack social power, if they were to "affirm" a dominant group, the act would be hollow and have little impact or meaning. However (and this reveals the insidiousness of heteronormativity), when a dominant group affirms a nondominant group, the social capitol of the dominant group is displayed and simultaneously reproduced.

Still not buying my argument? Then let me pose a few rhetorical questions: Should straight folks be seeking affirmation from queer folks? Do heterosexuals move through their world looking to be affirmed by sexual minorities? How bizarre might it sound if a man were to present for counseling and hear his counselor say, "I want you know that I affirm your male gender expression." And why aren't there scholarly articles calling for "heterosexual-affirming counseling?"

Furthermore, I suggest that there are assimilationist assumptions within the language of affirmation—that such language implicitly suggests that it is a good and benign thing for sexual and gender minorities to be embraced by the dominant heterosexual, cisgender culture. However, those who seek to decolonize heteronomativity reject these assumptions (Sedgwick 1990; Warner 2002; Wilchins 2004), because decolonization is at odds with the embrace of, or assimilation into, the heteronormative power structure (Stein & Plummer 1996). Ultimately, equity and justice for gender and sexual minorities will not be achieved through heterosexuals' accepting, affirming, or celebrating LGB and transgender individuals and communities. A truly equitable society can only be accomplished through the dismantling of the heteronormative hierarchy altogether (Smith et al. 2012).

Moving Toward "Anti-heteronormative" Counseling

Rather than utilizing the hierarchical language of affirmation that is grounded in the MCC paradigm, I invite the fields of counseling and psychology to adopt positive disposition language that is grounded in the struggle to interrupt heterosexual hegemony—let's take up the work of "anti-heteronormative counseling." Such a linguistic transformation would introduce a counter-discourse with the fields of counseling and psychology that would not only be a meaningful shift away from tacit support of the heterosexual hierarchy but also result in increased exposure of the discourse of heteronormativity and an emphasis on its interruption.

I believe that the fields of counseling and psychology will generate an entire literature of helpful, decolonizing models, action plans, and interventions when they enthusiastically operationalize anti-heteronormative counseling, but for starters I will offer just a few, albeit rather limited, concrete ideas. Anti-heteronormative counseling will entail changing the gender identity boxes on our intake forms. Anti-heteronormative counseling will result in replacing the pictures on the walls of our offices and changing the gender identity signs on the bathroom doors. Anti-heteronormative counseling will alter the assumptions we make when we see a client for the first time. Anti-heteronormative counseling will change the questions we ask regarding our client's partners, parents, sex life, and "marriage" history. Anti-heteronormative counseling will result in inviting clients to discuss how society's response to their sexual orientation and gender identity might connect to their current struggles. Anti-heteronormative counseling will mean that counselors who identify as heterosexual and cisgender will invite their queer clients to discuss what it is like for them to attempt to be vulnerable with a member of the oppressive majority. An anti-heteronormative approach will mean that counselors will ask their supervisors to assist them in examining how their internalized heterosexism is interfering in their work.

Conclusion

Within this chapter I have attempted to "queer" multicultural competence within counseling—to demonstrate how well-intended counselors grounded in the MCC model perpetuate heterosexual colonization within the fields of counseling and psychology at both the individual and systemic level. To aid this exploration, we looked at the narrative of one counselor who—with MCC training, beneficent intentions, curiosity, knowledge of the literature, and a close friendship with gay identified man—is lacking awareness of the discourse of heteronormativity and her internalization of it. Without such awareness, she perceives herself to be engaged in multiculturally competent practice with her LGB clients without having exposed and interrogated her disturbing negative attitudes, and all the while buttressing the heterosexual hierarchy.

Before anyone demonizes Nichole, let me add that there is nothing in her story that I do not personally connect with or have not heard repeatedly from the graduate students in my courses. Recognizing how my internalization of heteronormativity continues to produce ugly prejudiced attitudes, microaggressions, and colonizing behaviors on my part will be lifelong journey. Indeed, this is another piece of the MCC model that is insufficient: The fields of counseling need a model that underscores the notion that *the work of decolonizing ourselves and our profession will never cease*. Dominant discourses are too powerful and lodge too deeply in our collective psyches. The SJ model not only highlights the idea that the work of decolonizing ourselves will only be an aspiration and never an achievement but also that it is *within* the pain and struggle of this journey that healing and liberation occur.

Let me conclude by stating that I deeply admire the MCC model. We are all indebted to those scholars who took great personal and professional risk in putting forth the idea that culture is superordinate within all counseling. Their courageous work engendered nothing less than the fourth force in counseling and psychology.

We can celebrate the MCC model's achievements while also addressing its deficiencies: It is not a model that adequately fosters equity; it is not a model that is sufficient for the interruption of privilege and oppression; it is a model that can tacitly contribute to the maintenance of heterosexual hegemony.

The fields of counseling and psychology need to ground themselves in a model that presents awareness of dominant discourses as axiomatic. We need to move into a paradigm where there is a primary emphasis on the colonizing force of dominant discourses so that modern heterosexism is exposed, microaggressions are addressed, privilege is acknowledged, and all are interrupted. Moreover—20 years into the MCC paradigm—the field of counseling needs a model that will abort, not reproduce, the heterosexual hierarchy in the very language it uses to communicate a positive disposition toward sexual minorities.

We can do better. It is time to honor and integrate the lessons of the MCC paradigm while we move forward into an SJ paradigm. It is time to take up anti-heteronormative counseling. It is time to decolonize the fields of counseling and psychology.

Discussion and Reflection Questions

- Did you feel yourself become activated or defensive while reading this chapter? If so, what was that like?
- How are you like Nichole? How are you different? Please elaborate.
- For those of you who identify as heterosexual, how do you feel if someone mistakenly identifies you as lesbian, gay, or bisexual?
- What are manifestations of the discourse of heteronormativity in your daily experience?
- Discuss a time when you have participated (knowingly or unknowingly) in modern heterosexism or microaggressions?
- What are three things that you can do to interrupt heteronormativity to practice anti-heternormative counseling—in your work as a counselor or psychologist?

References

Basow, S. A., & Johnson, K. (2000). Predictors of homophobia in female college students. *Sex Roles, 42*(5–6), 391–404.

Bieschke, K. J., Hardy, J. A., Fassinger, R. E., & Croteau, J. M. (2008). Intersecting identities of gender-transgressive sexual minorities: Toward a new paradigm of affirmative psychology. In W. B. Walsh (Ed.), *Biennial review of counseling psychology* (Vol. 1, pp. 177–206). New York: Routledge.

Brondolo, E., Brady, N., Thompson, S., Tobin, J. N., Cassells, A., Sweeney, M., & Contrada, R. J. (2008). Perceived racism and negative affect: Analysis of trait and state measures of affect in a community sample. *Journal of Social and Clinical Psychology, 27,* 150–173.

Boysen, G. A. (2010). Integrating implicit bias into counselor education. *Counselor Education and Supervision, 49,* 210–227.
Chen-Hayes, S. F. (2005). Challenging multiple oppressions in counselor education. In J. M. Croteau, J. S. Lark, M. A. Lidderdale, & Y. B. Chung (Eds.), *Deconstructing heterosexism in the counseling professions: A narrative approach* (pp. 53–58). Thousand Oaks: Sage.
Cowan, G., Heiple, B., Marquez, C., Khatchadourian, D., & McNevin, M. (2005). Heterosexuals' attitudes toward hate crimes and hate speech against gays and lesbians: Old-fashioned and modern heterosexism. *Journal of Homosexuality, 49*(2), 67–82.
Dermer, S. B., Smith, S. D., & Barto, K. K. (2010). Identifying and correctly labeling sexual prejudice, discrimination, and oppression. *Journal of counseling & development, 88*(3), 325–331.
Greenleaf, A. T., & Bryant, R.M. (2012). Perpetuating oppression: Does the current counseling discourse neutralize social action. *Journal for Social Action in Counseling and Psychology, 4,* 18–29.
Herek, G. M. (2004). Beyond "homophobia": Thinking about sexual prejudice and stigma in the twenty-first century. *Sexuality Research & Social Policy, 1*(2), 6–24.
Hwang, W. C., & Goto, S. (2009). The impact of perceived racial discrimination on the mental health of Asian American and Latino college students. *Asian American Journal of Psychology, 1,* 15–28.
Israel, T., & Hackett, G. (2004). Counselor education on lesbian, gay and bisexual issues: Comparing information and attitude exploration. *Counselor Education & Supervision, 43,* 179–191.
Johnson, A.G. (2006). *Privilege, power, and difference* (2nd ed.). Boston: McGraw Hill.
Kim, H., & Pukilla, M. (2005). *GLBTTIQQ Q & A. A Q & A guide to GLBT diversity issues.* Waterville: Colby College.
McDowell, T., & Hernandez, P. (2010). Decolonizing academia: Intersectionality, participation and accountability in family therapy and counseling. *Journal of Feminist Family Therapy, 22,* 93–111.
McIntosh, P. (1992). White privilege and male privilege: A personal account of coming to see correspondences through work in womens studies. In M. L. Andersen & P. H. Collins (Eds.), *Race, class, and gender: An anthology* (pp. 70–81). Belmont: Wadsworth.
Nadal, K. L., Rivera, D. P., & Corpus, M. J. H. (2010). Sexual orientation and transgender microaggressions. In D. W. Sue (Ed.), *Microaggressions and marginality: Manifestation, dynamics, and impact* (pp. 217–240). Hoboken: Wiley.
Purdie-Vaughns, V., Davis, P. G., Steele, C. M., & Ditlmann, R. (2008). Social identity contingencies: How diversity cures signal threat or safety for African Americans in mainstream institutions. *Journal of Personality and Social Psychology, 94,* 615–630.
Robinson, T. L. (1999). The intersections of dominant discourses across race, gender, and other identities. *Journal of Counseling and Development, 77,* 73–79.
Rostosky, S., Riggle, E., Gray, B., & Hatton, R. (2007). Minority stress experiences in committed same-sex couple relationships. *Professional Psychology: Research and Practice, 38,* 392–400.
Russell, G. (2007). Internalized homophobia: Lessons from the mobius strip. In G. Russel (Ed.), *Narrative therapy: making meaning, making lives* (pp. 151–173). Thousand Oaks: Sage.
Sears, J. T. (1999). Teaching queerly: Some elementary propositions. In W. J. Letts IV & J.T. Sears (Eds.), *Queering elementary education: Advancing the dialogue about sexualities and schooling* (pp. 3–14). Lanham: Rowman & Littlefield.
Sedgwick, E. K. (1990). Epistemology of the closet. Berkeley: University of California Press.
Schiffman, J. B., Delucia-Waack, J. L., & Gerrity, D. A. (2006). An examination of the construct of homophobia: Prejudice or phobia? *Journal of LGBT Issues in Counseling, 1,* 75–93.
Sinclair, S. L. (2006). Object lessons: A theoretical and empirical study of objectified body consciousness in women. *Journal of Mental Health Counseling, 28,* 48–68.
Smith, L. C. (2009a). Struggling against heteronormativity: The narratives of seventeen heterosexuals. *Dissertation Abstracts International, 71,* 11A.
Smith, L. C. (2009b). The anxiety of affirming heterosexuals when negotiating heteronormativity. *Human Services Education, 29,* 49–58.

Smith, L. C., & Shin, R. Q. (2014). Queer blindfolding: Difference "blindness" towards persons who identify as lesbian, gay, bisexual and transgender. *Journal of Homosexuality, 61,* 940–961. doi:10.1080/00918369.2014.870846.

Smith, L. C., Shin, R. Q., & Officer, L. M. (2012). Moving counseling forward on LGB and transgender issues: Speaking queerly on discourses and microaggressions. *The Counseling Psychologist, 40,* 385408. doi:10.1177/0011000011403165.

Stein, A., & Plummer, K. (1996). I can't even think straight": "Queer" theory and the missing sexual revolution in sociology. In S. Seidman (Ed.), *Queer theory/sociology* (pp. 129–144). Cambridge: Blackwell.

Sue, D. W. (2010a). *Microaggressions in everyday life: Race, gender and sexual orientation.* Hoboken: Wiley.

Sue, D. W. (Ed.). (2010b). *Microaggressions and marginality: Manifestation, dynamics, and impact.* Hoboken: Wiley.

Sue, D.W., Arredondo, P., & McDavis, R. J. (1992). Multicultural counseling competencies and standards: A call to the profession. *Journal of Counseling and Development, 70,* 477–486.

Sue, D. W., Bucceri, J., Lin, A. I., Nadal, K. L., & Torino, G. C. (2009). Racial microaggressions and the Asian American experience. *Asian American Journal of Psychology, 1,* 88–101.

Swim, J. K., Aikin, K. J., Hall, W. S., & Hunter, B. A. (1995). Sexism and racism: Old-fashioned and modern prejudices. *Journal of Personality and Social Psychology, 68,* 199–214.

Warner, M. (2002). *Publics and counterpublics.* New York: Zone Books.

Wilchins, R. (2004). *Queer theory, gender theory: An instant primer.* Los Angeles: Alyson Books.

Winslade, J., Monk, G., & Drewery, W. (1997). Sharpening the critical edge: A social constructionist approach in counselor education. In T. L. Sexton & B. L. Griffin (Eds.), *Constructivist thinking in counseling practice, research, and training* (pp. 228–245). New York: Teachers College Press.

Chapter 4
Colonialism and Multicultural Counseling Competence Research: A Liberatory Analysis

Kevin A. Tate, Edil Torres Rivera and Lisa M. Edwards

The effort to advance the multicultural counseling movement has been hard-fought over the past few decades. We have made huge strides toward creating a more inclusive, relevant, and meaningful counseling experience for all clients. The multicultural counseling movement flowed out of the Civil Rights movement of the 1960s, and has focused the counseling profession on the importance of oppressed and marginalized clients' lived experience in and out of the counseling room (Arredondo et al. 2008). This movement has ushered the counseling profession from apathetic neglect of oppressed populations to acknowledgment of cultural differences for clients through the creation of specialized understanding of clients from various cultural backgrounds (Ponterotto 2010).

In recent years, important work has been done to further advance the multicultural counseling movement through the paradigm of social justice. Social justice has been posited as the fifth force in the counseling profession (Ratts 2009), and has added a more critical, systemic perspective to the framework of multicultural counseling (Lewis et al. 2003, 2011; Toporek et al. 2009). This contemporary movement toward social justice in counseling follows in the tradition of many previous critical thinkers and theories of sociopolitical inequity (e.g., Freire 1970; hooks 2000; Martín-Baró 1991, 1994) who have called into question the colonial and patriarchal foundations on which "truth" is built. Regarding the field of counseling, this social justice paradigm

K. A. Tate (✉)
Department of Counselor Education and Counseling Psychology, Marquette University,
PO Box 1881, 168G Schroeder Health Complex, Milwaukee, WI 53201, USA
e-mail: kevin.a.tate@gmail.com

E. T. Rivera
Department of Counseling, The Chicago School of Professional Psychology,
Room: 4089, 325 North Wells Street, Chicago, IL 60654, USA
e-mail: etorres-rivera@thechicagoschool.edu

L. M. Edwards
Counselor Education and Counseling Psychology, Marquette University,
168G Schroeder Health Complex, Milwaukee, WI 53201, USA
e-mail: Lisa.edwards@marquette.edu

R. D. Goodman, P. C. Gorski (eds.), *Decolonizing "Multicultural" Counseling through Social Justice,* International and Cultural Psychology, DOI 10.1007/978-1-4939-1283-4_4

calls into question the colonial structure in which notions of counseling competence in general, and multicultural counseling competence in particular, have been defined and investigated. In this chapter, we attempt to shine a critical light on these colonial foundations as they pertain to researching multicultural counseling competencies.

The purpose of this chapter is threefold. First, we will describe the colonial foundations of the counseling profession in general, and of the multicultural counseling competency paradigm specifically. Second, using liberation psychology (Martín-Baró 1994) as a lens, we will detail the implications these colonial foundations have for research on multicultural counseling competencies. Third, we will provide suggestions for decolonizing the process of research on multicultural counseling competencies. We aim to provide a map for rethinking multicultural counseling competencies and how the counseling profession might define and investigate such competencies in the future.

Counseling and Colonialism

The Colonization Process

In order to discuss the colonial nature of counseling and counseling competencies, it is necessary to define what we mean by colonization. Laenui (2000) suggests that colonization occurs through: (1) denial of subjects' cultures; (2) attempts to destroy the culture; (3) belittlement and insult of cultural values and practices; (4) token acceptance and accommodation of certain aspects of a culture; and finally (5) a co-opting and control of the expression of cultural values and practices *within* the dominating structure of the colonizer. This framework suggests that colonization is not a simple matter of real estate and political control. Rather, it is a complex process that also involves colonizing the psychological and social worlds of the colonial subjects. These subjects include both the original inhabitants of particular geographic areas and also those who come thereafter, subjugated by the colonizers' sociopolitical system. For example, Native American peoples were first called savages and assumed to have no culture of value (*denial of culture*), systematically killed and repeatedly relocated (*attempts to destroy*), forcibly educated about Western traditions and religion (*belittlement and insult*), allowed to sell cultural tokens or engage in native traditions under close watch (*token acceptance*), and finally their culture was folded into US culture through avenues such as popular media (e.g., "cowboy and Indian" movies) and sports team mascots (e.g., Florida State Seminoles and Washington Redskins; *co-opting within colonized structure*). We now turn to applying this framework of colonization to an analysis of counseling and counseling competencies.

Colonial Foundation of Counseling

Counseling's roots are in psychology, a discipline in which people sought to create "universal" notions of mental health and wellness. Although well-intentioned, psychology as a discipline excluded cultural values and practices that did not fit into a Western, reductionist, individualistic framework (Sue and Sue 2003). These origins of the counseling field can be understood in terms of Laenui's (2000) concept of cultural denial, in that it was assumed that there was no value in understandings of mental health and wellness outside of Western psychological traditions. As a field, psychology went on to actively pathologize cultures and peoples not of the colonial power structure. For example, in a discussion about the intellectual ability of African Americans, Pinter (as cited in Viteles 1928) stated that results from psychological studies "are sufficiently numerous and consistent to point to a racial difference in intelligence" wherein African Americans were assumed to be less intelligent than whites (p. 175). This psychological oppression fits with Laenui's (2000) idea of cultural insult and belittlement, as African Americans were "found," through psychological research, to be psychologically inferior to whites.

Later, scholars attempted to include non-Western cultural values by co-opting them *within* psychology's larger colonial structure. For example, cultural differences in the experience of anxiety have been researched (Heinrichs et al. 2006) by using an instrument (Social Interaction Anxiety Scale, SIAS; Mattick and Clarke 1998) that was constructed to filter subjects' responses through a predetermined, monocultural framework of anxiety. Such research can be understood in terms of Laenui's (2000) concept of co-opting and controlling cultural values and practices within the dominating structure of the colonizer. In studies such as this one, researchers and scholars began to investigate and define "multicultural" concepts, but the research was done through the Western lens of a universal framework of mental health and wellness, as defined by psychological "experts." As such, although such researchers would likely claim cultural responsiveness in their research design, using universal instruments such as the SIAS excludes and marginalizes the varying cultural constructions and expressions of anxiety.

Building on the counseling profession's colonial roots in psychology, counseling competence has also been defined and researched within a colonial framework. Several methods of researching counseling competence (e.g., Larson et al. 1992; Lent et al. 2003) posit that there are competencies that should be applied across all clients and counseling contexts in order to provide effective counseling services. These models include knowledge sets, communication skills, and conceptual frameworks for thinking about clients which are assumed to be crucial to basic counseling competence with any and all clients. The models of competence used to build these methods of research were constructed by counseling "experts," predominantly those in Western academia, that have dictated the frame through which counseling competence should be defined and researched. This colonial nature of contemporary formulations of counseling competence fits within Laenui's (2000) idea of cultural insult and belittlement, in that the client's particular cultural background is ignored, and hence belittled, in favor of counseling competencies that should be helpful to all clients regardless of cultural background. This flies in the face of widely varying differences in how people from marginalized groups might experience and benefit from counseling.

This critical analysis of the colonial nature of Western psychology in general, and notions of counseling competence in particular, shows us that the counseling field is nested within and complicit with the overarching maintenance of Western domination of social, psychological, and scientific thought. It follows from this analysis that the multicultural counseling competence paradigm, and the research conducted about these competencies, was also likely constructed within colonial confines. In order to test this assumption, we now turn to an analysis of the multicultural counseling competency paradigm using a critical social justice lens.

Decolonizing Multicultural Counseling Competence Research

In order to critically analyze the way in which multicultural counseling competence research fits within the larger colonial foundations of counseling, and how we might move toward the decolonization of this paradigm, we will apply liberation psychology (Martín-Baró 1991, 1994) as an analytical tool. The ideals of liberation psychology were first articulated by Ignacio Martín-Baró (1994), and have been developed in significant ways by others (Montero and Sonn 2009; Watkins and Shulman 2008). We begin our analysis by framing our discussion through a liberatory lens.

Reframing the Discussion: Searching for "Lost History"

Martín-Baró (1994) said that, in order to begin the process of liberation from colonial oppression, we must first look for "lost history." Specifically, we need to look for information that has been excluded or hidden by the colonization process. This is a crucial first step toward a decolonized understanding of counseling and mental health in that, without an understanding of the actual etiology of systemic oppression and subsequent problems, true understandings of any counseling issue cannot be attained. We will begin our search for lost information by analyzing unexamined patterns and assumptions embedded in multicultural counseling competence research.

Multicultural counseling competence (Arredondo et al. 1996) is a contemporary paradigm of counseling competence that is based on attaining knowledge, awareness, and skills that lead to effective counseling practice with people of various cultural backgrounds and identities. Multicultural counseling competence research has focused primarily on counselors' self-reported competence (e.g., Kim et al. 2003; Ponterotto et al. 2002) or on expert ratings of said competence (e.g., Cartwright et al. 2008; LaFromboise et al. 1991). Moreover, the frameworks and instruments used to research this type of competence are built on universal, expert-based notions of cultural competence. For example, the Multicultural Awareness, Knowledge, and Skills Survey-Counselor Edition-Revised (MAKSS-CE-R; Kim et al. 2003) and the Multicultural Counseling Inventory (MCI; Sodowsky et al. 1994) are psychometric instruments that were designed by academics who are deemed, via academic publications, expert in multicultural counseling competence. Further, these two instruments assess competence by asking counselors to rate their own skills, thereby placing the counselor in the expert position of defining competence. This reveals that such research methods are built on and perpetuate the colonial process of defining multicultural competence using a universal, expert-based approach supported by Western academic institutions. The question that arises here is, where are the voices of those that multicultural counseling competence is intended to benefit?

Given that the focus of multicultural counseling competence is on marginalized and oppressed clients, it might be expected that a significant amount research on this topic would include the voice of such clients. On the surface, there does seem to be a growing body of research in this area that includes voices of clients (e.g., Constantine 2002, 2007; Fuertes and Brobst 2002; Kim and Atkinson 2002; Kim et al. 2002; Kim et al. 2009; Owen et al. 2011). Upon deeper inspection though, one finds that these studies are also clearly based on universal, expert-based notions of cultural competence. For example, Lowe (2005) attempted to study Asian American counseling clients' experience of their counselors using an adapted version of the Cross-Cultural Counseling Inventory (CCCI-R; LaFromboise et al. 1991). Like the instruments discussed earlier, this instrument was designed by academics, and counseling clients are restricted in their ability to provide feedback due to the closed-ended, quantitative, limited response format of the instrument.

It seems that, although the voices of clients have been included in some controlled instances, multicultural counseling competence research exists within Laenui's (2000) last stage of colonization—the co-opting and control of clients' unique cultural values, practices, and perceptions (what they bring to counseling) *within* the dominating colonial structure (universal models of multicultural counseling competence). This pattern of systematically excluding clients from equal participation in the process of defining and researching multicultural counseling competence has been "lost" in the mainstream narrative about such research. As such, it is important to ask, why is this so, and what does it mean?

Analyzing Found Information: De-ideologization

Given that marginalized and oppressed clients have been systematically excluded from defining and investigating multicultural counseling research, we now turn to making sense of this state of affairs. Martín-Baró (1991, 1994) pointed out that dominant social and political forces (e.g., the Catholic Church, universities, media campaigns, and governmental bureaucracies) establish "realities" about the lived experience of oppressed peoples, and that these realities should be examined for their veracity. He termed this process of critical examination the *de-ideologization* of everyday dominant cultural messages. Applying this process to the topic at hand, we find that the paradigm of multicultural counseling competence has been constructed and researched based largely on the expert opinions of those within colonial power structures (e.g., universities and counseling centers). Even when the voices of clients have been included, they have been selectively filtered through expert-based, universal frameworks. As such, the implicit assumption that seems to underlie multicultural counseling research is that marginalized and oppressed clients do not have anything inherently valuable to offer in the research process. This is a paternalistic, colonial mindset in that oppressed clients' voices are only valuable when filtered through predetermined instruments and methods. This is particularly problematic given the strengths and wisdom such clients have to offer.

The Strength of the People: An Essential Component of Liberation

Marginalized and oppressed clients are not simply subjects to be studied or clients to be fixed by counselors and researchers. Rather, they have inherent strengths and gifts to offer in the defining and study of multicultural counseling competence. Martín-Baró (1994) described the strength of oppressed peoples of his own country, El Salvador, by marveling over "their ability to deliver and to sacrifice for the collective good, their tremendous faith in the human capacity to change the world, [and] their hope for tomorrow that keeps being violently denied to them" (p. 31). This strengths-based approach allows the social scientist to depend on those who are oppressed to produce the tools and energy that lead to liberation. Further, utilizing the strengths of oppressed peoples takes the tools that have been used to cope with oppressive circumstances for generations and transforms them into an indispensable tool for liberation.

In terms of investigating multicultural counseling competence, utilizing the strengths of oppressed populations means that we should include their unique and contextually accurate perspectives about multicultural counseling competence. To be more specific, oppressed and marginalized clients have what can be considered a more accurate view of counselors' multicultural counseling competence given that it is the sociopolitical position of such clients that necessitates such competencies. For example, certain cultural strengths, values, and experiences may contribute to well-being and may be unique to the lives of diverse individuals (Sue and Constantine 2003; Walters and Simoni 2002). As an illustration, bicultural individuals have been found to have flexible responses to contextual cues and are better able to adapt their behavior in cross-cultural settings than those who are monocultural (Benet-Martinez and Haritos 2005; Benet-Martinez et al. 2006; Hong et al. 2000). This "social savvy" is a potentially powerful source of information when attempting to investigate counselors' multicultural counseling competence, particularly given the centrality of the counseling relationship in culturally competent counseling (Roysircar, Hubbell, & Gard 2003). Applying this social intelligence, clients might provide us with as yet undiscovered aspects or frameworks of counseling competence. Such assets represent culture and context-specific strengths that flow from individuals' lived cultural experience as oppressed persons (Christopher and Hickinbottom 2008), but which have yet to be fully acknowledged as strengths to be utilized in the defining and investigation of multicultural counseling competencies. We must move away from co-opting clients' voices within predetermined frameworks, and toward research methods that systematically and collaboratively include such clients' voices in the research process.

Critical Collaborative Inquiry: Seeking Conscientization

Martín-Baró (1994) outlines an inquiry process called *problematization* that is directly relevant to researching multicultural counseling competence. Although Martín-Baró (1994) included problematization as a critical aspect of his theory, he and other liberation psychologists (e.g., Jiménez-Domínguez 2009; Montero 2009) point toward Freire (1970) as the originator of this concept. In short, problematization involves utilizing a de-ideologized understanding of lost history, along with the strengths of oppressed peoples, to investigate problems being faced by these peoples. This process, obviously, is closely related to a discussion of research process and methods. More specifically, using this as a method for investigating multicultural counseling competence means that we must, necessarily, include clients' unfiltered lived experience of, and opinions about, actual counseling sessions in the research process. By utilizing the unique strengths of such clients, it is possible to gain a more accurate understanding of marginalized and oppressed clients' *lived experience* of counseling. Such an understanding is, by nature, a tool for decolonization in that it systematically gives equal voice to individuals who have had their voices assimilated into a dominant framework. Egalitarian inclusion of clients in the research and defining of multicultural competence should also be considered an ongoing, recursive process of encountering and creating knowledge. The goal of this process is what Martín-Baró (1994) and Freire (1970) termed critical conscientization.

The traditional (i.e., colonial) goal of psychological and counseling research is to collect data, analyze the data within expert-based frameworks, and create static theoretical structures that should be applied across contexts and individuals. In opposition to this goal, a primary goal of liberation psychology is the awakening of critical conscientization (critical consciousness) in the person or group (Freire 1970; Martín-Baró 1991, 1994). Specifically, critical consciousness "is not simply becoming aware of a certain fact, but rather it is a process of change" (Martín-Baró 1991, p. 227). In other words, to become conscious of reality in this sense is to become aware of, and involved in, a process of continual discovery and action related to "truth." In the context of defining and investigating multicultural counseling competence, conscientization requires that counselors and scholars be engaged in an ongoing process of collaborative discovery that is centered on marginalized clients' actual experience of, and unfiltered input about, the counseling process. It is not enough to simply administer a psychometric instrument, calculate results, and assume one has arrived at some "truth." Instead, the research questions themselves should be based on unfiltered knowledge that is provided by oppressed and marginalized clients (Watkins and Shulman 2008). Further, such clients must be engaged in the analysis process in order to maintain the process of critical consciousness. In order to achieve and maintain critical consciousness about multicultural counseling competencies, it is necessary to avoid simply "harvesting" data from clients, and to continually engage these clients in our discovery process on this topic.

Given the comprehensive changes in the research process we are suggesting here, it is clear that current definitions of, and knowledge about, multicultural counseling competence must be reconsidered and critically analyzed. Further, such a comprehensive reconsideration should take the form we have just described—a collaborative, critical, cyclical inquiry process that is aimed at liberation from colonial constraints, and should lead to the formation of definitions that are rooted in the lived experience of counseling clients. Even so, in this process, we must also embrace the wisdom and efforts of professionals who have dedicated their careers to the multicultural movement in counseling.

Engaging the Wisdom of the Elders: Looking Back to Move Forward

In this chapter, we have proposed a possible method for the decolonizing the defining and research of multicultural counseling competence. This method is incomplete, though, if we exclude the effort and wisdom of those dedicated elders who have researched this topic in the past. Through a cyclical process of collaborative critical inquiry by scholars, counselors, and clients, it may be possible to look back with a critical eye at colonial histories in movement toward a liberated future. Watkins and Shulman (2008) describe this tension between a critical view of the past and a creative view of the future:

> One motion is deconstructive and critical, looking backward at what we have been doing and thinking that is dysfunctional, dissociative, and destructive; the other motion is moving forward, toward new capacities for imagining, voicing, connecting, empathizing, and celebrating self and others in community. (pp. 28–29)

In true egalitarian partnership, counselors, scholars, and clients may be able to throw off the colonial structures and assumptions of the past, and imagine a future in which counseling competence is defined and researched in service of those it was first intended to serve and support.

General and Multicultural Counseling Competence: A False Dichotomy

The process of conducting multicultural counseling competence research is, in theory, an effort to discover new knowledge that will inform effective, socially just counseling practice. But we have argued that such research is based on foundations that are colonial in form. So, there is a need for a transformative shift in how counseling competencies are defined and investigated. Researchers, counselors, and clients should come together in a collegial community to begin systematic dialogue about what constitutes competent counseling practice. It is at this point that we leave behind the term *multicultural* from the counseling competence discussion. This is intentional, as we believe our proposed mode of defining and researching competence is one that applies to the unique lived experience of all counseling clients across their multiple, intersecting identities and contexts (Burman 2003). So, we are further proposing the elimination of the false dichotomy between "multicultural counseling competence" and "general counseling competence" given the colonial structures that underlie them both. When asking what it means to be competent with a particular client, we should be systematically and collaboratively including the voice of such clients in this inquiry. This process of egalitarian inclusion in the research process becomes particularly important in regard to marginalized and oppressed populations, but is relevant to all clients given the inherent power differential present between clients and counselors, and clients and researchers. This philosophical shift has several implications for the counseling profession.

Implications

The Need for Transformation: A New Role for Counselors and Researchers

In order to engage in a decolonization and liberation, researchers and counselors also must be engaged in these liberating processes on a personal level. Specifically, there is no completely objective researcher or counselor. Instead, one's role

> becomes that of a convener, a witness, a coparticipant, a mirror, and a holder of faith for process through which those who have been silenced may discover their own capacities for historical memory, critical analysis, utopian imagination, and transformative social action. (Watkins and Shulman 2008, p. 26)

Such individuals would be primarily focused on the transformation of peoples and communities rather than on treatment adherence or improving credentials. As such, researchers must view themselves as collaborative partners, seeking to liberate both themselves and others from colonial constraints.

Research Methodologies

Traditional Methods

While traditional quantitative and qualitative research methods have been used to maintain the colonial status quo, it may be possible to use them in service of the process we have proposed in this chapter. For example, it may be possible to create quantitative instruments in collaboration with the clients with which they are intended to be used. Or, it might be possible to conduct qualitative inquiry with clients about their views on counseling competence. Although such methods may be useful, they must be couched in larger research frameworks that are liberatory in nature. One such method is participatory action research.

Participatory Action Research

Participatory action research (PAR) methodologies hold the most promise for decolonizing the process of researching counseling competencies. This method of research is broad in scope, and may include both quantitative and qualitative components (Creswell and Clark 2007). On a philosophical level, PAR is:

> A process in which people (researchers and participants) develop goals and methods, participate in the gathering and analysis of data, and implement the results in a way that will raise critical consciousness and promote change in the lives of those involved. (Kidd and Kral 2005, p. 187)

For example, PAR has been used to research and actively address the effect of deportation on Central American families (Lykes et al. 2011), to develop culturally-anchored understandings of native Alaskan alcohol use (Mohatt et al. 2004), and to engage urban youth in a collaborative description and transformation of their community (McIntyre 2000). At the base, PAR is designed to include the voices of marginalized and oppressed populations in an intentional process of collaborative social change, and liberation psychology has been often expressed through the PAR process. As Watkins and Shulman aruged, "Liberation psychologists are committed to co-creating *with* others contexts for inquiry that are dialogical and emancipatory."

PAR provides an ideal framework for developing a collaborative, systematic understanding of counseling competence that includes the voice of client, counselor, and scholar. One of the major challenges with PAR is that there are no manualized instructions for it. Rather, each study is specific to a particular context (Kidd and Kral 2005). When applied to the study of counseling competence, this means that researchers will need to choose a particular community/population and context, and develop a systematic method for collaborative inquiry about what constitutes competence. PAR also takes a significant amount of time to plan and conduct given that it is necessary to intentionally allow research participants to guide the process of asking research questions, collecting data, and analyzing data.

An example may be helpful in conceptualizing an application of PAR. Let us imagine a community organization that offers counseling services in a predominantly Latina/Latino area wherein many of the residents are recent immigrants to the USA. Further, most members of this community live on very meager wages, but also display a pronounced pride in their membership within the community. Applying PAR to studying counseling competence in this context would involve recruiting community members to join the research process in service of bettering the community for all residents. These community members would work with researchers to develop research questions that are relevant to mental wellness and counseling; collect data; and make sense of the data. Finally, the results would be used to change, or develop new, counseling practices that are relevant within the context of *this particular* community. Further, such a research process might provide opportunities for collaborative, system-level interventions that address sociopolitical sources of mental maladies. While the results and process of such research may certainly be applicable to other similar contexts, this would be a side-effect of such a study. The primary goal of PAR in this instance is collaborative inquiry aimed at producing meaningful changes for the particular community that was engaged in the research project. Specifically, a context-specific model of meaningful counseling interventions and counseling competence would have been developed, thereby informing counselors working within this community. Moreover, systemic changes may be made possible through such a process. To be sure, this is time consuming and complex, but powerful in its ability to empower the clients who have been marginalized and oppressed by colonial methods of research and counseling.

Counseling Practice

As discussed earlier, liberation psychology posits that there is no real division between theory and practice. This also applies to counseling practice, and applies to both practitioners and scholars. For counseling practitioners, the argument we have made suggests that a client should never be separated from the process of developing theories of counseling competence. Further, counselors should be including their clients in this process of theory development and research. Referring back to the example of PAR, counselors should be actively involved in designing and facilitating research projects. For counseling scholars, our argument suggests that they should be founding their research process and questions on the perceptions and expertise of both counselors and clients. Further, researchers should provide the resources (e.g., time, research expertise, funding) to which practitioners may not have access. In community, clients, counselors, and researchers may be able to erase the colonial barrier between theory and practice as well as that between researcher and subject. Practitioners serve a crucial role in this effort, as it is counselors who have the opportunity to continually and systematically engage their clients in a dialogue about counseling competence from the clients' perspectives.

Summary

The counseling profession has an opportunity to decolonize our understanding and definitions of counseling competence through collaborative engagement with our clients in the research process. The multicultural counseling movement was founded on the assumption that many clients were being treated unjustly within traditional, universal models of counseling practice. We are suggesting that the counseling profession needs to continue in the tradition of transformation through completely throwing off the assumptions of expert-based "truth" as the foundation for determining what counseling should look like. We value the contributions of researchers and counselors to this process, but without the equal inclusion of clients, we will remain locked within colonial sociopolitical structures.

References

Arredondo, P., Toporek, R., Brown, S. P., Jones, J., Locke, D. C., Sanchez, J., & Stadler, H. (1996). Operationalization of the multicultural counseling competencies. *Journal of Multicultural Counseling and Development, 24,* 42–78.

Arredondo, P., Tovar-Blank, Z., & Parham, T. (2008). Challenges and promises of becoming a culturally competent counselor in a sociopolitical era of change and empowerment. *Journal of Counseling and Development, 86,* 261–268

Benet-Martinez, V., & Haritos, J. (2005). Bicultural identity integration: Components and psychosocial antecedents. *Journal of Personality, 73,* 1015–1050.

Benet-Martinez, V., Lee, F., & Leu, J. (2006). Biculturalism and cognitive complexity: Expertise in cultural representations. *Journal of Cross-Cultural Psychology*, *37*, 386–407.

Burman, E. (2003). From difference to intersectionality: Challenges and resources. *European Journal of Psychotherapy, Counseling & Health, 6,* 293–308.

Cartwright, B. Y., Daniels, J., & Zhang, S. (2008). Assessing multicultural competence: Perceived versus demonstrated performance. *Journal of Counseling & Development, 86*(3), 318–322.

Christopher, J. C., & Hickinbottom, S. (2008). Positive psychology, ethnocentrism, and the disguised ideology of individualism. *Theory & Psychology, 18(5)*, 563–589.

Constantine, M. G. (2002). Racism attitudes, White racial identity attitudes, and multicultural counseling competence in school counselor trainees. *Counselor Education and Supervision, 41*(3), 162–174.

Constantine, M. G. (2007). Racial microaggressions against African American clients in cross-racial counseling relationships. *Journal of Counseling Psychology, 54*(1), 1.

Creswell, J. W., & Clark, V. L. P. (2007). *Designing and conducting mixed methods research.* Thousand Oaks: Sage.

Fuertes, J. N., & Brobst, K. (2002). Clients' ratings of counselor multicultural competency. *Cultural Diversity and Ethnic Minority Psychology; Cultural Diversity and Ethnic Minority Psychology, 8*(3), 214.

Freire, P. (1970). *Pedagogy of the oppressed.* New York: Continuum.

Heinrichs, N., Rapee, R. M., Alden, L. A., Bogels, S., Hofmann, S. G., Oh, K. J., & Sakano, Y. (2006). Cultural differences in perceived social norms and social anxiety. *Behavior Research and Therapy, 44,* 1187–1197.

Hong, Y. Y., Morris, M., Chiu, C.Y., & Benet-Martinez, V. (2000) Multicultural minds: A dynamic constructivist approach to culture and cognition. *American Psychologist, 55,* 709–20.

Hooks, b. (2000). *Feminist theory: From margins to center*. Cambridge, MA: South End Press

Jiménez-Domínguez, B. (2009). Ignacio Martín-Baró's social psychology of liberation: Situated knowledge and critical commitment against objectivism. In M. Montero & C. C. Sonn (Eds.), *Psychology of liberation: Theory and applications* (pp. 37–50). New York: Springer.

Kidd, S. A., & Kral, M. J. (2005). Practicing participatory action research. *Journal of Counseling Psychology, 52*(2), 187.

Kim, B. S., & Atkinson, D. R. (2002). Asian American client adherence to Asian cultural values, counselor expression of cultural values, couselor ethnicity, and career counseling process. *Journal of Counseling Psychology, 49*(1), 3.

Kim, B. S., Cartwright, B. Y., Asay, P. A., & D'Andrea, M. J. (2003). A revision of the multicultural awareness, knowledge, and skills survey-counselor edition. *Measurement and Evaluation in Counseling and Development, 36*(3), 161–180.

Kim, B. S. K., Li, L. C., & Liang, T. H. (2002). Effects of Asian American client adherence to Asian cultural values, session goal, and counselor emphasis of client expression on career counseling process. *Journal of Counseling Psychology, 49*(3), 342.

Kim, B. S. K., Ng, G. F., & Ahn, A. J. (2009). Client adherence to Asian cultural values, common factors in counseling, and session outcome with Asian American clients at a university counseling center. *Journal of Counseling and Development, 87,* 131–142.

Laenui, P. (2000). Processes of decolonization. In Battiste, M. (Ed.), *Reclaiming indigenous voice and vision* (pp. 150–160). Vancouver: University of British Columbia Press.

LaFromboise, T. D., Coleman, H. L., & Hernandez, A. (1991). Development and factor structure of the cross-cultural counseling inventory—revised. *Professional Psychology: Research and Practice, 22*(5), 380.

Larson, L. M., Suzuki, L. A., Gillespie, K. N., Potenza, M. T., Bechtel, M. A., & Toulouse, A. L. (1992). Development and validation of the counseling self-estimate inventory. *Journal of Counseling Psychology, 39*(1), 105.

Lent, R. W., Hill, C. E., & Hoffman, M. A. (2003). Development and validation of the counselor activity self-efficacy scales. *Journal of Counseling Psychology, 50*(1), 97

Lewis, J., Arnold, M. S., House, R., & Toporek, R. (2003). Advocacy competencies. http://www.counseling.org/resources/competencies/advocacy_competencies.pdf. Retrieved 1 Nov 2012.

Lewis, J. A., Ratts, M. J., Paladino, D. A., & Toporek, R. L. (2011). social justice counseling and advocacy: developing new leadership roles and competencies. *Journal for Social Action in Counseling and Psychology, 3*(1), 5–16.

Lowe, S. M. (2005). Integrating collectivist values into career counseling with Asian Americans: A test of cultural responsiveness. *Journal of Multicultural Counseling and Development, 33*(3), 134–145.

Lykes, M. B., Hershberg, R. M., & Brabeck, K. M. (2011). Methodological challenges in participatory action research with undocumented Central American migrants. *Journal for Social Action in Counseling and Psychology, 3*(2), 22–35

Martín-Baró, I. (1991). Developing a critical consciousness through the university curriculum. In J. Hasset and H. Lacey (Eds.) *Towards a society that serves its people: The intellectual contributions of El Salvador's murdered Jesuits* (pp. 220–244). Washington, DC: Georgetown University Press.

Martín-Baró, I. (1994). *Writings for a liberation psychology*. A. Aron & S. Corne (Eds.). Cambridge, MA: Harvard University Press.

Mattick, R. P., & Clarke, J. C. (1998). Development and validation of measures of social phobia scrutiny fear and social interaction anxiety. *Behaviour Research and Therapy, 36*, 455–470.

McIntyre, A. (2000). Constructing meaning about violence, school, and community: Participatory action research with urban youth. *The Urban Review, 32,* 123–154.

Montero, M. (2009). Models for liberation: Critical consciousness in action. In M. Montero & C. C. Sonn (Eds.), *Psychology of liberation: Theory and applications*. New York: Springer.

Montero, M., & Sonn, C. C. (Eds.). (2009). *Psychology of liberation: Theory and applications*. New York: Springer.

Mohatt, G. V., Hazel, K. L., Allen, J., Stachelrodt, M., Hensel, C., & Fath, R. (2004). Unheard Alaska: Culturally anchored participatory action research on sobriety with Alaska natives. *American Journal of Community Psychology, 33*(3), 263–273.

Owen, J., Leach, M. M., Wampold, B., & Rodolfa, E. (2011). Client and therapist variability in clients' perceptions of their therapists' multicultural competencies. *Journal of Counseling Psychology, 58*(1), 1.

Ponterotto, J. G. (2010). Multicultural personality: An evolving theory of optimal functioning in culturally heterogeneous societies. *The Counseling Psychologist, 38*(5), 714–758.

Ponterotto, J. G., Gretchen, D., Utsey, S. O., Rieger, B. P., & Austin, R. (2002). A revision of the multicultural counseling awareness scale. *Journal of Multicultural Counseling and Development, 30*(3), 153–180.

Roysircar, G., Hubbell, R., & Gard (2003). Multicultural research on counselor and client variables. Handbook of multicultural competencies in counseling and psy chology, 247–266.

Ratts, M. J. (2009). Social justice counseling: Toward the development of a fifth force among counseling paradigms. *Journal of Humanistic Counseling, Education and Development, 48*(2), 160–172.

Sodowsky, G. R., Taffe, R. C., Gutkin, T. B., & Wise, S. L. (1994). Development of the multicultural counseling inventory: A self-report measure of cultural competencies. *Journal of Counseling Psychology, 41,* 137–148.

Sue, D. W., & Constantine, M. G. (2003). Optimal human functioning in people of color in the United States. In B. W. Walsh (Ed.), *Counseling psychology and optimal human functioning* (pp. 151–169). New Jersey: Lawrence Erlbaum.

Sue, D. W., & Sue, D. (2003). *Counseling the culturally diverse*. New York: Wiley.

Toporek, R. L., Lewis, J. A., & Crethar, H. C. (2009). Promoting systemic change through the ACA advocacy competencies. *Journal of Counseling & Development, 87*(3), 260–268.

Viteles, M. S., (1928). The mental status of the Negro. *Annals of the American Academy of Political and Social Science, 140,* 166–177.

Walters, K. L., & Simoni, J. M. (2002). Reconceptualizing native women's health: An "Indigenist" stress-coping model. *American Journal of Public Health, 92,* 520–524

Watkins, M., & Shulman, H. (2008). *Toward psychologies of liberation*. New York: Palgrave Macmillan.

Chapter 5
A Liberatory Approach to Trauma Counseling: Decolonizing Our Trauma-Informed Practices

Rachael D. Goodman

> *Trauma is socially produced.* To speak of psychosocial trauma is to emphasize that trauma is produced socially and, therefore, that understanding and resolving it require not only treating the problems of individuals but also its social roots, in other words, the traumatogenic structures or social conditions. (Martín-Baró 1994, p. 125)

The term *trauma* is now commonly used both by mental health professionals and lay people, indicating widespread acknowledgement that traumatic experiences can have negative and lasting effects on individuals. The significant impact of traumatic events on mental and physical health is increasingly well documented in clinical research and can also be seen in our everyday lives when we turn on the news or hear stories of traumatic events, such as a school shooting, refugees displaced by political conflict, or rape on a college campus. While the Western study of traumatic events and their impacts is somewhat recent, these events are now commonly accepted as legitimate and important factors that may influence mental health. As such, clinical practice should not focus solely on intrinsic or intrapsychic causes of mental illness; rather, it should take into account the environmental factors that may cause harm. Counselors, psychologists, and other mental health professionals generally agree that we should work with our clients to identify the impacts of trauma and intervene to ameliorate these effects.

This increased focus on trauma has given rise to the concept of *trauma-informed* practices, a moniker that connotes attention to a client's traumatic experiences within human service provision generally, and mental health care specifically (Harris and Fallot 2001). In some ways, the creation of trauma-informed practices is a critical step forward in counseling and psychology because this framework acknowledges that trauma can have complex and long-lasting impacts on clients and must be addressed throughout all human services in order for our work to be effective. As noted, a plethora of research studies show that trauma may lead to problems in mental and physical health, personal relationships, educational achievement, and

---

R. D. Goodman (✉)
George Mason University, 4400 University Drive, Fairfax, VA 22030, USA
e-mail: rgoodma2@gmu.edu

R. D. Goodman, P. C. Gorski (eds.), *Decolonizing "Multicultural" Counseling through Social Justice,* International and Cultural Psychology, DOI 10.1007/978-1-4939-1283-4_5

more (e.g., Flaherty et al. 2006; Kerig et al. 2009). Commonly discussed symptoms of trauma include flashbacks, nightmares, avoidance, hyperarousal, depression, and anxiety (American Psychiatric Association 2013; Borja and Callahan 2009). Within the fields of counseling and psychology, the focus on understanding and healing trauma has greatly increased. We now see numerous scholarly publications and intervention programs on traumatology (the study and treatment of trauma). Furthermore, while these outcomes are of concern for all individuals, families, and communities who experience traumatic events, members of marginalized social groups (e.g., people of color, people living in poverty) are often impacted the most by traumatic experiences. Due to systemic injustices, members of marginalized social groups are at greater risk for experiencing traumatic events, and often experience greater difficulty recovering from such events due to differential recovery resources and ineffective services that do not address their unique experiences of trauma, which I will explore further in this chapter. As such, the rising focus on trauma in general has been coupled with a greater attention to the experiences of marginalized groups, so that we commonly link trauma-informed services with a focus on individuals from marginalized groups.

Consequently, there is a tendency, even among well-intentioned counselors and psychologists who serve marginalized clients, to believe that trauma-informed services inherently enact social justice simply because these practices address the impact of trauma. While the importance of addressing trauma is not in question, it is imperative that we critically examine the practices that are being operationalized as trauma-informed and question how and in what ways they might actually perpetuate injustice or a colonial perspective. In other words, we must ask, how is the concept of trauma-informed services being *enacted* in clinical settings and scholarly works? Indeed, upon closer examination, many of these well-intentioned trauma-informed practices operationalize a view of trauma that is flawed because of its narrowness and, therefore, fails to enact social justice. More specifically, the perspectives espoused by current scholarship on trauma-informed services are problematic in the following ways: (1) they fail to address the systemic injustices that create vulnerability to trauma (e.g., economic disparities that force working families to live in areas prone to flooding), (2) they do not include systemic or contextual sources of trauma (e.g., racist bullying encountered by a Haitian American child at school), and (3) they do not insist on addressing these systemic factors in order to prevent and ameliorate traumatic experiences (e.g., immigration policies that deport parents of young US-citizen children and separate families). Without addressing these three areas, trauma-informed practices perpetuate a *colonial* perspective in that they ignore societal factors and systemic forces that perpetuate injustice and they limit treatment of trauma (that is produced by these factors) to narrowly defined events and conventional (nonsystemic) inventions.

Rather than adhering to these limited views of trauma and trauma treatment, counselors and psychologists seeking to enact *decolonizing,* social justice-based clinical practice and scholarship should challenge these narrow frameworks and revise the current trauma-informed framework to include systemic understandings as central to trauma-informed work. Building on the growing attention to trauma-informed practices and their infusion in a variety of settings, social justice-minded counselors and psychologists must insist that a more systemic and comprehensive traumatology be used, including interventions that attend to systemic forces that engender trauma. Using that framework, in this chapter I outline the current perspectives that are generally used in trauma-informed practices; deconstruct the narrow view of trauma espoused by this and other frameworks; and provide a more comprehensive, social justice-orientated view of trauma and interventions.

Trauma-Informed Perspectives

Over the past 15 years, human service providers have begun using the term "trauma-informed" to describe the delivery of services that are informed by an understanding of trauma (Harris and Fallot 2001, p. 5). Trauma-informed human service systems (e.g., counseling or social work) are provided using a lens that acknowledges the complex and ongoing role of traumatic events in an individual's life. Trauma-informed service providers screen for a history of trauma and assess for trauma symptoms, including the ways in which trauma coping might manifest (Fallot and Harris 2001).

As I see it, trauma-informed perspectives have two important strengths. First, considering the fact that traumatic experiences are common but underreported, trauma-informed services can engender more comprehensive and effective mental health services by ensuring that practitioners conduct in-depth assessments of trauma (Drabble et al. 2013; Harris and Fallot 2001; Hodgon et al. 2013). This can help service providers address the underlying issues that clients do not initially identify but that certainly impact their mental health and ability to thrive. Trauma-informed services also have particular benefits when used in settings that are not focused on mental health since it is especially likely that trauma will be overlooked in these settings. One important example is the use in school settings where traumatic stress symptoms are hard to distinguish from other types of difficulties in children, including attention-deficit hyperactivity disorder, autism, and behavior problems (Goodman and West-Olatunji 2010; Levine and Kline 2007). As such, educators sometimes mistake signs of traumatic stress for other types of concerns, thus children who are in need of mental health services to address trauma are unlikely to receive these services. Instead, these students might be tracked for low ability, given discipline referrals, or provided with inappropriate special education services. Scholars have begun to show that using a trauma-informed perspective in schools can provide students with services that more appropriately acknowledge and address their mental health and learning needs (e.g., Dods 2013).

Second, trauma-informed scholars advocate for several positive changes in human service delivery. They posit that human service providers should attempt to address a client's underlying and interconnected concerns instead of only treating symptoms or seeing life events and concerns as separate and unrelated (Harris and

Fallot 2001). For instance, a boy is repeatedly sexually abused by his uncle and experiences anxiety and fear. As an adult, he begins drinking to numb the ongoing anxiety and has difficulty in romantic relationships. According to Harris and Fallot (2001), service providers should address these concerns as interrelated, including understanding how the traumatic events have ongoing impacts. The trauma-informed perspective also advocates for collaborative, strengths-based services that facilitate empowerment and an active role for trauma survivors (Drabble et al. 2013; Elliott et al. 2005). This is in contrast with what Harris and Fallot (2001) describe as traditional approaches that focus on clients' problems and create a hierarchical relationship in which the practitioner is in a position of power and the client is passive. Empowerment is often noted as a particularly important construct when working with trauma survivors because they are often disempowered by traumatic events and/or by post-trauma symptoms that continue to affect their lives. For instance, a woman who is raped in her college dorm then feels, rightfully, unsafe in her living space; she also fears going to places on campus that may be similarly unsafe and/or that might trigger flashbacks. This keeps her from attending her classes and being able to engage academically and socially as she would like, and it generates an overwhelming and continuing feeling of disempowerment.

Indeed, the importance of including a trauma-informed understanding in both clinical (e.g., counseling agencies) and community (e.g., nonclinical, schools) settings cannot be overstated. We cannot turn back; it is critical that scholarship and practice acknowledge the very real and significant impact that traumatic events can have on individuals, families, and communities. Even in clinical settings in which conceptualization and treatment of mental health concerns are the focus, clinicians may fail to assess for or treat trauma. For instance, a therapist counseling a family whose child is acting out might focus on treating the problem behaviors or developing healthy attachments without examining the underlying causes of the behaviors and attachment problems, such as traumatic experiences in early childhood or the impact of a parent's own trauma. A trauma-informed approach places the issue of trauma in the forefront, hopefully ensuring that clinicians *will* assess for and address any traumatic events that have occurred.

Unfortunately, despite the best of intentions, the ways in which trauma-informed practices are implemented have significant shortcomings. The growing popularity of trauma-informed services gives the false impression that this perspective is truly a comprehensive view that addresses traumatic experiences and that, as such, it naturally would help ameliorate a broad range of traumatic impacts, including those related to social injustices. In its current state, the trauma-informed literature describes individually focused interventions that fail to address the systemic factors related to trauma. This perspective is generated from the long-held narrow and limited view of trauma within the mental health fields. Next, I examine this narrow view of trauma, how it functions to perpetuate the status quo, and how it prevents a socially just trauma-informed practice.

A Narrow View of Trauma

Much of the Western study of trauma has been influenced by the inclusion of post-traumatic stress disorder (PTSD) in the American Psychiatric Association's (APA) *Diagnostic and Statistical Manual of Mental Disorders* (*DSM*) (Halpern and Tramontin 2007; Herman 1997). As such, the *DSM* definition of a traumatic event largely dictates what scholars and clinicians consider traumatic experiences. Further, the *DSM* criteria for PTSD frames the mental health symptoms expected to result from trauma, which then creates the basis for the tools and techniques that clinicians use to screen and assess for trauma among clients (e.g., asking a client about nightmares or difficulty concentrating).

In some ways, the inclusion of PTSD in the *DSM* was a significant step forward for the study and treatment of trauma. The diagnosis legitimized the experiences of trauma survivors and generated interest in and funding for traumatology. The PTSD diagnosis is unique from most other diagnoses in that it identifies an external source as the cause of the symptoms, rather than suggesting that the symptoms are intrinsic or intrapsychic.

However, the understanding of trauma has always been political, even before its inclusion in the *DSM*. As Judith Herman described in her landmark book, *Trauma and Recovery* (Herman 1997), Sigmund Freud was one of the earliest Western clinicians and scholars to study what was generally termed *hysteria* and viewed as an inherent weakness within women. In his study, he found that the underlying cause of this "character flaw" was actually rampant sexual abuse of women. This claim was shocking and controversial so Freud quickly succumbed to societal expectations, withdrew his theory, and developed a new theory attributing hysteria to women's dysfunctional sexual desires—a theory that is widely known, unlike his earlier findings.

This example, while historical, underscores that societies and those with power and control within societies have an interest in defining trauma in particular ways. To define a traumatic experience means to declare what is outside of the acceptable range of behavior. It also means to declare that reactions to such experiences are valid reactions to unacceptable experiences and that these reactions should not be pathologized or seen as intrinsic character flaws. If we shift the lens to look at what has *happened* to a person rather than focusing on what is *wrong* with a person, we are forced to consider society's ills and the ways in which unjust institutions, practices, and policies have actually *created* trauma. Indeed, we can no longer look at trauma symptoms without examining what in society prompted these symptoms.

Advocates for justice in a number of spheres have been attempting to do just that. In particular, the Veteran's and Women's movements of the 1960s and 1970s focused on lobbying for the inclusion of PTSD in the *DSM*, seeing it as a way to legitimize traumatic experiences as causes of mental health symptoms (Herman 1997). As such, when the *DSM-III* was published with PTSD included for the first time (APA 1980), it was considered a significant victory for clinicians and activists who had seen the horrific and long-ignored effects of trauma on individuals, including veterans and women.

This "victory," however, has fallen short of achieving justice in a number of ways. First, the PTSD definition of a traumatic event—and the understanding of trauma and trauma counseling that the PTSD produced—has been rife with problems. Even after several revisions, the definition continues to be problematic. The latest *DSM-5* defines a traumatic event as:

> Exposure to actual or threatened death, serious injury, or sexual violence in one (or more) of the following ways:
>
> 1. Directly experiencing the traumatic event(s).
> 2. Witnessing, in person, the event(s) as it occurred to others.
> 3. Learning that the traumatic event(s) occurred to a close family member or close friend. In cases of actual or threatened death of a family member or friend, the event(s) must have been violent or accidental.
> 4. Experiencing repeated or extreme exposure to aversive details of the traumatic event(s) (e.g., first responders collecting human remains; police officers repeatedly exposed to child abuse). (APA 2013, p. 271)

This definition maintains a focus on the individual and ignores the complex and multifaceted ways in which individuals and communities experience traumatic events. This exemplifies a colonial or Western/Eurocentric framework that focuses on the individual as a way to deflect attention from systemic factors. Instead, it is my focus in this chapter to offer a decolonizing perspective, one that turns attention *toward* systemic factors, including systemic oppression trauma (e.g., racism and discrimination) and transgenerational trauma, including historical and collective trauma. There is now significant research showing the impact of these traumatic events (which I will discuss further) and pointing to the need for clinicians to be prepared to identify and address them. This work shows the need for clinicians to take a social justice approach to counseling in which we identify and work against systems that are oppressive and harmful.

Another, and perhaps more fundamental, criticism of the *DSM* and its handling of PTSD lies in the creation of the diagnosis itself. While some scholars and advocates have focused their energy on expanding the *DSM* definition of trauma and criteria for PTSD to improve the diagnosis, others point to the problems inherent within the notion of psychiatric diagnosis itself. Therapist and scholar Bonnie Burstow (2003) urges practitioners and scholars to take what she calls a "radical understanding of trauma" (p. 1302), and asserts that by focusing attention on improving the diagnostic criteria, feminists and other well-meaning practitioners are actually colluding with the oppressive system. She argues that these actions are too limited, and actually maintain a deficit-oriented perspective by labeling the person who has experienced trauma and is exhibiting post-trauma symptoms as dysfunctional. As Burstow points out, individuals who have experienced trauma are likely to view the world as dangerous, which is actually a more accurate assessment since our world is, indeed, dangerous; however, using the traditional viewpoint, therapists might see this as problematic (diagnosable) and then work to correct this "distorted" view of the world.

In order to decolonize trauma-informed practice, we need a framework for viewing trauma and for including trauma throughout counseling and psychology services that (1) is inclusive of the multiple and systemic ways in which individuals and groups experience trauma and (2) rejects deficit-oriented, individualistic perspectives and incorporates strengths-based sociopolitical perspectives. It is important to clarify that using a strengths-based perspective points to rejecting the deficit-oriented perspectives that are so often used when characterizing socially marginalized communities (i.e., deficit-focused efforts assist these communities in *making up for* the deficits inherent in not being a member of a privileged group, such as middle class, heterosexual, White, and others). This is not sufficient, however, for decolonizing practice; we must not only reject the deficit focus, but also actively engage in understanding and working to eradicate the systemic forces that have created social injustice. Using these guideposts, I will offer a decolonized view of trauma-informed services that can produce counseling and other human services that are socially just; later in this chapter, I will describe how this approach may be operationalized in counseling practice.

Towards a Comprehensive View of Trauma

As noted, the way in which trauma is defined and conceptualized is based in a sociohistorical context, meaning that the way we view and understand trauma arises based on the world in which we live, our experiences, and our perceptions. As a counter to the *DSM*-based conceptions of trauma, scholars and clinicians have developed a number of different frameworks to address the shortcomings discussed above. Furthermore, while the Western scientific study of trauma is relatively recent and somewhat limited, trauma has been understood in other societies for centuries. As such, there are many ways in which we can expand our understandings of trauma to develop a trauma-informed approach that will decolonize rather than perpetuate colonial perspectives. In developing a framework for a more comprehensive view of trauma, I draw on the work of scholars who have examined historical and current-day experiences of trauma from both traditional and nontraditional (systemic) sources. In this section, I highlight the foundational work in these areas and describe an ecosystemic view of trauma as a framework for examining the multiple ways in which individuals, families, and communities are impacted by traumatic events (Goodman 2013). In broad strokes, there are two significant areas of literature upon which I draw: systemic oppression trauma and transgenerational trauma.

Systemic Oppression Trauma Over roughly the last 20 years scholars have produced a body of literature focusing on the ways in which systemic oppression (e.g., racism and discrimination) can cause suffering. In examining the impacts of discrimination on people of color, including African Americans, Latina/os, Asian Americans, and Native Americans, researchers in the fields of counseling, psychology, and public health have found harmful mental and physical health effects (Harrell et al. 2003; Paradies 2006; Williams et al. 2003). Researchers have found that the psychological impacts of discrimination for individuals from disenfranchised communities include higher levels of psychological distress (Broman et al. 2000; Forman 2003; Lightsey and Barnes 2007), lower levels of life satisfaction (Schultz et al. 2000), and lower emotional well-being (Deitch et al. 2003; Forman 2003). In addition to these findings, scholars have specifically examined how systemic oppression might lead to symptoms of PTSD; results from these studies indicate that systemic oppression can be a form of trauma despite the fact that it would rarely meet the narrow *DSM* criteria for a traumatic event (Carter 2007). Given that systemic oppression experiences would generally not meet the *DSM* criteria, scholars have suggested alternative frameworks. For instance, Carter (2007) noted that Carlson's (1997) definition of traumatic events (events that are sudden, negative, and uncontrollable) is more inclusive of systemic oppression trauma since this definition focuses on the individual's perception of an event and, while racism is common, it is not controllable by the individual who is being targeted.

Transgenerational Trauma Transgenerational trauma, also called intergenerational trauma, refers to the impact of traumatic events that is transmitted from one generation to the next (Dass-Brailsford 2007; Goodman and West-Olatunji 2008). While this type of trauma has been expressed in oral and written histories across cultures for many generations—as is the case with trauma in general—its study within the field of counseling and psychology is still nascent (Danieli 2007). The Western study of transgenerational trauma developed in large part in clinical work with the children of Holocaust survivors in the 1960s in which clinicians noted that symptoms of trauma were present in the children, even though their parents, and not them, had been exposed directly to a traumatic event (Danieli 1998; Dass-Brailsford 2007). As the understanding grew that trauma can be transmitted from one generation to the next, clinicians and scholars began to apply this framework in a number of ways, including to the cycle of domestic violence within families and child abuse (Frazier et al. 2009; Simons and Johnson 1998), the trauma experienced by families of soldiers (Rosenheck and Fontana 1998), and the trauma passed down to families who lived within repressive regimes (Baker and Gippenreiter 1998). Transgenerational trauma symptoms can arise at the individual, family, and community level, meaning that trauma may manifest and cause distress at any of these levels (Evans-Campbell 2008). There is also an important intersection between systemic oppression trauma and transgenerational trauma; for individuals who are from groups that have historically experienced discrimination, this type of trauma may be transmitted intergenerationally. One example is the transgenerational trauma for African American descendants of slaves, which intersects with present-day racism, and may engender trauma among African Americans (Cross 1998; Leary 2005).

The intersection between these types of traumas has also been discussed through scholarship on *historical trauma* and *collective trauma*. In particular, these concepts have been described among American Indian, Native American, or indigenous communities who have experienced genocide and the systemic destruction of their cultural practices for the benefit of those in power (namely, White European, land-owning colonists and their descendants). For instance, in the case of American Indians, boarding schools and bans against their cultural practices and languages were used to extinguish their cultures as a part of the attempted genocide (Evans-

Table 5.1 Ecosystemic view of trauma. (Adapted from Goodman 2013)

	Direct trauma	Indirect trauma
Traditional	Individual directly experiences trauma as traditionally (*DSM*) defined	Individual indirectly experiences trauma from traditionally (*DSM*) defined sources (transgenerational trauma)
	Examples: Car accident, abuse, death of loved one	Examples: Children of Holocaust survivors, Vietnam veterans, or hurricane survivors
Ecosystemic	Individual directly experiences trauma from nontraditional sources that are ecosystemic (systemic oppression trauma)	Individual indirectly experiences trauma from nontraditional sources that are ecosystemic (transgenerational systemic oppression trauma)
	Examples: Direct and traumatic experiences of racism (African Americans), heterosexism (lesbian, gay, bisexual, transgender, queer (LGBTQ) individuals)	Examples: Children of individuals who have experienced racism (African Americans)

Campbell 2008; Smith 2007). This has led to ongoing and intergenerational traumatic impacts, sometimes called a *soul wound*, among American Indian or Native American communities (Duran et al. 2008).

In Table 5.1, I offer a framework to illustrate how we need to expand our understanding of trauma beyond the narrow *DSM* definition that focuses on direct and individual experiences. In this table, trauma from both *direct* (e.g., experienced personally by the individual) and *indirect* (e.g., experienced indirectly via transmission from another person or the community) sources should be considered. This allows for a trauma framework that includes the important intergenerational experiences of trauma that have impacted families, cultures, and communities across one generation or more. *Traditional* trauma (characterized by the *DSM*) and *ecosystemic* trauma (systemic oppression) are also included. Without consideration of the harmful experiences of oppression, any assessment or intervention will fail to attend to the very real and harmful impacts of injustice.

A Liberatory Approach to Trauma Counseling

As I have discussed, a more comprehensive approach to trauma counseling and trauma-informed services requires a definition and conceptualization of trauma that is more inclusive and that explicitly attends to the sociopolitical nature of traumatic events. For counselors and psychologists, the act of articulating and utilizing such frameworks when working with clients and communities is a step toward more liberatory and socially just counseling services. However, we should go even further. If we are to embrace social justice-oriented trauma-informed services, we must enact a much more comprehensive and sociopolitical array of counseling and psychological services.

There are a number of counseling approaches that are particularly well suited to address the issues I have described. I mention a few of them below in hopes of offering some concrete ideas for practice. However, counselors and psychologists should not be limited to these practices, nor should these be seen as prescriptive. It is of utmost importance that any interventions be generated in a collaborative, critically conscious partnership with clients and community members; to do otherwise is usually ineffective and can exacerbate distress, particularly among people in marginalized communities who are often *provided* with solutions (without their consultation or consent) that are aimed at irrelevant problems or that fail to utilize indigenous healing practices. I highlight three approaches: deconstructing the sociopolitical context as a part of counseling practice, privileging indigenous ways of healing, and orienting toward resilience and resistance.

Deconstructing the Sociopolitical Context The work of Ignacio Martín-Baró, a social psychologist, priest, and scholar, was groundbreaking in its examination of the sociopolitical context and revisioning of the role of psychologists. Both of these aspects of his work are applicable to other mental health professions as well. In describing *liberation psychology*, he criticized his profession's complicity with social injustice, writing, "Psychology offers an alternative solution to social conflicts: It tries to change the individual while preserving the social order, or, in the best of cases, generating the illusion that, perhaps, as the individual changes, so will the social order—as if society were a summation of individuals" (Martín-Baró 1994, p. 37). He calls instead for psychologists to take on the task of transforming society for the good of people:

> This is not a question of whether to abandon psychology; it is a question of whether psychological knowledge will be placed in the service of constructing a society where the welfare of the few is not built on the wretchedness of the many, where the fulfillment of some does not require that others be deprived, where the interests of the minority do not demand the dehumanization of all. (Martín-Baró 1994, p. 46)

Key to transforming the profession and the work of psychologists, counselors, and other mental health professionals is the deconstruction of both historical and current sociopolitical contexts. Without deconstructing history and the sociopolitical context, some clients and practitioners may not be aware of these larger narratives or of the impact of social and political forces. Martín-Baró draws on the work of Paulo Freire, an educator, who worked with marginalized groups in Brazil and developed the concept of *concientizacion.* This revolutionary concept involved not just the traditional concepts of education (such as learning to read and write) but also a decoding of an individual's world and context, as well as the development of new knowledge and a sense of mastery and ability to take action to transform the world. In Martín-Baró's adaption of these concepts, he posited that concientizacion should be a core task of mental health professionals; in this way, psychologists and counselors could "attain a critical understanding of themselves and their reality" (p. 41).

When examining the trauma-informed work of counselors and psychologists, these concepts are particularly important. As I explained earlier, trauma does not occur in a vacuum; it arises in a sociopolitical context and is influenced and sometimes caused by systemic forces, such as political violence, racism, and economic inequality. However, by failing to deconstruct historical or current contexts, we embrace a very narrow view of trauma, why it has occurred, and how it might be healed or prevented. This leads to blaming survivors of trauma as inferior or failing in some way, and colludes with the dominant narrative that was created out of ignorance or to maintain the status quo for the benefit of those in power.

Trauma-informed practices that address the sociopolitical context include an exploration and interrogation of hegemonic narratives. There are a number of ways that counselors and clients can approach this deconstruction. In some cases, clients and counselors can co-investigate the sociopolitical context as part of their work together. One technique is to identify and highlight *counter-narratives*, or stories that challenge dominant narratives about disenfranchised communities that are often negative or stereotypical. A counter-narrative introduces different ideas and frameworks, illuminating the ways in which the dominant narrative is flawed or narrow. For example, while working with a Salvadoran American wife and husband who have had several close family members incarcerated or arrested (including the husband), the clinician should explore how this experience is reflective of bias in the criminal justice system that unfairly targets Latino American and African American men (Alexander 2010). This can shift the conversation in counseling to include an understanding of the systemic injustice the couple faces, and how this might be contributing the conflict in their relationship.

For counselors or psychologists, effectively preparing to engage in trauma-informed counseling that includes a deconstruction of the historical and current sociopolitical context requires a depth of knowledge and a commitment to continual learning, critical thinking, and dialoguing. Counselors and psychologists should seek out information that was developed by members of a community to learn about that community rather than relying on interpretations produced by outsiders. In my view, counselors have an obligation to consume relevant and critical information about the sociopolitical issues facing their clients, including the ways they are oppressed and their strengths; while we can look to our clients to inform us, we place an unfair burden on clients when we rely on them to educate us about the world, wasting their time and possibly furthering a sense of isolation among marginalized individuals by expecting them to take on the role of representative for their entire community (such as by speaking on behalf of the entire undocumented immigrant or Chinese American community).

In my work with residents of New Orleans following Hurricane Katrina, the importance of understanding the sociopolitical context was clear. We noted the dominant narratives, which tended to blame residents of New Orleans for not evacuating and were rife with racism; for instance, Black residents were described as "looting" while White residents engaging in similar behaviors were described as "finding" food (Jones 2005). These types of narratives can exacerbate the distress felt by the community, compounding historical experiences of racism with current-day systemic oppression trauma and disaster-related trauma. Further, the traumatic stress generated by ineffective disaster response by the government was compounded by historical experiences of disaster responses that privileged affluent communities by dynamiting levees in lower-income neighborhoods during Hurricane Betsy in 1965

(Brinkley 2006). As a counselor working with this community, failure to understand the sociopolitical contexts and the ways in which the dominant narratives are rife with racism would have resulted in ineffective counseling and the further marginalization of the lived experiences of the people of New Orleans, particularly within poor communities of color. Instead, through the process of deconstruction we can locate the source of inequity where it belongs: within the sociopolitical context rather than within an individual, family, or community. For individuals who might have internalized these negative messages, such a process can reduce personal blaming and a sense of inferiority. For counselors, this can shift their trauma-informed practices to be more accurate, effective, and just. Further, this could free up both clients and clinicians to take advocacy action on the sociopolitical context that influenced the traumatic event or aftermath (discussed later).

Privileging Indigenous Ways of Healing A second way in which we can enact trauma-informed practices that are decolonizing is to actively privilege indigenous ways of healing—meaning that these practices are central to trauma counseling instead of being relegated to secondary positions or adjunctive to mainstream models of counseling. This approach relies on some of the basic multicultural counseling competencies that are frequently referenced—knowledge, awareness, and skills related to the cultural practices of a particular cultural group (Sue et al. 1992)—but transcends some of the limitations inherent in the narrow focus of the multicultural counseling competencies.

We must recognize, first, that one of the critical assumptions is that all peoples have frameworks for wellness and ways of healing. Without this assumption, counselors and psychologists will view the community through a lens that may run contrary to beliefs held by community members; assessments will be inaccurate and interventions will be ineffective since the clinicians will misunderstand the various strengths, challenges, ways of healing, and beliefs about wellness of the community. Second, we must understand that this first assumption—and even knowledge about a community's beliefs—is not sufficient to achieve a decolonizing practice. Without *privileging* the community's beliefs and knowledge, clinicians still might see themselves as culturally competent, but could continue to use their own frameworks, such as those taught in Eurocentric counseling and psychology education programs, subjugating their understanding of the community to secondary or auxiliary knowledge. Often counselors believe they are culturally competent because they have some information about a particular identity group, such as their values or beliefs. However, this knowledge is not enough to actually engage with clients in a socially just way; it is often cursory or essentializing, and does not truly position indigenous views of health as primary. Moreover, this practice can further exacerbate hegemony-related distress that marginalized communities already experience. In communities with histories of marginalization, the active (if unintentional) marginalization of their worldviews and ways of healing *within* the counseling process itself represents another form of oppression and possible trauma instead of a form of healing from trauma.

Counselors and psychologists should, instead, privilege the viewpoints and practices that are meaningful to individual, families, and communities. One example from my own work occurred while working with the Lakota Sioux community in Pine Ridge Indian Reservation. Members of the community talked about historical trauma, ongoing injustice, and the very real traumatic stress outcomes within their community. Again and again, community members emphasized that they wanted others to know about the injustices and that they wanted the opportunity to address the traumatic impacts *themselves*. They indicated that they did not want pity or charity; they wanted justice, self-determination, and the resources to enact their own indigenous healing practices—not those imposed from the very groups who had caused the trauma to begin with.

Along with privileging indigenous perspectives, clients may choose to adjust or augment these practices. Often, trauma and oppression cause individuals, families, or communities to (consciously or unconsciously) constrict their responses, limiting what I term their *psychological range of motion*. One example discussed in the transgenerational trauma literature is the concept of the *conspiracy of silence* (Danieli 2007): parents who experience trauma will want to protect their children from this information, so they will not disclose information about traumatic events. In some cases, individuals might remain silent in order to protect others from persecution, as seen among Jewish communities due to the Nazi Holocaust. As such, trauma has the tendency to constrict lives, limiting the way people engage with others, what they share, and where they go. Trauma strains or damages the natural coping mechanisms within an individual or community while at the same time often limiting the resources upon which the individual or community is able to draw. As Watkins and Shulman (2008) wrote, "Oppressed communities have had their cultural traditions, values, history, and often even language diminished and assaulted" (p. 214). Communities might wish to explore how traditional ways of being or healing may have been distorted or have lost some of their effectiveness (usually due to oppression), as well as what new practices or traditions may have arisen or may be needed. This inquiry must be undertaken with caution on the part of the counselor or psychologist, as the professional tendency to pathologize or "fix" communities can arise despite our intention to be collaborative. As such, these efforts should be community-led and practitioners should continually interrogate the nature of our partnerships and work. We must reflect on how the work was initiated (by the community or by someone outside of the community), which will, in turn, drive the framework and agenda. Counselors and psychologists can help facilitate the process of determining how to revitalize or augment practices, but the ultimate power of determination must rest within the community, otherwise, facilitation turns into disempowerment and deficit-focused practice. This task requires that we continue to privilege indigenous viewpoints while also helping the community (1) explore the ways in which the psychological range of motion has been constricted in ways that are no longer helpful and (2) generate ideas about how their own practices can be revitalized or augmented. The practice of helping to restore culture, history, and language can, in and of itself, be a form of healing (see Gone 2013) that relies on the strengths of the community, as I shall discuss below.

Orienting Toward Resilience and Resistance Within the trauma literature, many scholars have emphasized the problems and "dysfunctions" that arise from experiencing a traumatic event. This is understandable because, in trauma-informed practices, it is important to identify the painful consequences of harmful events in order to encourage acknowledgment and healing. However, it is critically important that we do not make problems the sole focus and that we do not embrace a deficit view in trauma-informed counseling in which the person is seen as broken or weak. As Burstow (2003) pointed out, the way a person who has experienced trauma views the world might be more accurate than the perspectives of people who have not had traumatic experiences. Instead, we could say that the inability to recognize and acknowledge the sort of oppression that we do not personally experience is actually the "dysfunction" that should be addressed. Rather than focusing on responding to supposed deficits (that actually are symptoms and not causes of trauma), liberatory trauma-informed clinicians examine clients' unique strengths, including those that have been generated through the experience of trauma, either individual or collective. While returning a traumatized person back to pre-trauma functioning may seem like a worthy goal, it is problematic because it fundamentally ignores what could have surfaced or been generated through the traumatic experience, such as new strengths or meaning making. Of course, the strengths focus alone is not sufficient and must be coupled with a critical examination of oppressive conditions; furthermore, a strengths-focus can actually be a distraction from a more critical investigation of systemic conditions. Strengths based perspectives do not necessarily challenge the status quo, so practitioners must couple the strengths-based perspective with critical, systemic-focused interrogation, so as to not be complicit in perpetuating injustice.

Clinicians should examine individual, family, or community strengths that emerge following a traumatic experience. For instance, a clinician working with a refugee family might explore how the family was able to escape a dangerous situation and the ways in which they are supporting one another in a new country while encountering racism and xenophobia. Furthermore, looking beyond the individual or familial level, there is a long history of marginalized groups coming together to develop coping strategies and resilience in the face of systemic oppression or other socially produced types of trauma. Watkins and Shulman (2008) describe the power of what they term *communities of resistance*, in which groups of people who experience oppression come together to create spaces for healing, empowerment, and interconnection:

> Here the processes in the dominant culture that have attributed negative meanings to one's very existence are questioned and rejected. In their stead, positive meanings are encouraged that allow members of the community to recover from toxic internalizations and feelings of inferiority, emptiness, and meaninglessness. (p. 217)

While the term resistance often carries a negative connotation among counselors and psychologists—such as by describing a client as *resistant* or *noncompliant*—the concept can indicate a refusal to accept negative or limited narratives or harmful practices; from a liberatory perspective, resisting oppression is a healthy response to oppressive social conditions, not a "maladaptive" response. In trauma counseling, this resistance can be integral to the healing and recovery process.

Communities of resistance can also be spaces in which members take collective action in public spaces. Social action has been identified as important to trauma recovery in that it provides a vehicle for action following the disempowering experience of trauma; through social action, feelings of strength and empowerment might emerge as well as a sense of purpose through helping others or working to prevent future traumas (Herman 1997). Collective action might also take the form of community-wide healing interventions such as art making. One example of this that I observed when collaborating with a women's shelter in Botswana was the development of a book by the women in the shelter, in which women shared their narratives of abuse and resistance. The book was written both to provide an outlet for their stories and to support women who might be in abusive relationships. Counselors and psychologists can work with community members to develop ways of being together and co-creating projects that are meaningful and relevant for the community, such as talking circles, quilt making, or song and dance. These projects can provide vehicles to bring community members or trauma survivors together to discuss their shared struggles and also generate strategies for social action, which can be healing and also create a sense of community.

Finally, trauma-informed practices that are truly decolonizing require that clinicians take an active role in the process of decolonizing itself. This means that mental health providers should enter into the process of advocacy, activism, and social justice action. We must utilize whatever privilege we have to push for structural changes that not only better serve our clients but also, ideally, prevent harm from happening in the first place. We can take action at many different levels since many different levels of structures influence the well-being of individuals and communities. At the micro level, which includes the roles or settings in which we directly interact, we can examine how to reduce harm and promote a socially just, trauma-informed framework. This might include examining the policies and practices, either explicit or implicit, within organizations such as the schools or religious establishments we attend. In our interpersonal relationships with family members or peers, this might include addressing issues of injustice when they arise and giving voice to counter-narratives when we hear stereotypes.

At the macro level, we can examine how systems impact the sorts of traumatic stress that clients and communities experience. For instance, what are the policies of social services? Are services delivered in a trauma-informed manner? We can examine policies at local, national, and international levels. How might policies be creating or exacerbating traumatic stress? It is particularly important to investigate the ways that laws or policies impact marginalized groups, such as immigrants, women, and lesbian/gay/bisexual/transgendered individuals. Other issues we might investigate are working conditions and the minimum wage or housing policies and gentrification and displacement. We need to investigate where and how resources are distributed and whose interests are being protected—as clinicians, we are acutely aware of how these factors impact our clients and it is our ethical obligation to raise our voices and take action.

Conclusion

As I reflect on the limitations and possibilities within trauma-informed mental health services, I remain hopeful. I believe that the increased awareness around trauma and its impact offers us a unique opportunity to bring attention to the often-ignored social injustices in our world. We have a body of research that supports the painful consequences of these injustices and we have emergent frameworks that offer liberatory counseling practices. We must not be satisfied with the status quo; we must continually interrogate our clinical practice and generate frameworks and interventions that truly enact our social justice ideals.

Further, we must shift the lens from viewing those who have experienced trauma as problematic or "dysfunctional." Instead, we must shed a light on where the true "dysfunction" lies: with those who subjugate others for profit, put the benefit of the few above the well-being of the many, and dehumanize and sow seeds of hate for those who they see as different. Dr. Martin Luther King, Jr. pointed out the contradictory nature of a commonly used psychological term, "maladjustment." He insisted that people *should* be maladjusted to the injustices in society, stating in a 1963 speech:

> I say very honestly that I never intend to become adjusted to segregation and discrimination. I never intend to become adjusted to religious bigotry. I never intend to adjust myself to economic conditions that will take necessities from the many to give luxuries to the few. I never intend to adjust myself to the madness of militarism, to the self-defeating effects of physical violence. (Western Michigan University Archives, n.d., pp. 17–18)

Thus, in my view, as counselors and psychologists—people whose professions focus on the well-being and healing of individuals, families, and communities—we must be maladjusted to the limiting and narrow views that our professions take; we must identify injustice and its impact on the people we serve; and we must shift the lens from seeing the survivors of trauma as *having* a problem to seeing the perpetrators of trauma and the systems that perpetuate trauma as *being* the problem.

References

Alexander, M. (2010). *The new Jim Crow*. New York: New Press.

APA. (1980). *Diagnostic and statistical manual of mental disorders* (3rd ed.). Washington, DC: Author.

APA. (2013). *Diagnostic and statistical manual of mental disorders* (5th ed.). Washington, DC: Author.

Baker, D., & Gippenreiter, J. B. (1998). Stalin's purge and its impact on Russian families. In Y. Danieli (Ed.), *International handbook of multigenerational legacies of trauma* (pp. 403–434). New York: Plenum.

Borja, S. E., & Callahan, J. L. (2009). The trauma outcome process assessment model: A structural equation model examination of adjustment. *Journal of Child Sexual Abuse, 18,* 532–552. doi:10.1080/10538710903182685.

Brinkley, D. (2006). *The great deluge: Hurricane Katrina, New Orleans, and the Mississippi Gulf Coast*. New York: HarperCollins.

Broman, C. L., Mavaddat, R., & Hsu, S. (2000). The experience and consequences of perceived racial discrimination: A study of African Americans. *Journal of Black Psychology, 26,* 165–180.

Burstow, B. (2003). Toward a radical understanding of trauma and trauma work. *Violence Against Women, 9,* 1293–1317.

Carlson, E. B. (1997). *Trauma assessments: A clinician's guide*. New York: Guildford.

Carter, R. T. (2007). Racism and psychological and emotional injury: Recognizing and assessing race-based traumatic stress. *The Counseling Psychologist, 35,* 13–105.

Cross, W. E. (1998). Black psychological functioning and the legacy of slavery. In Y. Danieli (Ed.), *International handbook of multigenerational legacies of trauma* (pp. 387–400). New York: Plenum.

Danieli, Y. (1998). Introduction: History and conceptual foundations. In Y. Danieli (Ed.), *International handbook of multigenerational legacies of trauma* (pp. 1–20). New York: Plenum.

Danieli, Y. (2007). Assessing trauma across cultures from a multigenerational perspective. In J. P. Wilson & C. S. Tang (Eds.), *Cross-cultural assessment of psychological trauma and PTSD* (pp. 65–89). New York: Springer.

Dass-Brailsford, P. (2007). *A practical approach to trauma: Empowering interventions*. Los Angeles: Sage.

Deitch, E. A., Barsky, A., Butz, R. M., Brief, A. P., Chan, S. S. Y., & Bradley, J. C. (2003). Subtle yet significant: The existence and impact of everyday racial discrimination in the workplace. *Human Relations, 56,* 1299–1324.

Dods, J. (2013). Enhancing understanding of the nature of supportive school-based relationships for youth who have experienced trauma. *Canadian Journal of Education, 36,* 71–95.

Drabble, L. A., Jones, S., & Brown, V. (2013). Advancing trauma-informed systems change in a family drug treatment court context. *Journal of Social Work Practice in the Addictions, 13,* 91–113. doi:10.1080/1533256X.2012.756341.

Duran, E., Firehammer, J., & Gonzalez, J. (2008). Liberation psychology as the path toward healing cultural soul wounds. *Journal of Counseling & Development, 86,* 288–295.

Elliott, D. E., Bjelajac, P., Fallot, R. D., Markoff, L. S., & Reed, B. G. (2005). Trauma-informed or trauma-denied: Principles and implementation of trauma-informed services for women. *Journal of Community Psychology, 33,* 461–477. doi:10.1002/jcop.20063.

Evans-Campbell, T. (2008). Historical trauma in American Indian/Native Alaska communities. *Journal of Interpersonal Violence, 23,* 316–338.

Fallot, R. D., & Harris, M. (2001). A trauma-informed approach to screening and assessment. In M. Harris & R. D. Fallot (Eds.), *Using trauma theory to design service systems* (pp. 23–31). San Francisco: Jossey-Bass.

Flaherty, E. G., Thompson, R., Litrownik, A. J., Theodore, A., English, D. J., Black, M. M., Dubowitz, H., et al. (2006). Effect of early childhood adversity on child health. *Archives of Pediatrics and Adolescent Medicine, 160,* 1232–1238.

Forman, T. A. (2003). The social psychological costs of racial segmentation in the workplace: A study of African Americans' well-being. *Journal of Health and Social Behavior, 44,* 332–352.

Frazier, K. N., West-Olatunji, C., St Juste, S., & Goodman, R. D. (2009). Transgenerational trauma and CSA: Reconceptualizing cases involving young survivors of child sexual abuse. *Journal of Mental Health Counseling, 31,* 22–33.

Gone, J. P. (2013). Redressing first nations historical trauma: Theorizing mechanisms for indigenous culture as mental health treatment. *Transcultural Psychiatry, 50,* 683–706. doi:10.1177/1363461513487669.

Goodman, R. D. (2013). The transgenerational trauma and resilience genogram. *Counselling Psychology Quarterly, 26,* 386–405. doi:10.1080/09515070.2013.820172.

Goodman, R. D., & West-Olatunji, C. A. (2008). Transgenerational trauma and resilience: Improving mental health counseling for survivors on Hurricane Katrina. *Journal of Mental Health Counseling, 30,* 121–136.

Goodman, R. D., & West-Olatunji, C. A. (2010). Educational hegemony, traumatic stress, and African American and Latino American students. *Journal of Multicultural Counseling and Development, 38,* 176–186.

Halpern, J., & Tramontin, M. (2007). *Disaster mental health: Theory and practice*. Belmont: Thompson Brooks/Cole.

Harrell, J. P., Hall, S., & Taliaferro, J. (2003). Physiological responses to racism and discrimination: An assessment of the evidence. *American Journal of Public Health, 93,* 243–248.

Harris, M., & Fallot, R. D. (2001). Envisioning a trauma-informed service system: A vital paradigm shift. In M. Harris & R. D. Fallot (Eds.), *Using trauma theory to design service systems* (pp. 3–22). San Francisco: Jossey-Bass.

Herman, J. (1997). *Trauma and recovery*. New York: Basic Books.

Hodgon, H. B., Kinniburgh, K., Gabowitz, D., Blaustein, M. E., & Spinazzola, J. (2013). Developing and implementation of trauma-informed programming in youth residential treatment centers using the ARC framework. *Journal of Family Violence*. Advance online publication. doi:10.1007/s10896-013-9531-z.

Jones, V. (2005). Black people "loot" food…White people "find" food. *The Huffington Post*. Retrieved from http://www.huffingtonpost.com/van-jones/black-people-loot-food-wh_b_6614.html. Accessed 31 July 2014.

Kerig, P. K., Ward, R. M., Vanderzee, K. L., & Moeddel, M. A. (2009). Posttraumatic stress as a mediator of the relationship between trauma and mental health problems among juvenile delinquents. *Journal of Youth Adolescence, 38,* 1214–1225. doi:10.1007/s10964-008-9332-5.

Leary, J. D. (2005). *Post traumatic slave syndrome*. Milwaukie: Uptone.

Levine, P. A., & Kline, M. (2007). *Trauma through a child's eyes: Awakening the ordinary miracle of healing*. Berkeley: North Atlantic Books.

Lightsey, O. R., & Barnes, P. W. (2007). Discrimination, attributional tendencies, generalized self-efficacy, and assertiveness as predictors of psychological distress among African Americans. *Journal of Black Psychology, 33,* 27–50.

Martín-Baró, I. (1994). *Writings for a liberation psychology*. Cambridge: Harvard University Press.

Paradies, Y. (2006). A systematic review of empirical research on self-reported racism and health. *International Journal of Epidemiology, 35,* 888–901.

Rosenheck, R., & Fontana, A. (1998). Transgenerational effects of abusive violence on the children of Vietnam combat veterans. *Journal of Traumatic Stress, 11,* 731–742.

Schultz, A., Williams, D., Israel, B., Becker, A., Parker, E., & James, S. A. (2000). Unfair treatment, neighborhood effects, and mental health in Detroit metropolitan area. *Journal of Health and Social Behavior, 41,* 314–331.

Simons, R. L., & Johnson, C. (1998). An examination of competing explanations for the intergenerational transmission of domestic violence. In Y. Danieli (Ed.), *International handbook of multigenerational legacies of trauma* (pp. 553–570). New York: Plenum.

Smith, A. (2007, March 26). Soul wound: The legacy of Native American schools. *Amnesty International Magazine*. Retrieved from http://www.amnestyusa.org. Accessed 31 July 2014.

Sue, D. W., Arredondo, P., & McDavis, R. J. (1992). Multicultural counseling competencies: A call to the profession. *Journal of Counseling and Development, 70,* 477–486.

Watkins, M., & Shulman, H. (2008). *Toward psychologies of liberation*. New York: Palgrave Macmillan.

Western Michigan University Archives. (n.d.). *MLK at Western*. Retrieved from http://www.wmich.edu/sites/default/files/attachments/MLK.pdf. Accessed 31 July 2014.

Williams, D. R., Neighbors, H. W., & Jackson, J. S. (2003). Racial/ethnic discrimination and health: Findings from community studies. *American Journal of Public Health, 93,* 200–208.

Chapter 6
Decolonizing Psychological Practice in the Context of Poverty

Laura Smith and Carissa Chambers

> From the vantage point of the colonized, a position from which I write and choose to privilege, the term "research" is inextricably linked to European imperialism and colonialism. The work itself, "research," is probably one of the dirtiest words in the indigenous world's vocabulary. (Smith 1999, p. 1)

The name Linda Tuhiwai Smith may not be a familiar one to many mental health professionals, but her work (quoted above) is a fitting point of departure for counselors and psychologists who wish to counteract the potential harm that can be done via the use of dominant-culture practices within marginalized social groups. In this chapter, we will extend the metaphor of colonized practice to counseling work that takes place in the context of poverty, and in so doing, Smith will not be the only scholar outside the conventional counseling literature upon whose work we will draw. Scholarship from community psychology and educational theory will help frame our contention that the harmfulness of poverty goes beyond its material deprivation—and that helping professionals who do not understand the multidimensional nature of poor people's marginalization may not be helping them as much as they think. Throughout this discussion, we will supply linkages between our argument and the works of counselors and other mental health professionals.

Why will we be referring to dominant-culture counseling practices as *colonized*? Writing as an indigenous researcher and professor in New Zealand's Western-style university system, Smith (1999) offered a pathbreaking explication of the ways that conventional scientific paradigms have reflected and perpetuated objectification and oppression in the lives of indigenous peoples around the world. The Western researchers who imposed their conceptual frameworks and methodologies upon indigenous communities were not aware of themselves as colonizers; as Smith pointed out, they often thought of themselves as acting on behalf of the good of all humanity, or even in service of a particular emancipatory goal held by the people they studied. Nevertheless, the imposition of outsider conceptual frameworks upon

L. Smith (✉) · C. Chambers
Department of Counseling and Clinical Psychology, Teachers College, Columbia University, 525 West 120th St, Box 102, New York, NY 10027, USA
e-mail: S2396@tc.columbia.edu

R. D. Goodman, P. C. Gorski (eds.), *Decolonizing "Multicultural" Counseling through Social Justice,* International and Cultural Psychology, DOI 10.1007/978-1-4939-1283-4_6

indigenous life and the clinical diagnosing of community life (including the damage done by oppression itself) as individual pathology have, over time, produced devastating consequences:

> [C]onstant efforts by governments, states, societies, and institutions to deny the historical formations of such conditions have simultaneously denied our claims to humanity, to having a history, and to all sense of hope. To acquiesce is to lose ourselves entirely and implicitly agree with all that has been said about us. To resist is to retrench in the margins, retrieve what we were, and remake ourselves. (Smith 1999, p. 4)

Smith's (1999) work helped to bring the term *colonization* into usage as a term connoting the ways that dominant-culture ideologies and assumptions can pervade professional theory and practice to the detriment of people in marginalized social groups—even when those professionals intend to be helpful. People living in poverty belong to such a social group, and as helping professionals, counselors' and psychologists' altruistic intentions on behalf of the poor are often in evidence, such as through proffers of volunteer crisis intervention services. These intentions and the charitable actions that accompany them often seem necessary and appropriate, given the incontrovertible material deprivation that accompanies poverty—but is it possible that even the *help* dispensed by professionals to the neediest among us bears critical analysis? In the following section, we will preface this question by presenting poverty as more than a condition of diminished financial resources—rather, it is the marginalized social location on the bottom-most rung on the social class ladder. We will unpack traditional conceptions of "help" offered to the poor by relatively class-privileged professionals, and we will offer a framework that points the way toward innovative, decolonized actions by which counselors psychologists can partner with people living in poverty.

Poverty as a Social Class Location

The case that we will offer for the decolonization of counseling and psychological services for the poor begins with a way of understanding poverty that includes but goes beyond material deprivation and differences in purchasing power. It emerges from an understanding of social class dynamics, a topic that receives little concerted attention among mental health professionals. Counselors and psychologists are not alone in this regard; however, in her reflections on social class in the USA, the feminist social critic bell hooks wrote, "the closest most folks can come to talking about class in this nation is to talk about money" (2000, p. 5). Even in professions that more frequently address social class disparities, conceptualization and measurement of social class are inconsistent. In public health, for example, the health disparities literature demonstrates that "conceptually coherent and consistent measures of socioeconomic position…remain rare" (Krieger et al. 1997, p. 341). In the absence of coherent, consistent measures, social class is often represented by proxies, such as income or socioeconomic status (SES). SES is a ranked hierarchical measure often modeled as a continuous variable with numerical cutoff points determining different categories. Representing social class via a continuum implies that social class is simply a function of money and/or other resources—it does not account for the social, cultural, political, and interpersonal power that differentiates people in different class groups (Smith 2010). Moreover, such cutoffs are frequently driven by the data under examination and therefore differ depending on the samples in various studies (Krieger et al. 1997).

If social class is more than income or SES, what is it? As explicated by sociologists and political scientists (e.g., Bourdieu 1984), social class theory extends beyond numeric representations to encompass structures of power, privilege, status, advantage, access, agency, and influence over distribution of resources (Smith 2010). People whose social class positions lie near its lower rungs (poor and working-class people) have less socioeconomic power than those nearer the top (middle- and owning-class people), which is the power associated with wealth, property, and the means of economic production. Powerful people—owning-class people—own the resources by which others make a living, and may own enough property and wealth that they need not work at all. Less powerful people must work to support their basic needs, and have varying degrees of autonomy and power in the workplace. Middle-class people may hire and fire others, and/or have some freedom to choose for themselves the precise content and pace of their workday; working-class people often have neither of those opportunities. At the bottom are the poor, who may spend parts of their lives entirely outside socioeconomic structures and who do not have sufficient income to support their families' basic needs.

As is the case with social hierarchies corresponding to race, gender, and sexual orientation, a characteristic form of oppression is associated with the social class hierarchy and is called *classism* (Lott and Bullock 2001). Classism operates so that life at the bottom of the hierarchy is harder not only due to the material deprivation but also due to the prejudicial beliefs that confront poor people on a daily basis. Poor people are more likely to be thought of and portrayed in the media as lazy, dirty, and dysfunctional compared to people at more privileged social class positions (Bullock et al. 2001), a shaming vision of themselves that even young children living in poverty have already internalized (Weinger 1998). The damage inflicted by this imagery has been called *symbolic violence* by the French sociologist Pierre Bourdieu, and he considered its impact to be as real and as damaging as literal physical violence (Bourdieu 1984).

Social Class Oppression as Social Exclusion

This interrelated, systemic view of social class, therefore, positions poverty as the social location that is most distant from sources of socioeconomic power. According to this conceptualization, the poor are at the farthest margins of the social circles of power and influence—the centers of economic, political, and cultural life where power is held and decisions are made. In this way, they can be thought of as society's ultimate outsiders. They have little or no voice in the decisions that affect their families' access to health care, education, and housing. They own little or nothing; they do not hire or fire other people; much of their lives are spent outside the familiar places, spaces, and experiences that characterize life at other social locations. This class-derived, relational dimension of life in poverty is referred to as *social exclusion.*

The social exclusion of the poor can be contrasted with the insider positions that owning-class people occupy with regard to most social institutions and structures. Owning-class people make most of the political decisions in the USA and they control the corporations that dominate the economic life of society. They own the preponderance of cultural and media outlets, whether they are newspapers, movie studios, or art galleries. The public is fascinated with their marriages, wardrobes, and dinner parties; television programs are frequently devoted entirely to their pursuits. Middle-class people do not carry as much socioeconomic clout as these owning-class people do, yet, as compared to poor or working-class people, they enjoy more opportunities to take part in culturally esteemed social and educational experiences, and can more often be found participating in the US system of participatory democracy.

People with more social class privilege, therefore, have greater ability to be social insiders in every sense of the word. Examples of insider privileges contrast vividly with the ways that social exclusion can be manifested in the lives of the poorest people. One of the most concrete examples of this exclusion concerns the sheer physical presence (or absence) of poor people's bodies in shared public space. In a report entitled "Homes Not Handcuffs," The National Law Center on Homelessness and Poverty and The National Coalition for the Homeless (2009) documented the rise in national civic actions that prohibit poor people from occupying public property. These ordinances restrict the sharing of food, make it illegal to sit or sleep in public spaces, and/or otherwise drive homeless people away from public areas. Referring to this trend as "the criminalization of poverty" (para. 2), Ehrenreich (2009) went on to describe the double jeopardy that racism introduces into the experiences of poor people of color:

> By far the most reliable way to be criminalized by poverty is to have the wrong-color skin. Indignation runs high when a celebrity professor encounters racial profiling, but for decades whole communities have been effectively "profiled" for the suspicious combination of being both dark-skinned and poor.... Flick a cigarette in a heavily patrolled community of color and you're littering; wear the wrong color T-shirt and you're displaying gang allegiance. (para. 11)

People living in poverty do, unfortunately, face this marginalization in systems that are supposed to be of help to them, such as the mental health system. Poor women, for example, are much more likely to be without medical insurance than are higher income women (APA 2003). Individuals without insurance are more likely to receive services only on an emergency basis, and, in these situations, have little choice about their therapist and the duration of their treatment—assuming that they see a therapist. Some individuals repeat the acute care process numerous times with little or no opportunity to build rapport with a therapist or participate in treatment planning for their own well-being. In this cycle, mental health clients are often prescribed solutions instead of being regarded as the experts on what they most need to alleviate their suffering (Smith 2010).

Decolonizing "Help" for the Poor

A social exclusion framework for poverty has special relevance for counselors and psychologists interested in decolonizing their practice in that it is a relational perspective—it refers explicitly to relationships between people. Understanding the ways in which mainstream society pushes the poor out toward the margins is a first step toward seeing how class oppression pervades taken-for-granted assumptions about what is "normal" in psychological theories, interventions, and other expressions of professional intentions to help. Manifestations of these assumptions have been elaborated sporadically by the handful of psychologists who have attended to the well-being of poor clients in conventional therapy.

Psychotherapeutic distancing with regard to people living in poverty has been described and critiqued within the mental health literature since the 1970s (e.g., Jones 1974; Lorion 1973, 1974). Javier and Herron (2002) labeled it a fear of the poor that stemmed from therapists' own social class strivings. Schnitzer (1996), a family therapist who practiced in a low-income Boston community, observed that her clinic's accessibility was limited not only by clients' financial constraints but also by her colleagues' "thinking about who 'they' are and why 'they' don't come in" (p. 572). She furthermore speculated that clinician's alienation from the life experiences of the poor not only created barriers to service but also likely undermined the usefulness of conventional services for poor clients who did make use of them:

> Clinical work within poor communities offers another perspective on the question of why "they don't come in": perhaps our poorest clients do not think their appointments are *worth* keeping. This possibility naturally leads to the question of how clinical methods can be rendered more meaningful to people in poor communities who are struggling with the practical issues of making ends meet. (p. 579)

bell hooks (2000) also explored the notion that we may be hesitant to stand alongside people in poverty because of our own class strivings. Her perspective also highlights the suspicion with which professionals may regard poor and working clients:

> To stand in solidarity with the poor is no easy gesture at a time when individuals of all classes are encouraged to fear for their economic well-being. Certainly the fear of being taken advantage of by those in need has led many people with class privilege to turn their backs on the poor. (p. 46)

hooks's words call to mind an expression that many counselors and others will have heard: "working the system." When clients misreport personal information with the intention of getting resources that they need, it is regarded with distrust—and with the assumption that poor clients are attempting to "take advantage" as they perhaps place the helping professional at a disadvantage. A more socially just perspective may be to reflect upon the times clients seem to be "working the system" by placing scrutiny on the system itself. What is wrong with the system that it needs to be bent or broken for clients to actually obtain needed resources?

Although the language of decolonization was not in use within mainstream US psychology at that time, one of the most notable early supporters of the deconstruction of "help" for the poor was former American Psychological Association president George Albee. Albee spoke explicitly of the need for psychologists to address the suffering of the poor and disenfranchised through innovations in practice, and to train psychologists in settings where poor clients were more likely to be seen (Albee 1969). However, Albee did not call psychologists to help the poor in conventional "charitable" ways. He emphasized that part and parcel of this work was the establishment of a social platform by which the causes of poverty themselves could be addressed. Such work, he maintained, required identification of and confrontation with established power structures. How much longer, he asked his readers, could psychologists' silence on these issues be bought? Albee was articulating what a decolonization framework has to teach us today: that empathy and competent services for the poor are essential, but unless we frame these within an explicit analysis of power relations and a willingness to address our own participation within them, our efforts will merely reproduce and perpetuate the *power over* dynamic that exists between poor clients and ourselves. While such efforts could certainly be considered charitable, charity does not itself constitute social justice.

Albee's call to his profession echoed what another revolutionary helper of the day—this one an educator—had to say about the potential danger in the unexamined "help" offered to the poor. This educational theorist was Paulo Freire (1970), who wrote of what he referred to as "the false generosity of the oppressor." This "generosity," according to Freire, is not genuinely helpful at all—in fact, it is part of the problem. It is the help offered by privileged people to the oppressed in the *absence* of any attempt to acknowledge or address the sources of oppression themselves. The privileged helpers then have the opportunity to experience themselves as beneficent and dissociated from systems of oppression even as those systems continue their unfettered, unexamined operation—thus ultimately serving to perpetuate the privileged positions enjoyed by the "helpers." As helping professionals, it is important that we constantly reflect upon and seek supervision and peer consultation around this very issue. Counselors and psychologists concerned with the liberation of their clients should strive toward becoming intimately aware of when they enjoy being the expert and/or bestowing advice upon a grateful client. These dynamics are not necessarily helpful in contexts with economically marginalized clients, as they may not privilege the voices and opinions of the clients themselves. In an effort to privilege the voices of our clients, it may help to reframe how we typically think of "insiders" and "outsiders" as Freire does:

> …the oppressed are not "marginal," are not men living "outside" society. They have always been "inside"—inside the structure that made them "beings for others." The solution is not to "integrate" them into the structure of oppression, but to transform that structure so that they can become "beings for themselves." (p. 56)

It is safe to say that conventional psychological interventions offered to the poor do *not* typically incorporate attempts to acknowledge or address sources of oppression—which implies that counselors' and psychologists' professional attempts to help may do as much to perpetuate an inequitable status quo as they do to relieve the suffering and exclusion of the poor within that status quo. This, in fact, is a pivotal point within the scholarship of another indispensable commentator on the embeddedness of colonial/oppressive ideologies within mainstream psychological thought: Isaac Prilleltensky (1989). To contrast with status quo professional operations, Prilleltensky (2003) proposed a framework by which innovative, liberatory psychological interventions could be developed and gauged. Within this framework, an intervention or a research project would be evaluated according to its *psychopolitical validity*. To attain psychopolitical validity, an intervention must incorporate an accounting of the relevant power dynamics operating at psychological and political levels as well as catalyze change toward liberation within personal, interpersonal, and structural domains.

A Framework for Decolonizing Psychological Practice in the Context of Poverty

What new practices could enable psychologists and counselors to begin to subvert the social exclusion of people living in poverty? How could we transform the colonized "helpful" interactions that most graduate students are trained to deliver into decolonized, psychopolitically valid practice? We work toward this goal from a framework that includes (1) transformed psychotherapeutic practices, (2) co-created interventions, and (3) community praxis to challenge the one-up/one-down dynamics that often exist in counseling by explicitly locating the work within a social, cultural, historical, and political context (Smith 2010).

Transformed Psychotherapeutic Practice

A decolonized perspective on conventional psychological practice reveals that White, Western, class-privileged perspectives are embedded deep within the practices of many counselors and other mental health professionals who work in poor communities. David Blustein, a vocational psychologist put it this way:

> [O]ur specialty, like much of applied psychology, has been profoundly shaped by classism, which remains a major stumbling block in the growth of a relevant and comprehensive psychology.... Classism refers to prejudicial beliefs about individuals based on their social class; typically, it encompasses implicit or explicit attempts to ignore, marginalize, or silence the voices of working-class and poor people. (Blustein 2001, p. 175)

At the same time, many clinicians are currently practicing in settings where they are required to provide conventional services, which most often means offering 50-minute talk therapy hours.

How can individual therapists begin to transform this quintessentially conventional practice modality? First on our list is the suggestion that therapists expand their knowledge of theoretical orientations that explicitly address power dynamics within the therapeutic dyad—and which offer therapists opportunities to break the silence that typically surrounds them. Relational-cultural therapy (RCT) is one of these. A feminist psychotherapeutic technique, RCT was developed at the Jean Baker Miller Training Institute at Wellesley College and is based upon mutuality and power sharing. In fact, as Jordan (2000) explained, *both* members of the dyad are understood to grow and change as part of the best psychotherapy: "Both people bring strengths, wisdom, gifts, troubles, and blind spots to this relationship. The therapist holds some special expertise in the area of mental suffering and relationships. Patients bring knowledge about themselves, wisdom about many matters, and even insights about the therapist that are invaluable" (p. 1011). In addition to transforming their roles within the conventional consulting room, psychologists can remain open and flexible regarding the incorporation of diverse elements of support and advocacy within their individual work (Vera and Speight 2003). Examples include, using a session to practice for a job interview, providing a referral to a food bank, accompanying a client to court, or meeting a client for a session in a local YMCA, church, or homeless shelter.

Co-created Interventions

Many class-aware therapists will recognize that they have knowledge deficits in areas where poor clients are experts. Frequently, features of everyday life in a poor community will be unfamiliar to middle-class professionals; for example, Cote summarized studies that suggested that lower-income individuals "have more egalitarian values, provide more help to a stranger in distress, and trust others more than their higher-class counterparts" (Cote 2011, p. 53). Therapists often know little about the labyrinthine intricacies of welfare applications and reviews, or about the lack of taken-for-granted resources (like grocery stores) in the neighborhood. Given this culture gap, interventions that are co-created with people living in poverty can empower clients, enact a more egalitarian value system, and result in more relevant interventions for poor communities. In its Resolution on Poverty and SES, APA supported this contention, stating a commitment to advocating for

> research that identifies and learns from indigenous efforts by low-income people to work together to solve personal and shared problems or create organizations that advocate effectively for social justice…[as well as] early interventions…that are strengths based, community based, flexible, sensitive to culture and ethnic values of the family, and that have a long-lasting impact (APA 2003, p. 103).

Conventionally trained therapists may find it disorienting at first to regard poor clients and other nonprofessionals as collaborators, but innovative, effective practices and programs have evolved in just this way. Examples have included group counseling modalities based on poetry and spoken word performances (Smith et al.

2009) and peer-led psychoeducational groups to address depression in the context of poverty (Goodman et al. 2007).

Interventions that can encourage such co-creation include inviting community members to sit in and/or fishbowl during program and service development meetings. Clinicians could create leadership positions for clients and community members on clinic and hospital decision-making boards and open mental health centers to focus groups, town halls, and fund-raising strategy brainstorm sessions. The fact that these actions would be considered unconventional merely underscores the degree to which the opinions and expertise of people in poor communities are usually disregarded. Many mental health agencies attempt to brainstorm ways to better serve the community only to run into dead ends regarding utilization and feasibility. Honoring and giving voice to community members so that new interventions reflect their input not only subverts conventional power dynamics but also opens the door to more genuinely helpful interventions in the future.

Community Praxis

The term *praxis* is derived from Freirian pedagogy. As Freire explained it, "[O]ppression is domesticating. To no longer be prey to its force, one must emerge from it and turn upon it. This can be done only by means of *praxis*: reflection and action upon the world in order to transform it" (Freire 1970, p. 36). Praxis, then, is an ongoing cycle; as a consequence, transformative efforts are themselves reflected upon, and the cycle continues. True reflection should always lead to action, according to Freire, as it highlights the injustice and oppression at work in society. Isaac Prilleltensky (2001) expressed the connection between a community's engagement in praxis and the wellness of that community:

> Value-based praxis begins with the identification of a set of values that is capable of promoting personal, collective, and relational wellness. The next step is to engage in the cycle of praxis and ask ourselves what should be the ideal for a community, what is the present state of affairs, what is desired by members of the community, and what can be done to close the gap between the ideal and the actual states of affairs. (2001, p. 774)

Mental health practitioners who see engagement and action as components of well-being, and who therefore partner with poor communities to engage in praxis, have ventured the farthest afield in their commitment to decolonized practice. Although, as Prilleltensky suggested, they are still using their skills to promote emotional well-being, they are *not* so much offering interventions to people as they are engaging alongside community members in practice/actions that explicitly connect individual and community well-being to the larger sociocultural context. In fact, community praxis constitutes a way of understanding mutual support, critical-consciousness-raising, and social action as the primary ingredients of individual and community wellness (Smith 2010). With its explicit identification of oppression and exclusion as pathogenic influences in the lives of poor people, community praxis reaches a high level of psychopolitical validity through its inherent potential to contribute to social action.

How can psychologists and counselors participate in community praxis? Participatory action research (PAR) represents a promising vehicle. PAR is most broadly an approach to research by which professionals do not conduct studies *on* community members; they conduct studies *with* community members on issues of local interest and urgency. It is, therefore, a process of research, reflection, and action in which conventional distinctions between the researcher and the researched are challenged (Brydon-Miller 1997). Its collaborative approach makes possible the production of knowledge that represents worldviews other than those characteristic of university settings and other elite-class locations—which aligns it with the deepest commitments of decolonized approaches to knowledge creation. Psychologists and community members participate as co-researchers and co-seekers in PAR, a process that challenges everyone involved to create mutual engagement and to interrogate obstacles to that mutuality. And just as Prilleltensky explained, PAR can be an emotionally growthful experience for everyone involved, as has been referenced within many descriptions of PAR (Law 1997; Lykes 2000; Smith and Romero 2010). Along these lines, Mexican activist Arturo Ornelas summarized his PAR experience as one of deep personal healing:

> You begin by recognizing a need and knowing it well. Then you start taking action. Reflecting on that action with the others, maybe every day for a half hour or more, a dialogue starts about the need and about the action.... The Spanish for word for knowledge, *saber*, comes from the Latin *sabor*, meaning flavor. In order to know, you need to taste, to eat. In my culture, you cannot separate these things.... You are nourished by knowledge. You achieve intimacy by doing a deep analysis of your inner being and celebrating that analysis by dialoguing with others. It is an act of creation and re-creation. (Debbink and Ornelas 1997, p. 19)

Conclusion

Understanding poverty within a social class framework reveals it to be a marginalized social location that is vulnerable to harm via professionals' colonized attitudes—unless they consciously act to the contrary. Conventional therapists and their clients can occupy different positions of power within therapeutic dyads even when both are middle or owning class. When the client lives in poverty, that discrepancy is magnified, and proffers of help can actually function as reproductions of privilege. Decolonized practice in the context of poverty requires us to stand in a new place as we think about the poor and the operations of classism: it means seeing ourselves as part of a broad, dynamic system wherein our circumstances and well-being exist in dialectic relationship to the circumstances and well-being of the poor (Smith 2010). Psychologists and counselors who accept the challenge of re-*visioning* their professional roles can contribute their practice toward the "researching back," "writing back," and "talking back" that Linda Tuhiwai Smith (1999) described as lying at the heart of anti-colonial work (p. 7).

References

Albee, G. W. (1969). Who shall be served? *Professional Psychology, 1,* 4–7.

APA (American Psychological Association). (2003). Resolution on poverty and socioeconomic status. *Roeper Review, 25*(3), 103–105.

Blustein, D. L. (2001). Extending the reach of vocational psychology toward and inclusive and integrative psychology of working. *Journal of Vocational Behavior, 59,* 171–182. doi:10.1006/jvbe.2001.1823.

Bourdieu, P. (1984). *Distinction: A social critique of the judgment of taste*. Cambridge: Harvard University Press.

Brydon-Miller, M. (1997). Participatory action research: Psychology and social change. *Journal of Social Issues, 53,* 657–666.

Bullock, H. E., Wyche, K. F., & Williams, W. R. (2001). Media images of the poor. *Journal of Social Issues, 57,* 229–246.

Cote, S. (2011). How social class shapes thoughts and actions in organizations. *Research in Organizational Behavior, 31,* 43–71. doi:10.1016/j.riob.2011.09.004.

Debbink, G., & Ornelas, A. (1997). Cows for campesinos. In S. E. Smith, D. G. Willms, & N. J. Johnson (Eds.), *Nurtured by knowledge* (pp. 13–33). New York: Apex.

Ehrenreich, B. (9 Aug 2009). Is it now a crime to be poor? *The New York Times*, New York Edition, p. WK9.

Freire, P. (1970). *Pedagogy of the oppressed.* New York: Continuum.

Goodman, L. A., Litwin, A., Bohlig, A., Weintraub, S. R., Green, A., Walker, J., et al. (2007). Applying feminist theory to community practice: A multilevel empowerment intervention for low-income women with depression. In E. Aldarondo (Ed.), *Advancing social justice through clinical practice* (pp. 265–290). Mahwah: Lawrence Erlbaum.

Hooks, B. (2000). *Feminist theory: From margin to center*. London: Pluto Press.

Javier, R. A., & Herron, W. G. (2002). Psychoanalysis and the disenfranchised: Countertransference issues. *Psychoanalytic Psychology, 19,* 149–166.

Jones, E. (1974). Social class and psychotherapy: A critical review of research. *Psychiatry, 37,* 307–320.

Jordan, J. V. (2000). The role of mutual empathy in relational/cultural therapy. *Journal of Clinical Psychology, 56,* 1005–1016.

Krieger, N., Williams, D. R., & Moss, N. E. (1997). Measuring social class in U.S. public health research: Concepts, methodologies, and guidelines. *Annual Review of Public Health, 18*(3), 341–378. doi: 0163-7525/97/0510-0341.

Law, M. (1997). Changing disabling environments through participatory action research. In S. E. Smith, D. G. Willms, & N. J. Johnson (Eds.), *Nurtured by knowledge* (pp. 34–58). New York: Apex.

Lorion, R. P. (1973). Socioeconomic status and traditional treatment approaches reconsidered. *Psychological Bulletin, 79,* 263–270.

Lorion, R. P. (1974). Patient and therapist variables in the treatment of low-income patients. *Psychological Bulletin, 81,* 344–354.

Lott, B., & Bullock, H. (2001). Who are the poor? *Journal of Social Issues, 57*(2), 189–206.

Lykes, M. B. (2000). Possible contributions of a psychology of liberation: Whither health and human rights? *Journal of Health Psychology, 5,* 383–397.

National Law Center on Homelessness and Poverty and The National Coalition for the Homeless. (2009). Homes not handcuffs. http://nlchp.org/content/pubs/2009HomesNotHandcuffs1.pdf.

Prilleltensky, I. (1989). Psychology and the status quo. *American Psychologist, 44,* 795–802.

Prilleltensky, I. (2001). Value-based praxis in community psychology: Moving toward social justice and social action. *American Journal of Community Psychology, 29,* 747–778. doi:0091-0562/01/1000-0747.

Prilleltensky, I. (2003). Understanding, resisting, and overcoming oppression: Toward psychopolitical validity. *American Journal of Community Psychology, 31,* 195–201.

Schnitzer, P. K. (1996). "They don't come in!" Stories told, lessons taught about poor families in therapy. *American Journal of Orthopsychiatry, 66,* 572–582.

Smith, L. T. (1999). *Decolonizing methodologies*. New York: Zed Books.

Smith, L. (2010). *Psychology, poverty, and the end of social exclusion: Putting our practice to work*. New York: Teachers College Press.

Smith, L., & Romero, L. (2010). Psychological interventions in the context of poverty: Participatory action research as practice. *American Journal of Orthopsychiatry, 80,* 12–25.

Smith, L., Chambers, D. A., & Bratini, L. (2009). When oppression is the pathogen: The participatory development of socially-just mental health practice. *American Journal of Orthopsychiatry, 79,* 159–168.

Vera, E. M., & Speight, S. L. (2003). Multicultural competence, social justice, and counseling psychology: Expanding our roles. *The Counseling Psychologist, 31,* 253–272. doi:10.1177/0011000002250634.

Weinger, S. (1998). Poor children "know their place": Perceptions of poverty, class, and public messages. *Journal of Sociology and Social Welfare, 25,* 100–118.

Chapter 7
Story Sciencing and Analyzing the Silent Narrative Between Words: Counseling Research from an Indigenous Perspective

Eduardo Duran and Judith Firehammer

Terms like multiculturalism, competency, and sensitivity have been overused in research and clinical practice in counseling and psychology. As long as these terms are defined by an epistemology that is not from the community under investigation, the practice of research will merely be one of ongoing neo-colonialism. Researchers, including those doing supposedly "multicultural" scholarship, generally adhere to the requirements imposed by academia or funding sources that are not situated within the communities at the center of their inquiries and that have little or no contact with the communities. When this is the case, researchers may be required to engage in the research process and to report findings in a manner that does not reflect the investigative needs of disenfranchised communities on whose backs they are building their careers, furthering a process of marginalization and colonization.

Relying on empirical methodologies, ethical standards, and procedures that are not based in the lived experience of communities being studied can be a great detriment to acquiring knowledge that is actually beneficial to the community. For example, a Native community may have done research for millennia through the use of oral traditions, such as storytelling; however, researchers from a Western, non-Native perspective may not see these as valid research methods and may, instead, insist that these practices should be validated by a Western rationality framework. This is in itself a hegemonic, colonizing practice: it is a great imposition on communities to insist that their methodologies should be subjected to and validated by Western empiricism. Unfortunately, this practice is so commonplace and so accepted—even in the world of "multicultural" counseling and psychology research—that most researchers never entertain the thought that their research may be undermining or even causing harm to the population being studied.

E. Duran (✉) · J. Firehammer
Seventh Direction, 37 Ea. Main st. Ste. 7, Bozeman, MT 59715, USA
e-mail: soulhealing16@yahoo.com

J. Firehammer
e-mail: judefire@aol.com

R. D. Goodman, P. C. Gorski (eds.), *Decolonizing "Multicultural" Counseling through Social Justice,* International and Cultural Psychology, DOI 10.1007/978-1-4939-1283-4_7

Another problem in much of the research being conducted in Indigenous communities—often by scholars who see themselves as progressive advocates—is that the research must adhere to Western standards of ethical guidelines. This becomes problematic in relation to tribal etiquette and exchange of information. I know of specific instances in which community elders, through the practice of oral tradition, have shared valuable data that could be used to help their communities. Funding sources, however, will not allow the data to be used unless there is clearance from a human subjects board and signed written consent forms. This requirement can be deeply offensive to the community leaders who often are operating from spiritual frameworks; any future possibility of further investigation may not be possible because of such a breach in "multicultural manners."

In this chapter, we delineate some methods that can be useful when pursuing research in Indigenous communities. Data collection as well as data analysis will be explored from an Indigenous framework in the hope that these ideas may begin to shift the research paradigm towards one that is community-based. The hope is that "participatory research method" is not just used as jargon, but represents a real shift in the power dynamics of how new knowledge is pursued within communities. In particular, some marginalized communities have been over-researched and have developed research fatigue. This occurs in large part because of the way that knowledge is sought from a Western framework. As such, communities have become resistant to any further investigation.

Research in Aboriginal communities has been a method of colonization due to the illusion that science is neutral and objective (Duran 2006). Many of the studies conducted in Aboriginal/Native communities represent replicas of Western paradigms that are imposed on Native communities, and thus perpetuate hegemony disguised as an attempt to "help." Sinha (1984) illustrates this point:

> [M]odern psychology has been a product of the West and has been imported wholesale to Third World countries.... Too often, problems taken up for research have been mere replications of whatever had been done in Europe or the United States with little relations to the needs of the country. Such unimaginative replications of Western research have been decried and called caricatures of Western studies...one is disappointed by their artificiality, triviality, and lack of relevance to real life psychological phenomena. (pp. 20–21)

Murray (1991) and Said (1978) make the point that many of these studies are invalid because the methods employed intrude into Native lifeworlds and fail to contribute to the community's liberation.

Fortunately, there are changes on the research horizon and new approaches and methods are being developed that honor communities (Wilson 2008). Aboriginal researchers, clinicians, and theorists are developing research processes that are more relevant to Native research needs, especially as they apply to transforming the lifeworld through liberation (Duran 2006; Martin 2003; Rigney 1999; Steinhauer 2002; Wilson and Pence 2006). Unfortunately, despite this movement there is still pressure from academia and funding sources to comply with a strict scientific method that is entrenched in Western philosophy. Therefore, the Native researcher finds herself or himself in a quandary, wanting to acknowledge Tribal research methods, while needing to conduct research within restrictions and controls imposed by Western-oriented institutions.

Many Indigenous researchers attempt to fill the paradigmatic gap between the Western logical positivistic mindset and traditional forms of epistemological understanding by conducting qualitative research. This is done at the risk of not being considered a *real* scientist. At times, qualitative researchers compromise further by gathering data using qualitative methods, and then "crunching" the meaning into thematic units through "sophisticated" statistical methods. Applying such quantitative methods can drain most of the soul from the precious narrative collected through qualitative means from the holders of knowledge within the community. (This is the worst case scenario. There are instances in which this does not occur or may not occur as deeply so as to remove the soul from the data.) Recently, however, there have been important evolutionary developments in these methodologies that are aligned with a decolonizing perspective on research.

Towards Analyzing the Silent Spaces Between the Words

Most qualitative research can be categorized into one of five areas of inquiry that rely on analyzing or making meaning of spoken or written narrative (Creswell 1998). These include:

- Biographical study, which is described by Denzin (1989) as the "use and collection of life documents that describe turning points in an individual's life" (p. 69).
- Phenomenological study, in which the researcher is trying to get at the essence of reality as experienced in human consciousness as the things in themselves (Polkinghorne 1994). This is an ambitious form of research in that the researcher is using the psyche to explore itself. One of the main tenets of this method is that the researcher attempts to suspend all bias through what is known as "bracketing" (Stewart and Mickunas 1990).
- Grounded theory, which attempts to develop or find a theory that is explanatory (Creswell 1998).
- Ethnography, which requires that the researcher gathers information through participant observation, immersing herself or himself in the lifeworld of the group being studied (Creswell 1998). This method has been used in many Native communities.
- Case studies, which focus on understanding a unique person or program. In some cases, these can be seen as throwbacks to the medical model of grand rounds in which physicians gathered around the table and dissected cases in order to achieve an informed diagnosis, leading to a relevant intervention.

Once the narrative data are gathered, there are many methods to which they can be subjected to in order to uncover their meaning for the community and researcher. A common approach to analyzing narrative data is thematic interpretation, wherein content is the exclusive focus (Riessman 2008). Thematic analysis has its roots in phenomenology.

In our high-tech world, there are computerized algorithms that use artificial intelligence to interpret narratives. Although this might help solve the problem of bias, it introduces another problem by excluding the human reflective component that is critical to knowing the essence of the phenomenon being examined.

Structural analysis is not only concerned with thematic content but also is attentive to the narrative form (Riessman 2008). In this method of analyzing data, the structure of language and how humans communicate are important to the understanding of the narrative. When working with different Tribal communities, it becomes apparent that meanings of words in the English language vary from one group to the next. Merely subjecting narrative from different communities to simple thematic analysis would miss a large part, if not all, of the meaning being transmitted in the narrative. To understand the nuances of how narrative is expressed, the researcher must have a deeply rooted understanding as a participant observer so that the researcher does not have to translate these ideas. This point speaks to the fact that Native researchers—who do not have to take this quantum leap into the linguistic nuances of the Tribal world—would be better at interpretation and more efficient. It can take non-Native researchers a long time to learn how to interpret these fine linguistic meanings, and it is unlikely that computerized models would be able to accomplish this task.

The third option of interpretive analysis is what Riessman (2008) calls dialogic or performance analysis:

> [Dialogic analysis] interrogates how talk among speakers is interactively (dialogically) produced and performed as narrative. More than the previous two, this method requires close reading of contexts, including the influence of the investigator, setting, and social circumstances on the production and interpretation of the narrative. Simply put, if thematic and structural approaches interrogate "what" is spoken and "how," the dialogic/performance approach asks "who an utterance may be directed to," "when," and "why," that is for what purposes? (p. 105)

Dialogic analysis considers the presence of the investigator as well as the importance of the interaction. This method allows for cultural nonverbal communication to be analyzed, making it more valid in analyzing narratives from Aboriginal people where much of the communication occurs in the silent spaces between words. In order to interpret the silence between the words, the researcher, or story scientist, must have a deep connection to and understanding of the meanings of these the silences.

An example of how some Native people interpret the communication encounter is apparent in an experience I had during a hiring interview with a Tribal council. During the interview, few questions were asked and most of the conversation was friendly and not job-related. The council had my resume in which my experience and publications were provided. A few weeks later an elder from the council approached me and told me that she did not know I had written a particular book. The fact that she did not ask anything during the interview and the fact that she did not know about the book indicated that she had not read my resume. At that point, I realized that she had resorted to another type of narrative interpretation because I had been offered the job. When I investigated the matter further, I learned why she thought I would be a good selection: she saw the way I moved and this told her that I could do the job. This was a clear example of how dialogic analysis was part of her lifeworld and she took into account much more than the verbal or written narrative I presented.

Research Transference

Although the latest research trend in Indigenous communities involves community-based participatory research (CBPR) methodologies, this approach is not necessarily free of power and colonial influence. The mere fact that most inquiry originates in university settings demonstrates the one-sidedness of research because, at some level, it is serving the needs of the university or the university-based researcher. This is not to say that there are not some benefits to the community being studied, but power differentials continue to feed the distrust in Indigenous communities. As long as power rests with the individuals designing and implementing the study, and the community has little power to influence the course of events and research, the process of participatory research will continue to be hindered in its ability to be pro-justice (Nelson and Prilleltensky 2005). This aspect is challenging because power dynamics are not always obvious because of their sometimes-subtle nature (Nel 2010; Nelson and Prilleltensky 2005).

CBPR is usually conducted on a continuum of participation modes (Cornwall 2003). According to Nel (2010), "This continuum of participatory approaches starts with *functional* participation at the conservative end, followed by *instrumental* and *consultative* modes of participation. At the radical end of the continuum is *transformative* participation" (p. 106). Transformative participation occurs when research findings bring about change from within communities, such as alleviating problems and suffering (Kelly and Van der Riet 2003). Unfortunately, very few studies, even within the realm of multicultural counseling and psychology, attain transformative or liberation levels of participation (Cornwall and Jewkes 1995).

Transformative processes can be restricted or impaired when communities do not have power over the methods or analyses used in researching their communities. In addition, transformative/liberation research cannot occur if the analysis is restricted to Western concepts and metaphors. The use of Western empirical jargon at the grant-writing phase and the implementation phase of research is a barrier to achieving the full ideal of participatory research in most instances (Duran 2006). Further, economic advantage becomes an issue that distorts the perception of balance in most university-led research projects. It is an accepted practice that the academic institution can gain in excess of 50 % of the research budget for overhead costs. Most of the time the "participatory community" is not privy as to how these funds are used and the academic institution uses these funds for an all-encompassing item called "overhead." The economic issue has more than symbolic significance to most Native communities that are dealing with serious economic disparities. When a Native community realizes that an academic institution is gaining one-half or more of a five-million-dollar research project, the community feels used, which in turn impacts the research results and sets up the community for future lack of participation. Again, the lack of economic participation adds to the feeling of lack of power and participation in all of the research process. This area is usually ignored by researchers because it is merely a university policy that is out of their control. From the community point of view, however, this is not acceptable; tribal communities are beginning to resist this practice and exercise their power by not allowing research to occur if the economic issue is not made participatory.

As long as the research has a linear method in which data have to be extracted and analyzed, the participation will be less than transformative regardless of whether the method is quantitative or qualitative in nature. A different conceptual framework that fits the community's conceptual life-world needs to be made part of the method in order for the community to begin feeling that their way of seeing the world is congruent with the research process. The fact that much research conceptualization is done in the mind of the principal investigator as a follow-up of previous research increases the existing trust barrier in the minds of tribal and community members and a feeling of subtle colonization ensues. For example, if the research proposal must be substantiated by what already exists in the research literature, then the foundation of the proposal is research that is based on Western empiricism and underlying that method is Western philosophy, which in many instances is felt as a tool of social control and colonization. The fact that the funding sources also have a predisposed idea of what they will fund and what method is acceptable to them is problematic because the proposal itself will have a trajectory that is not participatory from the start, and this will affect the process through the end of the project. Again, this leaves the community feeling used and the results of the research will not give the community or tribe the needed transformative power that is so direly needed in many of these communities in order for them to heal from some of the health, economic, and other issues present in their lifeworld.

As it is practiced presently, most CBPR projects can be categorized as instrumental and consultative modes of participatory research (Cornwall 2003). The instrumental mode of participatory research occurs when community ideas are included in the research aims and some responsibilities are delegated to community members. The consultative mode views the community as a stakeholder and the aim of the research is to enhance awareness and understanding by the community (Nel 2010). Community participation is limited in both the instrumental and consultative modes in that final authority rests with the academic entity that is operating at the discretion of funding sources that are usually far removed from the community and their concerns. In most research projects that are conducted in Native communities, the principal investigator is an academic and not a community member or someone who has been involved in community work over an extended period of time. Communities that have been colonized and subjected to many types of hegemony from the academy react with silent distrust that creates a negative transference to the process. Psychological transference, the unconscious redirecting of feelings, can have a deep impact on the process of research while no one is aware that there is an ongoing resistance to historical processes that are triggered by hegemonic memories that become transference reactions. Lately, some of these communities are finding their voice and demanding agency in all facets of research.

Story Science as an Approach

In order for participatory methods to become liberating and transforming, the overall approach needs to be changed. This new approach can best be defined and categorized at this point as *Story science* (Kubo 2011, personal communication). Story science is an approach to understanding issues in communities and within individuals and a way of achieving insight through narrative. Narratives that inform insight have been part of Indigenous oral traditions for millennia and are an integral part of how Indigenous peoples perceive their world. Yet, dominant society's empirically based research has privileged literacy and numeracy over oral traditions, thus invalidating the most basic way to make sense of the Indigenous lifeworld.

What we can write down or count is perceived as more valid and credible than what we can convey interpersonally (Kubo 2011, personal communication). Maynes et al. (2008) wrote:

> Scholars in the social sciences have often regarded life histories with unease and suspicion…. Within positivist strains of social science, life stories are reduced to the status of the anecdotal, adding color or personal interest but unreliable as a basis for generalization. (p. 5)

For example, we no longer make deals based on a conversation or a handshake—we need a written legal contract instead. American and Canadian Indigenous oral histories, as well as dominant-culture-written histories, attest to how Native people were presented with written contracts that made no sense to Natives and were then used to confiscate land and resources. Furthermore, until statistics, such as the percentage of land and resources taken from Native peoples, can be used to validate what we, as Native people, may already feel inside (i.e., that stark inequities exist in our society), we may not be taken seriously. In short, we have stopped relying on our intuitive ways of knowing, and stopped practicing our most fundamental human ways of communicating with one another.

Storytelling is fundamentally human, and narrative is a basic frame of being human (Young and Saver 2001). Our brains are wired for stories. Human beings begin to attend more to spoken language when we hear what we know is the typical beginning of a story: phrases like, "a long time ago," or "it happened that way." Neuroscience informs us that stories are where the most deeply ingrained belief systems are manifested. Young and Saver (2001) wrote, "recent advances in cognitive neuroscience suggest a regionally distributed neural network mediates the creation of narrative in the human central nervous system" (p. 72). Young and Saver note that once we lose our ability to construct narrative, we lose ourselves. This loss of self has been experienced in many Native communities through the process of historical trauma; as such, it is critical that storytelling and narrative be revitalized in communities in order to restore self-identity as well as communal/tribal identity. Storytelling is the oldest form of narrative and occurs in the direct and active interaction between storyteller and listener.

Without realizing it, most of us shape our decisions and actions based on the cultural narratives or stories that surround us. Even though most Aboriginal communities have suffered tremendous devastation to their culture, language, and environment, the stories have prevailed through oral tradition. These stories have been the lifeline that have provided resiliency that has allowed our communities not only to survive but also to reconnect and reinvent what it is to be Aboriginal within the context of historical trauma and the horrendous symptoms that this has brought onto our communities. One surviving story in Aboriginal country is how Aboriginal science was practiced and how the insights of these studies were used to improve the community as well as to ensure survival.

The power and value of story science lie in its capacity to reach deeper levels of understanding and uncover new knowledge that traditional literate and numerate scientific inquiry is less effective at detecting and communicating. By using narrative frameworks as devices of inquiry, story science evokes authentic information about human experiences. For example, an interview protocol could invite participants to "tell a story about a time long ago and what mothers did when they found out they were pregnant." This allows researchers to listen to and interpret that information from within their own deeply human schema, connecting researchers with the subject of their inquiry on an emotional and historical level, as well as on a formal cognitive level (Kubo 2011, personal communication).

The experience for researchers and participants is entirely different from administering a survey to gather the same type of data. Story science requires that the researcher give up the control that she or he has in a fixed interview format that is designed for efficiency, and instead to encourage equality in the process of telling and hearing a story (Devereux 1967). Story science will produce another level of anxiety for researchers who have been socialized into the "efficient" fixed interview or quantitative data gathering and analysis methods when working with Native people.

Further, many of the people from tribes of North and South America have a different way of communicating verbally than do most English-speaking researchers. There is a cadence and set of rules that are part of the Native style of communicating, especially among elders and members of the community who still live in a traditional lifeworld. This cadence requires that the researcher be very mindful of the slightest intent to speak on the part of the storyteller, and that the researcher pays close attention to the nonverbal narrative during the silence that occurs in between words. Most communication between people in the USA and Canada requires that there be very little or no space for silence. The exact opposite is true when speaking with key informants in Native communities. When speaking to elders, there are times that the silence in between exchanges may take several minutes; there are instances where the silence may even require days before a response is given. Many researchers find this excruciating and they invariably try to fill in the silence. Once they slip into this familiar turf of filling the silence, the discussion is essentially over. The elder/informant will know that the method of communicating is not what she or he understands as the process of communication and will respond politely from this point on, but there may be little substance offered in the conversation.

Another consideration that researchers interested in story science must be aware of is that Western linearity may be replaced by random curvilinearity. Random curvilinearity occurs when a Native speaker does not adhere to the spatio-temporal rules of relating that are found in most conversations held in Euro-American day-to-day verbal exchanges. The Native speaker may start in the middle of a story and tell a parallel story that may seem to be tangential, and then end the story by telling the beginning with or without a parallel story that also may start in the middle, beginning, or end. Maynes et al. (2008) write, "Confusion and misunderstanding can occur when participants in a conversation do not share the convention of temporal ordering of a plot" (p. 5). If the researcher tries to re-direct the informant towards their own level of spatio-temporal comfort, the informant will more than likely be polite and comply, but the hidden essence of the phenomenon that is being sought will more than likely be lost.

Story science considers the layers of belief systems embedded within stories as a framework for data analysis; as such, it reveals patterns of experience of a subgroup within a society. Trends and patterns revealed in a set of stories from a community may challenge the validity of dominant societal belief systems, or illustrate the ways in which a dominant narrative may denigrate people's lived experience and may even cause harm within otherwise functional communities (Kubo 2011, personal communication). It is also worth noting that within Aboriginal understanding "the story" is a live entity and has a spirit. Therefore, a person is not telling the story per se; instead, the story is telling itself and, in this way, the story takes on a quality that brings life into the process. The story does not entail merely content which objectifies the story, as in Western cosmology. As the story comes to life in the process of telling, it transforms the material world as well as the human participants.

A story scientist will analyze the stories contained in interviews and field observations in the context of other layers of narrative present in the culture, community, and larger society, rather than presenting a qualitative analysis in isolation (Kubo 2011, personal communication). The presentation of findings from a story science-based inquiry will take a narrative form, such as a set of stories presented to an audience, a film, or a website containing a range of stories in multimedia formats. At times, the life-force of the story itself will provide a different layer of story which may allow for the story scientist as well as thc community participant to bring insightful analysis to the community situation that is being explored and transformed.

A story science framework presents many opportunities for CBPR—community residents can help develop interview protocols, administer them, and participate in analysis and reporting. But the essential element of any story science inquiry is the opportunity for stories to be told, and to transform behavior and beliefs of participants, researchers, and audiences of practitioners. Yes, at the risk of sounding heretical, the transformation that is possible through story science is not just for the community being researched. The research paradigm that dictates that the community is "being researched" places the community in the place of the same age-old place as the research "subject" that is the sine que non of social science research (i.e., you must have a subject in order for inquiry to occur). Once you place the community as the research subject, the narrative message becomes clear to the community: "We must have a problem or are sick and in need of being a research subject in the study." This sentiment rings true regardless of how much community participation is gained in the research project. Story science transcends the idea of having a subject–object relationship; and only the entity of the story remains, which transforms both the (so-called) subject and object of the research. The process, then, is truly participatory because both participants and researchers are servants of the story and not the "research project."

Story sciencing takes the approach that the community has had and continues to have traditional methods of pursuing inquiry. Research or story sciencing then becomes an organic process in which it will be difficult to distinguish the researcher from the research. From the very beginning, the people who are taking a lead in the inquiry must be able to give up their position of privilege and power in order for the silent spaces between the words to emerge from the community; this enables their ideas and needs for inquiry to emerge to the forefront. At this point, the old-style academic researcher can take on the role of advisor when needed or perform such functions that the community story scientists may need assistance with. A possible protocol or research outline may take on the following form:

- Through contact with the Tribe/community a need will be made known. These needs could be related to physical health, mental health, economic concerns, administrative issues, and many others.
- Once the need is known, it is important that the reason for the need is understood in a historical context. A question that can be asked at this point is: "If this were 1491, would we be having to create this project/intervention/prevention?" Asking about a time before colonization or historical community trauma will then elicit memories and knowledge of historical events that have led the community to have a need to address the particular issue. This in turn will help the community objectify the problem and realize that the problem is not the culture or who they are as Native people. Many projects fail at this point in that they persist in pathologizing the community. In turn, the projected pathology is internalized by the community. This internalizing of the projected pathological model can become part of the belief that it is the culture that is at fault, which can lead people to lose hope that there can be a solution.
- After the community becomes aware of historical trauma and its effects and impact on their lifeworld, the community can then begin to develop their method of inquiry into developing a pre-postcolonial intervention.
- The intervention development must rely on knowledge that needs to be revived by accessing the keepers of knowledge through oral tradition. At this point, the process of gathering stories and narratives that directly inform the issue at hand needs to follow methods that are congruent with traditional forms and etiquette of gathering such information. It is imperative that community experts/ethnographers are central to this process because they know the method that will yield the information that is needed in order for the process to be valid. The ethnographers should be able to make sense of the spoken word as well as the silence between the words.
- Initial analysis and results of the narratives should be presented to the keepers of knowledge and oral traditional history for their further validation of the results. This step is what is usually called *member checking* and is left out in many of the studies.

- At this point, the results of the narrative analysis can be integrated into a model that will yield a culturally responsive intervention that adheres to traditional etiquette as to how the intervention is to be presented. It is important to consider using words other than *intervention* because the word itself may imply pathology. If the word is used, it must be explained that the word is only being used as metaphor and not as a possible descriptor as to what the community has to receive in order for harmony to be restored. The intervention must also be phrased in a way that the community understands that this intervention is needed in order to reverse the effects of historical trauma. By phrasing the intervention as such, the historical context is again taken into account and the community will be more open to change and transformation.

Engaging in Story Sciencing

It appears that the issues that are discussed in this paper may make true participatory or transformative inquiry more difficult because, at times, it takes a leap of faith to go from theory to praxis. How is the Aboriginal researcher to write a proposal that follows the form of inquiry and search for answers in their community if all she has at her disposal are the rules of research imposed by academia and federal funding sources? In order to try to be of assistance to the community, the prospective scientist will have to resort to the rules of science as prescribed by the prevailing system of doing science. Once the researcher is forced into this paradigm, the ideal has been compromised. Not all is lost though, because the researcher can be truthful with the tribe or community and let them know that there are underpinnings of colonization in the proposed inquiry. These underpinnings can then be examined by the community or tribe and perhaps they can be addressed during the actual data gathering. In this manner, consciousness about the intent of the study and any problematic underpinnings will allow for the project to come closer to the ideal of true participatory research.

Another way of circumventing the needs for scientific colonial jargon on the part of the funding source and university is for the researcher to translate the proposed inquiry into language that is congruent with the community/tribal traditional form of inquiry. Either way, the people involved in doing the inquiry will have substantially more work than if they just succumb to the usual way of conducting research. The fact that researchers are tied to time constraints because of their academic responsibilities makes the extra interpretation problematic, especially if the researcher is on a tenure-track trajectory in which their work will be judged in terms of quantity to the point of how many actual research papers are published in refereed journals. (Refereeing poses yet another colonial imposition that should be obvious and not dealt with at length in this chapter.) When academia and funding agencies continue with the practices of not deferring to traditional tribal approaches to inquiry, they are adding to the ongoing historical trauma and the effects. It is ironic that most attempted research in Aboriginal communities, at least in their wording, are designed to remedy the impact of the effects that historical trauma has imposed on Aboriginal peoples, while actually perpetuating this trauma.

Story sciencing researchers in Aboriginal communities should consider the methodological notions put forward in this paper. In gathering data, researchers must understand not only methodology, but also the historical context of the community in which they are working. It does not suffice to study phenomena out of context because most of the people living in Native communities have a deep understanding of how history has impacted them, including the trauma imposed by research that was intrusive and meaningless. Through the implementation of story science approaches—including taking the interpretation of text beyond the bounds of dialogic analysis—knowledge attained will be more valid and will also help bring a new transforming narrative to the community.

Challenges abound in the area of research, and we should be working towards actual solutions that come from the tribes or communities with whom we are working. Funding sources and academia should take notice that social problems continue to abound. The social contract that is unwritten is that academia is to serve the society. Funding sources, which are mostly taxpayer funded, also have a social responsibility to be responsive to the community or tribe, not just in providing funding but also in providing funding in a culturally responsive manner. Achieving these ideals requires that academics and people in charge of funding sources make an attempt to learn what is needed in tribal communities. In addition to learning about the needs, they should make an attempt to learn and immerse themselves into the lifeworld of the community on whose behalf they are making sometimes life- and death-funding decisions. If these simple recommendations are developed and implemented, we will be on the road to a new trajectory in which we will be making participatory transformative research a reality.

References

Cornwall, A. (2003). Whose voices? Whose choices? Reflections on gender and participatory development. *World Development, 31,* 1325–1342.

Cornwall, A., & Jewkes, R. (1995). What is participatory research? *Social Science & Medicine, 41,* 1667–1676.

Creswell, J. W. (1998). *Qualitative inquiry and research design: Choosing among five traditions.* Thousand Oaks: Sage.

Denzin, N. K. (1989). *Interpretive biography*. Newbury Park: Sage.

Devereux, G. (1967). *From anxiety to method in behavioral sciences.* The Hague: Mouton.

Duran, E. F. (2006). *Healing the soul wound.* New York: Teachers Press.

Kelly, K., & Van der Riet, M. (2003). Participatory research in community settings: Processes, methods, and challenges. In M. Seedat (Ed.), N. Duncan & S. Lazarus (Con. Eds.), *Community psychology. Theory, method and practice. South African and other perspectives* (pp. 159–188). Cape Town: Oxford University Press.

Martin, K. (2003). *Aboriginal people, Aboriginal lands and Indigenist research: A discussion of re-search pasts and neo-colonial research futures*. Unpublished masters thesis, James Cook University, Townville.

Maynes, M., Pierce, J. L., & Laslett, B. (2008). *Telling stories: The use of personal narratives in the social sciences and history*. Ithaca: Cornell Press.

Murray, D. (1991). *Forked tongues: Speech, writing and representation in Native North American text*. Bloomington: Native American University Press.

Nel, W. (2010). *Developing a model of education support for the Komani San School Community*. Unpublished doctoral thesis, University of the Western Cape, South Africa.

Nelson, G., & Prilleltensky, I. (Eds.). (2005). *Community psychology. In pursuit of liberation and well-being*. New York: Palgrave Macmillan.

Polkinghorne, D. E. (1994). Reaction to special section on qualitative research in counseling process and outcome. *Journal of Counseling Psychology, 41,* 510–512.

Riessman, C. K. (2008). *Narrative methods for the human sciences*. Los Angeles: Sage.

Rigney, L. (1999). *Internationalisation of an Indigenous anti-colonial cultural critique of research methodologies: A guide to Indigenist research methodology and its principles*. Paper presented at the Herdsa Annual International Conference, Adelaide, SA.

Said, E. W. (1978) *Orientalism*. New York: Random House Publishers.

Sinha, D. (1984). Psychology in the context of third world development. *International Journal of Psychology, 19,* 17–29.

Steinhauer, P. (2002). Thoughts on an Indigenous research methodology. *Canadian Journal of Education, 25,* 183–187.

Stewart, D., & Mickunas, A. (1990). *Exploring phenomenology: A guide to the field and its literature* (2nd ed.). Athens: Ohio University Press.

Wilson, A., & Pence, E. (2006). U.S. legal interventions in the lives of battered women: An indigenous assessment. In D. E. Smith (Ed.), *Institutional ethnography as practice*. Lanham: Rowman and Littlefield, 199–226.

Wilson, S. (2008). *Research is ceremony: Indigenous research methods*. Halifax: Fernwood.

Young, K., & Saver, J. L. (2001). The neurology of narrative substance. *Annals of Internal Medicine,30*(1 & 2), 72–84.

Chapter 8
Decolonizing Alterity Models Within School Counseling Practice

Lance C. Smith and Anne M. Geroski

School Task Force: A Case Vignette

The school board of a local, predominantly White high school appointed a task force to examine issues of diversity, equity, and achievement. The school counselors in the district all identified as White, egalitarian, culturally pluralistic, and inclusive, and all had training in the profession's multicultural counseling competencies (MCCs; Sue et al. 1992) and were trained in master's programs that emphasized the ASCA National Model (ASCA 2012). The counselors were aware of cultural nuances germane to the community, such as a willingness to integrate spirituality into their work with students, and had historically promoted the annual Martin Luther King, Jr. Day school-wide celebration. They prided themselves in fostering a school community that celebrated diversity. When working with their Latina/Latino students, the counselors were sensitive to cultural values regarding the importance of elders and familial unity. Recently, a few of the school counselors sponsored a workshop for the teachers to develop knowledge regarding the cultural differences between students of Puerto Rican and Mexican descent. They took seriously their call to provide knowledge to teachers, staff, and students about differences in their school.

The school counseling faculty felt fairly confident that the task force would identify areas for improvement, but that overall the evaluation would be favorable—they had done exactly what their training had asked of them. However, the task force found that significant disparities existed within the school along racial lines—specifically with regard to dropout rates, graduation rates, mathematical achievement, and disciplinary actions. The task force report, which was published subsequently

L. C. Smith (✉) · A. M. Geroski
The University of Vermont, 102 Mann Hall, 208 Colchester Ave, 05405 Burlington, VT, USA
e-mail: lance.smith@uvm.edu

A. M. Geroski
e-mail: ageroski@uvm.edu

R. D. Goodman, P. C. Gorski (eds.), *Decolonizing "Multicultural" Counseling through Social Justice,* International and Cultural Psychology, DOI 10.1007/978-1-4939-1283-4_8

in the town newspaper, made references to "subversive and institutional racism." The predominantly White faculty in the school felt scolded for not working hard enough and judged for being incompetent. Parents of color praised the report for identifying the unequal academic "playing field" within the school.

The task force findings also caused quite a stir in the proudly liberal and progressive community who demanded accountability on the part of the school. Others in the community, however, expressed frustration along the lines of the sentiment expressed in an op-ed piece in the local newspaper which rang out, "Why can't students of color be held individually responsible for discrepancies in achievement? They are given more resources than other students—maybe they just don't want to achieve." A small number of students of color organized a protest and walked out of class claiming that their needs were identified in the task force report and that the school and community were not taking them seriously.

Not wanting to exacerbate tensions and not clear on how to resolve the larger problems unveiled in the report, the school counselors empathized with the students of color who felt marginalized as well as those in the community who were complaining that the task force report would result in new mandates and higher taxes; thus they publicly took a position of neutrality.

Alterity is defined as the state of being *Other* (Bauman and Gingrich 2006). Addressing alterity means dealing with the social processes that position some identities on the social margins, on the outside looking in—those forces that imbue certain identities with "otherness" as opposed to "sameness" or "belonging." Models of alterity identify the existence of othering and address working with and for those who have membership in nondominant, traditionally undervalued, and underrepresented social groups. This chapter will argue that the current models that guide the field of school counseling in addressing alterity—the American Counseling Association's (ACA) multicultural counseling competency model (MCC; Sue et al. 1992), the American School Counseling Association's (ASCA) National Model (ASCA 2012), and the ASCA Position Statement: The Professional School Counselor and Cultural Diversity (ASCA 2009)—are problematic. They are insufficient for addressing the needs of students from traditionally underrepresented and undervalued groups. We will present the case that the guiding assumptions upon which these models were created reinforce colonizing practices, and call for replacing these models with a social justice model.

Multicultural Counseling Competencies

Etiology of the MCC Model

In the late 1980s and early 1990s, the counseling and counseling psychology professions established the still-emerging multiculturalism movement as the "fourth force" in the history of counseling (Lee and Richardson 1991; Sue 1991). Finally, there was unstoppable momentum within the field towards acknowledging alterity as axiomatic to the profession. The upswell of this fourth force culminated in the drafting and adoption of the MCCs by the ACA. The MCCs attempted to operationalize the awareness, knowledge, and skills necessary for counselors to work with individuals from diverse racial, ethnic, and cultural backgrounds (Sue et al. 1992). The MCC movement quickly spread into the field of school counseling (Pedersen and Carey 1994).

The primary purpose of the MCC model was to replace monocultural counseling practice with multicultural counseling practice (Sue et al. 1992). No longer would diverse cultural and ethnic approaches to mental health, emotional well-being, and human development be ignored. Inclusion would supplant exclusion and become the new norm. All of the various cultural and ethnic threads of the human experience would be woven into the tapestry of counseling and psychology, adding greater richness and complexity to what had been a rather bland quilt of Euro-Western cultural uniformity.

Substituting the paradigm of monoculturalism with multiculturalism was a significant and long-overdue undertaking. While the MCC model was cutting edge for its time, we will see that the model's assumptions do not adequately deal with alterity because they do not focus on interrupting the discourses that promote cultural hegemony. Indeed, the tapestry of counseling, however colorful and diverse it has become, still serves as a colonizing shroud for those from traditionally underrepresented groups. In the words of Figueira (2007), "The reality is that before any theory of alterity can be successful (be it multiculturalism, postcolonialism, transnationalism, posthumanism, or the Global South), there needs to occur a decolonization of the other" (p. 144).

Assumption of Cultural Pluralism

Early on, the set of ideas that encapsulate multiculturalism was also referred to as *cultural pluralism* (Anderson and Collins 2006; Rothenberg 2007). The premise of both "multiculturalism" and "cultural pluralism" is linguistically self-evident: Both constructs underscored the fact that "multiple" and a "plurality" of cultures are present in the human experience. They affirm that more than one single cultural approach to the human experience needs to inform the fields of counseling, psychology, and school counseling. The movement away from monoculturalism and towards multiculturalism entails an egalitarian assumption—that everyone benefits from cultural plurality, therefore we must preserve, protect, promote, and respect cultural variance and heterogeneous expressions of ethnicity (Manning 2009). In its simplest form, this set of ideas is expressed by the bumper sticker "Celebrate Diversity."

What is important for us to understand is that the premise of multiculturalism requires an *egalitarian pursuit* of inclusion. As stated by the National Coalition for Cultural Pluralism in 1973, "Each person must be aware of and secure in his [or her] own identity, and be willing to extend to others the same respect and rights that he [or she] expects to enjoy himself [or herself]" (as cited in Manning 2009, p. 15). If the aims of multiculturalism are to be met, then there must exist a level playing field and a social context of good faith—that rather than being threatened by inclusion, the dominant culture must act beneficently and make room for others. In other words, if the goal is to have a society-wide celebration, then everyone in the society must experience an equal degree of hospitality and safety. To state this from one more angle: Multiculturalism is anchored in the assumption that there *is not* a large, powerful, and subversive force that seeks to subjugate all nondominant cultural expressions.

American School Counselor Association

At around this same time, in the late 1980s, the profession of school counseling was working to identify its scope of practice. Its professional organization, ASCA (a division of ACA at the time), was attempting to distinguish itself from other counseling organizations. To this end, a series of position statements, including one on cultural diversity, were drafted and have been continually revised, updated, and officially adopted by the organization's governing body. Furthermore, in the late 1990s a task force was charged by ASCA to draft a more cohesive and comprehensive directive outlining the full scope of practice of school counselors. The results of these efforts were the ASCA Position Statement: The Professional School Counselor and Cultural Diversity (ASCA 2009) originally published in 1988 and The ASCA National Model (ASCA 2012), which was originally published in 2003.

ASCA—Pluralism, Egalitarianism, and Advocacy Position Statement

Within the ASCA Position Statement: The Professional School Counselor and Cultural Diversity (ASCA 2009), one can clearly see the assumptions of cultural pluralism carried over from the MCC model. Within this single-page document, phrases that speak to "embracing," "welcoming," "appreciating," and "celebrating," cultural diversity abound. In addition, the position statement underscores an egalitarian premise that school counselors "collaborate with *all* stake holders" to meet the needs of "*every student*" and "*all students*" [italics added]. Finally, the position statement calls on school counselors to take up the role of an advocate—a function not articulated in the MCC model. School counselors are to advocate for students "who are marginalized," particularly, "students of culturally diverse, low socioeconomic, and other underserved and underperforming populations" and to "address inequities within schools."

ASCA National Model

The pluralistic assumptions of the MCC model are clearly evident in the ASCA National Model (ASCA 2012) as well. The National Model specifically addresses "multicultural competence" (p. 14) and "cultural sensitivity" (p. 38). School counselors are called upon to improve their "cultural awareness, knowledge, and skills," to "value, respect, and be responsive" to diversity (p. 37), and to "create a vibrant school climate where cultural richness and strengths are celebrated" (p. 38). An egalitarian approach to school counseling is strongly emphasized–language that underscores meeting the needs of "every student" and "all students" occur no less than 55 times. The National Model further highlights the role of advocacy within the profession. School counselors are called upon to engage in the work of advocacy to "identify systemic barriers to student achievement" (p. 8) and "remove barriers to access" (p. 9) so that "equity and access to rigorous education [is possible] for every student" (p. 1).

Benefits of the MCC and ASCA Models

The shift toward multiculturalism within the profession of school counseling has been generative. Now, all counselors are expected to approach their work with the understanding that individuals have different ways of defining and experiencing mental health and wellness, that there are culturally variant paths toward healthy development, and that they all have value. The MCC model has been infused into counselor education standards (CACREP 2012) as well as ethical standards (see ACA 2005; APA 2002; ASCA 2010).

Specifically regarding school counseling, the integration of these models has fostered beneficial reflection, questions, and actions. For example, as these models of cultural "competence" spread throughout the field, school counselors began to advocate for "diversity days" within their local schools, assuring that the cultural heritage of students from "minority" groups is recognized and celebrated. Multiculturalism resulted in school counselors adding images of students of color in their offices and hallways, updating their play therapy toys to include nonwhite figures and heterogeneous ethnic symbols. Rainbow stickers were displayed on office doors. Advocacy efforts on behalf of students who identify as lesbian, gay, or bisexual (LGB) resulted in gay/straight alliances (GSAs) being formed in some schools around the country. Advocacy efforts taken on behalf of students with disabilities resulted in older school buildings being remodeled to be more accommodating, including improvements such as the installation of elevators and incorporation of wireless audio networks.

Publications in the flagship journal of the profession of school counseling also suggest that school counselors are beginning to explore the ways in which the work of school counselors can be culturally informed. A recent volume of the *Professional*

School Counseling (Dec 2012, 16(1)), the flagship journal of the ASCA, has articles about obesity among Latino/Latina youth, counseling "multiple heritage" adolescents, college readiness for youth with autism-spectrum disorders, and issues related to achievement and self-esteem in a population of English language learners.

With this important paradigm shift, monoculturalism has been sufficiently problematized. Counselors are no longer granted a free pass to assume that traditional counseling practices created, implemented, and measured by a homogeneous or dominant social group are relevant or effective for persons of ethnically heterogeneous backgrounds and diverse social identities. Thanks to the MCC model, *Other* cultural and ethnic identities are being included, celebrated, studied, and honored within the fields of counseling, psychology, and school counseling. Thanks to the ASCA model, school counselors now see advocacy for marginalized students as a part of their professional identity. And yet—and this cannot be emphasized enough—institutional apartheid thrives (Bemak and Chung 2005; Shin and Kindall 2013).

Significant Flaws

We will now lay out the argument that the assumptions of cultural pluralism and egalitarianism found within the MCCs, the ASCA National Model, and the ASCA Position Statement are inadequate for addressing alterity within the field of school counseling. Moreover, in our minds they are anemic and far too easily allow school counselors to unintentionally collude in the oppression of students from traditionally undervalued and underrepresented groups. Models of alterity that are built on the assumptions of cultural pluralism and egalitarianism are problematic because they neither directly identify nor account for the forces that are advancing inequality and cultural hegemony in our schools. That is to say, the existing models not only ignore but also aid in veiling from our awareness the social, institutional, and structural powers that drive colonization; they allow these forces to remain concealed, uninterrupted, and thereby protected.

Discourses and Discursive Positioning

The prevailing forces at work within individuals, institutions, and social systems that seek to defend cultural hegemony, to subjugate nondominant cultural expressions, and to maintain power for the powerful have been identified as colonizing, dominant discourses. The term *discourse* refers to the culturally constructed set of "truths" that serve as the structuring "rules" governing social practices (Winslade and Geroski 2008). That is, discourses are what we take for granted that (1) allow us to know how to act in social situations, (2) become the structuring ideas that allow us to make meaning of our experiences in the world, and (3) construct our identity—how we see ourselves in the world. According to Foucault (1972), "Whenever, between objects, types of statement, concepts, or thematic choices, one can define a regularity (an order, correlations, positions and functionings, transformations), we will say…that we are dealing with a discursive formation" (p. 38).

Furthermore, discourses are integral to social power (Foucault 1980). They are not neutral. They are webs of meaning that serve to shape and constitute the world in ways that inevitably promote or undermine social power. They are stories and frameworks about the human experience that are prescriptive, not descriptive. And they are everywhere, all the time, creating "[t]he ways in which people act on the world and the ways in which the world acts on individuals" (Robinson 1999, p. 73).

Narrative theorists use the term *discursive positioning* to describe the ways in which discourses are acted on and circulated within a culture (Monk et al. 1997). The term *dominant discourses* refer to the set of social "truths" that are so salient in a given culture or community, they tend to drown out other discourses. Many of the dominant discourses that are awarded social capital in contemporary US society are colonizing, in that they reinforce positions of power for those that are already powerful: those who occupy commanding social locations, including Whites, men, heterosexuals, the wealthy, the nondisabled, and those who are cisgender (persons comfortable with the gender identity assigned to them at birth). Simultaneously, colonizing dominant discourses position those with nondominant identities—persons of color, women, persons who identify as LGB or transgender, persons with disabilities, and the poor—as subordinate, less than, and *Othered*. What is particularly insidious about colonizing dominant discourses is that they generally go unnoticed and are particularly invisible to those in power. The term *counter-discourses* refer to the stories and social truths that interrupt, problematize, complicate, and question the dominant discourse.

The concept of colonizing dominant discourses offers an explanatory account of the unequal social playing field in our schools and communities: Playing fields that privilege those from dominant social locations and disadvantage those from nondominant social locations. Media accounts of Hurricane Katrina provide stark evidence of how the colonizing dominant discourse of White supremacy privileges whites while subjugating persons of color. When news footage displayed images of White people making off with goods and supplies taken from merchants without permission, they were discursively positioned as "residents" and "survivalists." Captions of persons of color engaged in the *exact* same activity framed the subjects as "looters" and "criminals" (Jones 2005).

Discourses tell the story of people even before actions and events take place. In the school setting, we consistently witness colonizing dominant discourses telling different stories about persons depending upon their social identity. For example, when a male principal becomes visibly frustrated and raises his voice during a staff meeting, the colonizing dominant discourse of patriarchy discursively positions him as a "strong leader." When a female principal behaves in the same manner, however, she is storied as "demanding," "out of control," and perhaps, a "bitch." During lunch in the teacher's lounge, when a heterosexual school counselor announces her recent engagement, the colonizing dominant discourse of heteronormativity frames the announcement as celebratory. When a lesbian woman or gay man expresses the same sentiment, she or he is discursively positioned as pushing a political agenda.

In another example, the colonizing dominant discourse of cisgender normativity was at work when a gender-nonconforming student in one of our schools approached the middle school counselor complaining of bullying and harassment. With great empathy, the school counselor invited the student and the student's parents to consider how certain behaviors (a gender-neutral haircut and clothing) were a provocation to others and the cause of the problem. Rather than attempting to interrupt systemic discrimination against this transgender student, the school counselor provided the student with social skills training.

If models of alterity are to have any substantive effect, they have to deal directly with the power of colonizing dominant discourses. As captured by Monk et al. (2008), "If counseling practice is not based on addressing the effects of power relationships, we do not believe it is adequately multicultural" (p. 49).

Dominant Discourses and Cultural Pluralism

As we saw earlier, the MCC model is reliant upon the assumption of societal good faith and an egalitarian playing field. The influence and pervasiveness of colonizing dominant discourses shatters this critical central assumption. That is to say, the assumption that those with social power—both individuals and institutions—will extend to the *Other* the same cultural capital that they themselves enjoy is erroneous. The notion that there is an egalitarian playing field upon which cultural pluralism can take root and grow is fallacious.

Colonizing dominant discourses are mighty; they are intractable. The colonizing dominant discourse of sexism continues to secure the power of men while subjugating women (Bernstein 2010; Johnson 2010). The colonizing dominant discourse of White supremacy remains successful at advancing White dominance over all other ethnic identities (Lipsitz 2010; Wise 2005). The discourse of heteronormativity has been highly successful in maintaining legal sanctions against persons identifying as LGB (Human Rights Campaign 2014). The dominant discourse of the cisgender normativity perpetuates an abominable rate of hate crimes and violence against transgender and gender-nonconforming persons: 40 % have experienced physical assault and over 50 % have reported sexual assault (Stotzer 2009). Colonizing dominant discourses grant power to the powerful, and they are, in turn, sustained by those with the power. It cannot be assumed that institutions and systems will relinquish their power beneficently. As stated by Douglass (1857/1985), "Power concedes nothing without a demand. It never did and it never will."

The central notion of cultural pluralism, while admirable and desirable, will never be possible until colonizing dominant discourses are identified and interrupted.

Understanding that dominant discourses advance some "truths" while marginalizing others is crucial to the practice of school counseling. Operating from a model of alterity that pretends that a social context of good faith exists and that ignores how colonizing dominant discourses position students from undervalued groups not only hinders the efficacy of school counseling, but, in effect, colludes in protecting these discourses. For example, engaging a school-wide celebration of Dr. Martin Luther King on January 21st that positions the civil rights movement as an event that only occurred during the 1950s and 1960s, suggests that racial inequality is a thing of the past. The dominant discourse of White supremacy fosters the belief that systemic racism died with martyrdom of Dr. King. Celebrating Dr. King's birthday is the ideal opportunity to introduce a counter-discourse. To better address the force of racism in the present, the day should include events like a school-wide essay or art project on how covert racism manifests itself in the halls and classrooms; a staff meeting wherein teachers and faculty are asked to examine instructional methods to be sure that they accurately account for a broad range of experiences, styles, and understandings; a lesson on microaggressions (Sue 2010) in each and every classroom; and an in-service training on White privilege (Johnson 2006).

Dominant Discourses, Egalitarianism, and the Unequal Playing Field

At first glance, the egalitarian principles found within the ASCA National Model (ASCA 2012) and ASCA Position Statements (ASCA 2009) may seem highly appropriate, if not enlightened. It goes without saying that the profession of school counseling should value "all" students, approach "every" student regardless of their social location with equal respect, and construct a comprehensive program that considers everyone's needs equitably. However, upon looking more closely, one can notice the subtle influence of colonizing dominant discourses here. A narrative strategy that emphasizes "any," "all," and "every" student(s) assumes a level playing field: that all students regardless of social location or identity, upon receiving equal effort and resources, will develop in a relatively equitable way. Colonizing dominant discourses remain concealed when we think that "every" student has a fair share in society, that "all" students were dealt an equitable set of cards. The evidence suggests otherwise.

To unpack the production of an unequal playing field in our society and schools, we will focus specifically on how the colonizing dominant discourse of White supremacy positions students of color in schools. We realize that the idea of white supremacy relating to the field of school counseling may sound like a radical and even absurd statement to many readers. Let us clarify that by White supremacy we do not mean the overt, fascist ideology that brings to mind images of swastikas white hoods, and burning crosses. No, the form of white supremacy that we are talking about, and that we will now unpack, is virtually invisible. It is subtle. Covert. It is a way of living that secretly yet insidiously positions "Whiteness" as supreme to all other ethnic and cultural identities. It produces a playing field that advantages White students and disadvantages students of color. And it is maintained by some of the nicest, most beneficent school counselors you are likely to ever meet.

As a result of the social and economic conditions that are produced by the dominant discourse of White supremacy, students of color must contend with a litany of contextual factors that will impede success in schools. For example, diminished economic opportunity—unemployment or jobs that pay less than a living wage and lack benefits—have a direct correlation with low academic achievement (Alliance for Excellent Education 2003). Compared to their White counterparts, students of color tend to grow up in households with far less wealth and far greater rates of unemployment, poverty, and insufficient healthcare (Hines and Boyd-Franklin 2005). Due to the legacy of *formerly legal* racist economic policies like the Homestead Act and the FHA Home Loan Program that privileged Whites and discriminated against Blacks, the typical college-degreed Black couple begins life with one fifth the net worth of the typical White couple (Council of Economic Advisers 1998). With identical resumes, parents of White children are twice as likely as parents of Black children to receive a callback for a job interview (Bertrand and Mullainthan 2004). Young Black college graduates earn on average 11% less than their White counterparts, and by the time they retire the gap grows to 42% (Roth 2012). The recent recession has hit families of color much harder than White families, with the rate of unemployment for college-degreed Blacks being twice that of college-degreed Whites (U.S. Congressional Joint Economic Committee 2010). The economic deck has been stacked against families of color, affecting their children's ability to achieve in school.

Inequities in the criminal justice system illustrate another way in which the playing field is not equal. White supremacy propagates an unjust prison industrial complex that targets persons of color (Bonilla-Silva 2001; Brewer and Heitzeg 2008) and we know that having a parent in prison has a significant effect upon a child's success in school (Kjellstrand et al. 2012; Merenstein et al. 2011). Compared to White families, parents of students of color are twice as likely to be pulled over by police; and if pulled over, they are twice as likely to be arrested; and if arrested, they are twice as likely to be prosecuted; and if prosecuted, they are twice as likely to be sentenced to jail (Johnson 2006). For students of color in our schools, White supremacy results in a prison rate for their parents five times that of Whites (Mason 2012).

As these examples illustrate, White supremacy disadvantages students of color before they ever arrive at the school's front door, and equally harms them when they walk in. Students of color navigate school environments that are filled with stereotypes, discrimination, and unconscious teacher bias (Moore et al. 2008). White supremacy produces inequitable suspension and expulsion policies in schools that directly inform the school-to-prison pipeline (Brown 2007; Casella 2003; Fenning and Rose 2007). In studies that control socioeconomic status, placement for African Americans in special education classrooms is disproportionate to that of their White peers (Moore et al. 2008). Unconscious teacher bias results in lower teacher expectations for students of color (Colorblindness: The new racism? 2009; Gorski 2007). The educational achievement gap between African American and White high school students is unmistakenly large (Dillon 2009). African American students are twice as likely as Whites to drop out of high school (Chapman et al. 2011), Latina/Latinos five times as likely, and Native Americans four times as likely (U.S. National Center for Education Statistics 2010).

If the field of school counseling approaches the work in a myopic egalitarian manner, devoting equal time and equal energy to "every" and "all" student(s), then we are tacitly supporting the inequitable status quo. Ignoring the unequal playing fields produced by dominant discourses is equivalent to giving some runners a two-lap head start in a five-lap race and blithely cheering along for "any" and "all" runners as if the race were fair.

Dominant Discourses and Unnamed Advocacy

Finally, we see the power of colonizing dominant discourses at play, even in ASCA's call for advocacy. Recall that the National Model (ASCA 2012) calls upon school counselors to engage in the work of advocacy to identify systemic barriers to student achievement" (p. 8) and "remove barriers to access" (p. 9) that impede the success of "any" student. It is commendable that ASCA is promoting the role of advocacy within the profession of school counseling. However, even in ASCA's call for advocacy, colonizing dominant discourses have yet again succeeded in cloaking themselves. Given that the ASCA National Model addresses "systemic barriers" and "equity and access issues" over 30 times, it is severely problematic that these constructs go unnamed and unspecified.

Why the ASCA model fails to name the "systemic barriers" is a bit of a mystery. There is no shortage of scholars that have clearly identified the systemic barriers that promote inequality, marginalization, and oppression (For more on this topic, see Aldarondo 2007; Johnson 2006; Shin and Kindall 2013; Smith et al. 2012). By refusing to name these systems as White supremacy, heteronormativity, patriarchy, classism, and ableism, the ASCA National Model buttresses the invisibility of these colonizing discourses, thereby colluding in their sustainment. A model that ignores the dominant discourse of white supremacy—along with such corresponding constructs, such as White privilege, modern racism (Bonilla-Silva 2003), and microaggressions (Sue 2010)—yet calls upon school counselors to address "disproportionate discipline rates for [...] students of color" (ASCA 2012, p. 15) or the "underrepresentation of students of color in advanced courses" (p. 16) is predisposed to maintain the status quo of White supremacy. We need a model of alterity that does not hesitate to name these forces for what they are and that promotes a discussion about the role of colonizing dominant discourses in schools and the effect that they are having on our students.

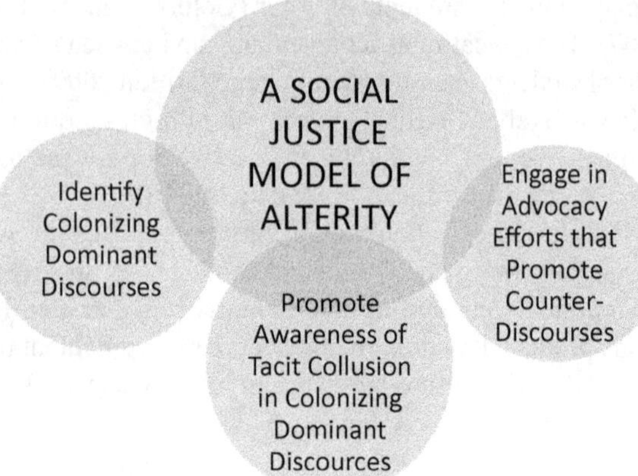

Fig. 8.1 A social justice model of alterity for school counseling

A Social Justice Model of Alterity

We call on the field of school counseling to make a commitment to work from a social justice model of alterity (Fig. 8.1). You see, the school counselors in our case vignette did not have a model of alterity that would aid them in recognizing the influence of the colonizing dominant discourse of White supremacy within their school. In other words, they lacked a working model that:

- Identifies colonizing dominant discourses
- Promotes awareness of tacit collusion in colonizing dominant discourses
- Calls for advocacy efforts that promote counter-discourses

Identifying Colonizing Dominant Discourses

Colonization occurs when school counselors are standing on the sidelines, unaware of the shaping effects of discourses. Refusing or failing to identify colonizing dominant discourses is perhaps *the most* significant way in which cultural hegemony is buttressed and reproduced. But acknowledging dominant discourses is not easy (Kiselica 2004). It is uncomfortable to sit with the pain that comes from accepting the disparity and oppression that some of our students experience and it is difficult to concede that inclusion and the celebration of diversity will not adequately interrupt colonization. Honoring diversity while letting systemic barriers go unnamed can be easier and more comfortable than social justice.

Had the counselors within our vignette been working from a social justice model, the institutional apartheid identified by the diversity task force would have been much less of a surprise. This is because colonizing dominant discourses like White supremacy would already have been named and defined. The school counselors would have had a clear understanding of how White privilege, modern racism, and microaggressions impact the lives of their students of color. The school counselors would have already been working to expose White supremacy as part of their mission.

Promoting Awareness of Tacit Collusion

While they may focus on inclusion and celebrating their students' ethnicities, if school counselors ignore the uneven playing field, they are tacitly colluding in the powerful forces that perpetuate inequality and oppression. Howard Zinn famously made the argument that one cannot be neutral on a moving train (Ellis and Mueller 2004). In our case vignette that opened this chapter, the uneven playing field resulting from the discourse of White supremacy is the train.

A social justice model asks us to examine how we tacitly support hegemony by not speaking up, how we buttress colonization by not calling attention to dominant discourses that result in an unequal playing field, and how we reproduce suffering by choosing not to invite conversations about institutional apartheid. A social justice model requires us to recognize how colonizing dominant discourses situate those of us from dominant social locations in positions of power and it asks us to interrupt our own positions of privilege. And, of course, taking up a social justice approach often results in pushback and even sanctions from our families, friends, colleagues, and employers.

With regard to identifying tacit collusion, a social justice minded school counselor would recognize that elementary school libraries without children's books that normalize same-sex parenting (such as *And Tango Makes Three* by Richardson and Parnell 2005) are libraries that tacitly reinforce the colonizing discourse of heteronormativity and devalue children of same-sex parents. Within a social justice model, the absence of gender-neutral bathrooms in the school will be recognized as an act that promotes the colonizing discourse of cisgender normativity, marginalizing gender-nonconforming students. School counselors who are alert to the colonizing discourse of classism will understand that offering parent–teacher conferences during the workday, when hourly wage earners have to take off from work in order to visit with their children's teachers, reinforces the discourse of classism and the oppression of working-class parents. A school counselor that is trained in a social justice model will understand that in the absence of any discussion of white privilege or modern racism, the ASCA National Model's well-intended emphasis on "achievement gaps for African-Americans" (p. 26) or "boys of color [who are] over represented in special education" (p. 16) will likely result in blaming the victim, wherein the problem is attributed to the student's parents or "ghetto" communities.

Advocacy that Promotes Counter-Discourses

Finally, colonization will continue as long as school counselors are untrained in how to promote counter-discourses. In terms of advocacy that introduces counter-discourses, a social justice model of alterity would have had the school counselors in our case vignette foster awareness among the teaching staff and the larger community about the unequal playing field for students from traditionally underrepresented groups and advance an understanding that not "every" student is granted equal societal privileges. To promote a counter-discourse, the school counselors could provide in-service training to colleagues or psychoeducational lessons to students on topics like White privilege (McIntosh 1992), dominant discourses (Greenleaf and Bryant 2012), internalized racism (Johnson 2006), and mircoaggressions (Sue 2010). They could write op-ed pieces in the local paper to promote counter-discourses and raise awareness. They could work with the principal in developing a coordinated schoolwide response to the issues raised. Moreover, when their students of color walk out of class in a display of activism against White hegemony, a social justice model would incite the counselors to interrupt their own White privilege and join their students on the sidewalk in solidarity.

School counselors who desire to write counter-discourses can offer critical consciousness groups for students from marginalized and devalued social locations (Shin et al. 2010). They can be intentional about forming school counseling advisory committees with members from traditionally undervalued and underrepresented groups. Social justice-minded school counselors will conduct annual needs assessments that seek data from students with marginalized social identities, such as students who identify as LGB, transgender or questioning, those who identify as multiracial, and those students with a significant religious identity. School counselors operating from a social justice model understand that referring to students from nondominant social locations as "minorities" contribute to their marginalization, but that referring to such students as "traditionally underrepresented" or "traditionally undervalued" subtly exposes and flattens identity hierarchies.

Conclusion

Let us be clear that we are not condemning or disparaging the school counselors in our case vignette or any other school counselor who has yet to take up a social justice vision. Such an act would be overtly hypocritical, as we, the authors—who both identify as occupying the dominant social locations of White, heterosexual, cisgender, educated, and nondisabled—continue to recognize our own colonization practices. We, too, have spent far too much time riding the train of colonizing dominant discourses while assuming positions of beneficence, pluralism, and neutrality. Learning how to more effectively decolonize our practice will be a lifelong endeavor for all of us.

As discussed in the introduction of this book, colonization occurs when counselors *knowingly or unknowingly* promote a dominant cultural belief and practice that has the effect of maintaining dominant group positions of power and influence (McDowell and Hernandez 2010). Integrating a social justice model of alterity in school counseling means acknowledging that no matter how inclusive we are, how egalitarian we are, or how much we seek to honor and celebrate the *other*, we often collude with the forces that marginalize and devalue our students from nondominant social locations. A social justice model will acknowledge that a "politically neutral" approach to school counseling contributes to the inequity experienced by students from traditionally underrepresented groups. A social justice mode of school counseling acknowledges that the race to academic success is rigged. We join Figueira (2007) in stating that without decolonization, "all theories and pedagogies of alterity serve as mere dogma and orthodoxies" and contribute to "institutional apartheid" (p. 144) within the profession of school counseling.

References

ACA. (2005). *Ethical Codes*. Alexandria: ACA.

Aldarondo, E. (Ed.). (2007). *Advancing social justice through clinical practice*. Mahwah: Lawrence Erlbaum.

Alliance for Excellent Education. (2003). *Fact sheet: The impact of education on health and well-being*. Washington: Alliance for Excellent Education.

Anderson, M. L., & Collins, P. H. (Eds.). (2006). *Race, class and gender: An anthology* (6th ed.). Belmont: Thomas Wadsworth.

APA. (2002). Ethical principles of psychologists and code of conduct. *American Psychologist, 57,* 1060–1073.

ASCA. (2009). The professional school counselor and cultural diversity. In *ASCA position statements* (pp. 19–20). Alexandria: ASCA.

ASCA. (2010). *Ethical standards for school counselors*. Alexandria: ASCA.

ASCA. (2012). *The ASCA national model: A framework for school counseling programs* (3rd ed.). Alexandria: ASCA.

Bauman, G., & Gingrich, A. (Eds.). (2006) *Grammars of identity/alterity: A structural approach.* New York: Berghahn.

Bemak, F., & Chung, R. (2005). Advocacy as a critical role for urban school counselors: Working toward equity and social justice. *Professional School Counseling, 8,* 196–202.

Bernstein, A. (2010). Women's pay: Why the gap remains a chasm. In M. Adams, W. J. Blumenfeld, C. R. Castaneda, H. W. Hackman, M. L. Peters & X. Zuniga (Eds.), *Reading for diversity and social justice: An anthology on racism, anti-semitism, sexism, heterosexism, ableism, and classism* (2nd ed., pp. 347–348). New York: Routledge.

Bertrand, B., & Mullainthan, S. (2004). Are Emily and Greg more employable than Lakisha and Jamal?: A field experiment on labor market discrimination. *American Economic Review, 94,* 991–1013.

Bonilla-Silva, E. (2001). *White supremacy and racism in the post–civil rights era*. Boulder: Lynne Rienner.

Bonilla-Silva, E. (2003). *Racism without racists: Color-blind racism and the persistence of racial inequality in the United States*. New York: Rowman & Littlefield.

Brown, T. M. (2007). Lost and turned out: Academic, social, and emotional experiences of students *excluded* from school. *Urban Education, 42,* 432–455.

Brewer, R. M., & Heitzeg, N. A. (2008). The racialization of crime and punishment: Criminal justice, color-blind racism, and the political economy of the *prison* industrial complex. *American Behavioral Scientist, 51,* 625–644.

CACREP. (2012). *Vision, mission and core values*. Retrieved July 30, 2014 from http://www.cacrep.org/about-cacrep/vision-mission-and-core-values/.

Casella, R. (2003). Punishing dangerousness through preventive detention: Illustrating the institutional link between school and prison. In J. Wald & D. J. Losen (Eds.), *New directions for youth development: Deconstructing the school-to-prison pipeline* (pp. 55–70). San Francisco: Jossey-Bass.

Chapman, C., Laird, J., Ifill, N., & KewalRamani, A. (2011). *Trends in high school dropout and completion rates in the United States: 1972–2009* (NCES 2012–006). U.S. Department of Education. Washington: National Center for Education Statistics. http://nces.ed.gov/pubsearch

Colorblindness: The new racism?. (2009 Fall). *Teaching tolerance*. Retrieved July 30, 2014 from http://www.tolerance.org/magazine/number-36-fall-2009/colorblindness-new-racism.

Council of Economic Advisers. (1998). *Changing America: Indicators of social and economic well-being by race and Hispanic origin*. Retrieved July 30, 2014 from http://w3.access.gpo.gov/eop/ca/pdfs/ca.pdf.

Dillon, S. (2009, Apr 28). 'No child' law is not closing a racial gap. *New York Times*. Retrieved July 30, 2014 from http://www.nytimes.com/2009/04/29/education/29scores.html.

Douglass, F. (1857/1985). "The significance of emancipation in the West Indies." Speech, Canandaigua, New York, August 3, 1857. In John W. Blassingame (Ed.), *Speeches, debates, and interviews, 1855–1863: Series One. The Frederick Douglass papers* (Vol. 3, p. 204). New Haven: Yale University Press.

Ellis, D., & Mueller, D. (2004). *Howard Zinn: You can't be neutral on a moving train* [Motion Picture]. United States: Icarus Films.

Fenning, P., & Rose, J. (2007). Overrepresentation of African American students in exclusionary *discipline*: The role of school policy. *Urban Education, 42,* 536–559.

Figueira, D. (2007). The global south: Yet another attempt to engage the other. *The Global South, 1,* 144–152.

Foucault, M. (1972). *Archeology of knowledge*. (trans: A. M. Sheridan Smith). New York: Pantheon Books.

Foucault, M. (1980). *Power/Knowledge: Selected interviews and other writings, 1972–1977*. New York: Pantheon Books.

Gorski, P. (2007). The question of class. *The Education Digest, 73,* 30–34.

Greenleaf, A. T., & Bryant, R. M. (2012). Perpetuating oppression: Does the current counseling discourse neutralize social action. *Journal for Social Action in Counseling and Psychology, 4,* 18–29.

Hines, P. M., & Boyd-Franklin, N. (2005) African American families. In M. McGoldrick, J. Giordano, & N. Garcia-Preto (Eds.), *Ethnicity and family therapy* (3rd ed.). New York: Guilford.

Human Rights Campaign. (2014). Maps of State Laws and Policies. Retrieved July 30, 2014 from http:www.hrc.org/resources/entry/maps-of-state-laws-policies.

Johnson, A. G. (2006). *Privilege, power, and difference* (2nd ed.). Boston: McGraw Hill.

Johnson, A. G. (2010). Patriarchy, the system: An it, not a he, a them, or an us. In M. Adams, W. J. Blumenfeld, C. R. Castaneda, H. W. Hackman, M. L. Peters, & X. Zuniga (Eds.), *Reading for diversity and social justice: An anthology on racism, anti-semitism, sexism, heterosexism, ableism, and classism* (2nd ed., pp. 332–336). New York: Routledge.

Jones, V. (2005, 1 September). Black people "loot" food, White people "find" food. *The Huffington Post*. Retrieved July 30, 2014 from http://www.huffingtonpost.com/van-jones/black-people-loot-food-wh_b_6614.html.

Kiselica, M. (2004). When duty calls: The implications of social justice work for policy, education, and practice in mental health professions. *The Counseling Psychologist, 32,* 838–854.

Kjellstrand, J. M., Clearley, J., Eddy, J. M., Foney, D., & Martinez, C. R. (2012). Characteristics of incarcerated fathers and mothers: Implications for preventative interventions targeting children and families. *Children and Youth Services Review,* 34, 2409–2415.

Lee, C. C, & Richardson, B. L. (1991). *Multicultural issues in counseling: New approaches to diversity*. Alexandria: American Association for Counseling and Development.

Lipsitz, G. (2010). The progressive investment in whiteness. In M. Adams, W. J. Blumenfeld, C. R. Castaneda, H. W. Hackman, M. L. Peters & X. Zuniga (Eds.), *Reading for diversity and social justice: An anthology on racism, anti-semitism, sexism, heterosexism, ableism, and classism* (2nd ed., pp. 79–87). New York: Routledge.

Manning, K. (2009). Philosophical underpinnings of student affairs work on difference. *About Campus, May–June*, pp. 11–17. doi:10.1002/abc.284.m.

Mason, C. (2012). *Dollars and detainees: The growth of for-profit detention*. The Sentencing Project website: Retrieved July 30, 2014 from http://sentencingproject.org/doc/publications/inc_Dollars_and_Detainees.pdf.

McDowell, T., & Hernandez, P. (2010). Decolonizing academia: Intersectionality, participation, and accountability in family therapy and counseling. *Journal of Feminist Family Therapy, 22,* 93–111.

McIntosh, P. (1992). White privilege and male privilege: A personal account of coming to see correspondences through work in women's studies. In M. L. Andersen & P. H. Collins (Eds.), *Race, class, and gender: An anthology* (pp. 70–81). Belmont: Wadsworth.

Merenstein, B., Tyson, B., Tilles, B., Keays, A., & Rufffolo, L. (2011). Issues affecting the efficacy of programs for children with incarcerated parents. *The Journal of Correctional Education, 62*(3), 166–174.

Monk, G., Winslade, J., Crocket, K., & Epston, D. (Eds.). (1997). *Narrative therapy in practice*. San Francisco: Jossey-Bass.

Monk, G., Winslade, J., & Sinclair, S. (2008). *New horizons in multicultural counseling*. Los Angeles: Sage.

Moore, J. L., III, Henfield, M. S., & Owen, D. (2008). African American males in special education: Their attitudes and perceptions toward high school counselors and school counseling services. *American Behavioral Scientist, 51,* 907–927.

Pedersen, P. B., & Carey, J. (1994). *Multicultural counseling in schools*. Needham: Allyn and Bacon.

Richardson, J., & Parnell, P. (2005). *And Tango makes three*. NY: Simon & Schuster.

Robinson, T. L. (1999). The intersections of dominant discourses across race, gender, and other identities. *Journal of Counseling and Development, 77,* 73–79.

Roth, M. (2012, 3 July). Recession has taken a toll on black families. *Pittsburgh Post-Gazette*. Retrieved July 30, 2014 from http://www.post-gazette.com/stories/local/neighborhoods-city/recession-has-taken-hidden-toll-on-black-families-300882/?p=0.

Rothenberg, P. S. (2007). *Race, class, and gender in the United States: An integrated study* (7th ed.). New York: Wadsworth.

Shin, R. Q., & Kindall, M. A. (2013). Dropout prevention: A (re)conceptualization through the lens of social justice. In E. M. Vera (Ed.), *The Oxford handbook of prevention in counseling psychology* (pp. 213–225). New York: Oxford University Press.

Shin, R. Q., Rogers, J., Silas, M., Smythe-Brown, C., Stanciu, A., & Austin, B. (2010). Advancing social justice in urban schools through the implementation of transformative groups for youth of color. *The Journal for Specialists in Group Work, 35*(3), 230–235.

Smith, L. C., Shin, R. Q., & Officer, L. M. (2012). Moving counseling forward on LGBT issues: Speaking queerly on discourses and microaggressions. *The Counseling Psychologist, 40,* 385–408.

Stotzer, R. L (2009). Violence against transgender people: A review of United States data. *Aggression and Violent Behavior, 14,* 170–179.

Sue, D. W. (1991). A conceptual model for cultural diversity training. *Journal of Counseling & Development, 70,* 99–105.

Sue, D. W. (2010). *Microaggressions in everyday life: Race, gender and sexual orientation*. Hoboken: Wiley.

Sue, D. W., Arredondo, P., & McDavis, R. J. (1992). Multicultural counseling competencies and standards: A call to the profession. *Journal of Counseling & Development, 70,* 477–486.

U.S. Congressional Joint Economic Committee. (2010). *Understanding the economy: Long-term unemployment in African American community*. Retrieved 12 Aug 2012, from http://www.jec.senate.gov/public/index.cfm?p=Reports1&ContentRecord_id=b5fa595ee61a-42ac-86ed-e8eb127f8c7d&ContentType_id=efc78dac-24b1-4196-a730d48568b9a5d7&Group_id=c120e658-3d60-470b-a8a16d2d8fc30132&MonthDisplay=3&YearDisplay=2010.

U.S. National Center for Education Statistics. (2010). *Digest of education statistics: 2009*. Washington: U.S. Department of Education. Retrieved 13 Nov 2010 from http://nces.ed.gov/pubs2010/2010013.pdf.

Winslade, J., & Geroski, A. (2008). A social constructionist view of development. In K. L. Kraus (Ed.), *Lenses: Applying lifespan development theories in counseling* (pp. 7–51). Boston: Houghton Mifflin.

Wise, T. J. (2005). *Affirmative action: Racial preferences in black and white*. New York: Routledge.

Chapter 9
De-colonizing Multicultural Counseling and Psychology: Addressing Race Through Intersectionality

William L. Conwill

Essentialist notions of race, such as the characteristically US Black/White racial binary, portray race as something individuals have. An intersectionality approach, on the other hand, views race as a system of inequality and as a vector of privilege and oppression that interacts with other systems and vectors, like those related to gender and class, to advantage or disadvantage groups of people. Essentialist notions of race in supposedly "multicultural" counseling and psychology paradigms are colonizing; that is, they help perpetuate practices that support inequities and injustices stemming from institutionalized White racism and White supremacy. Intersectionality, on the other hand, can be a decolonizing corrective to essentialist notions of race.

In this chapter, I examine the roots of the US's brand of racism, critique the colonizing nature of essentialist notions of race in supposedly "multicultural" counseling and psychology, point the way toward a more critical, transformative multiculturalism, and present intersectionality as a metadisciplinary framework incorporating a critical perspective on race that can decolonize multicultural approaches to counseling and psychology. Finally, I apply intersectionality in a case example featuring a domestic violence intervention with an economically disadvantaged Black couple.

Colonial and Early American Roots of the Essentialist Racial Binary

The essentialist understanding of traditional US racism portrays Black people as inferior to White people. Blackness and its opposite, Whiteness, are understood as inherent elements within an individual person. These constructions of group identity emerged from historical material circumstances and social interaction in the

W. L. Conwill (✉)
Harrison Conwill Associates, 7819 S. Merrill Ave., Chicago, IL 60649, USA
e-mail: wconwill@gmail.com

R. D. Goodman, P. C. Gorski (eds.), *Decolonizing "Multicultural" Counseling through Social Justice,* International and Cultural Psychology, DOI 10.1007/978-1-4939-1283-4_9

early 1600s. The principal influences on American White racism came from English plantation owners in the West Indies. In an effort to stabilize their labor force of indentured European and enslaved African workers in the extremely prosperous colony of Barbados, the planter class instituted the Barbados Slave Code of 1661, declaring that people of African descent were slaves for life and that the slave status was hereditary according to the condition of the mother. This strategy provided incentive to indentured European laborers, as they gained "White" privilege, to remain loyal to the institutionalization of slavery.

Many formerly indentured laborers of European descent, experienced in Slave Code enforcement, migrated north to the American mainland to seek a better life. They helped establish and maintain White supremacy as the symbolic order of the new nation (Gupta et al. 2007). The descendants of enslaved Africans became, in effect, an internal colony within the USA (Conwill 2007).

Essentialist Notions of Race as Colonizing

Reactions against counselors and psychologists who dare to speak out against the remnants of these historical systems in the form of White racism and White supremacy can be brutal. Of course, these reactions do not stand up well to analysis and appear, for the most part, to be an evidence of the racism they mean to deny. For example, when Derald Wing Sue received an award for his contributions to the study of multicultural issues in psychology, Thomas et al. (2005) unleashed a diatribe against Sue's (2004) critique of White privilege and ethnocentric monoculturalism. They dismissed Sue's anti-racism advocacy as "race-baiting," as though the lack of such analysis is less critique-worthy than the analysis itself.

The attack was astounding in its lack of understanding racism, especially in its social and institutional forms. For example, in response to Sue's critique, the authors stated defensively, "one is damned regardless of whether he or she makes distinctions between people of different races or treats them all the same" (p. 50). Making the distinctions and using them to advantage some and to disadvantage others is the real issue, I argue. The authors used universal statements to produce a Straw Man argument, as in this statement: "[e]vidently, Dr Sue and all other people of color have a more enlightened worldview than White psychologists and they have superior empathy skills, as well" (p. 50). They also presented an *ad hominem* argument:

> All of these charges are offered as though White people constitute a homogeneous, racially biased, and unfairly privileged group with few within-group differences. To propose such universality among White people suggests an extremely limited life experience. It also constitutes what can only be labeled as racial bias, since it would be grossly inappropriate, if not professionally unethical, for a White psychologist to level such charges against members of any other race. (p. 51)

Thomas et al. (2005) used obvious psychological projections in crafting their argument. Despite the publications of noted authors on White, middle-class, male privilege (e.g., Liu et al. 2007; McIntosh 2002) dating back more than 25 years, Thomas, et al. complained that Sue did not spell out what he meant by what they called "unearned 'White privilege'" and insinuated that it was Sue who grew up in isolated backwaters. Ignoring the history of ostracism endured by the people of color in the American Psychological Association and the American Counseling Association for decades, the authors contended, "it is extremely rare in the multicultural literature for dissenting opinions to be published. Stated bluntly, advocates of multiculturalism, ironically, are less likely than most psychologists to tolerate intellectual diversity" (p. 50).

Culture Wars: The Ploy of "Blacks Are Just One Ethnic Group Among Many"

Over time, many reactionary forces rallied against challenges to the US brand of internal colonialism that racialized people of African descent. At the beginning of the Black Power movement, for instance, Daniel Moynihan's *The Negro Family: the Case for National Action* (1965) conflated race and culture and intimated that Blacks would not fare better economically until American White society and Black culture changed. Moynihan was the Assistant Secretary of Labor under the Kennedy and Johnson administrations.

Moynihan and his colleagues hoped to divert attention away from Blacks' outcries against White supremacy by introducing culture and ethnicity into the White/Black binary discourse. During the 1960s' backlash against the push for Black civil rights, they encouraged Whites to see themselves as European ethnics who also had suffered injustice in the US, with an attendant right to redress wrongs. Through invidious comparisons between Blacks and people of other racial or ethnic identities, they ushered in the age of the hyphenated American, as Kilson (1975) illustrated, with the people of White ethnicities purported to have risen from poverty through individual effort and industry:

> Unlike the ethnicity of White social groups, black ethnicity lacked until recently the quality of authenticity—that is, a true and viable heritage, unquestionable in its capacity to shape and sustain a cohesive identity or awareness. Anti-African attitudes, widespread among most Afro-Americans until recently, were fundamental to this situation. Thus, black ethnicity has the status in American society of a curiously dependent cluster: it borrows from White society much, though by no means all, of its culture-justifying ingredients. (p. 243)

The above statement wilts in the face of the historical record. It masks the White intentionality in the disruption of African cultures, solidifying a permanent class of formerly enslaved laborers (Pitman 1926). Their specious reasoning ignored panoramic job discrimination, the destruction of successful Black communities, and state-sponsored Black prison labor forces, among other conditions—the same conditions ignored by Thomas et al. (2005) in their attempted dismissal of Sue's work.

Culture Wars in Multicultural Counseling and Psychology

By the late 1960s, counselors in the Association for Non-White Concerns and psychologists in the Association of Black Psychologists committed themselves to resisting peers who attempted to derail the struggle against White racism and White supremacy. They charged members of their own professions as culprits in the oppression of Black citizens. They directed their efforts primarily and directly against their parent organizations and exposed tainted psychological theories and national practices based on White supremacy. They rebuked peers who acted out their Whiteness on the basis of alleged superiority or who assumed that all persons with dark skin felt inferior because of their color.

Their charges were serious. Downplaying the significance of White supremacy and adopting the rhetoric of cultural differences, with race as just one factor among many that are vying for attention, ensures inadequate attention to racial injustice and, by extension, it ensures the perpetuation of racism. Avoiding contestations about White racism and White hegemony by emphasizing Black resilience and Black middle-class success narratives similarly obscures the real, underlying issue of White racism. It is, in effect, "playing nice" with the White people who might fear the implications of racial justice. Unfortunately, such an approach dominates discourses on multicultural counseling and psychology today.

To press this assessment, I present a commentary on Vontress and Jackson's (2004) "Reactions to the multicultural counseling competencies debate." spurred on by Arredondo et al. (1996) a decade earlier. I choose to focus on it not because of its singularity, but because it includes several elements of the "Blacks are just one ethnic group among many" argument.

Vontress and Jackson (2004) expressed sentiments common among many people who oppose social activism in the counseling and psychology professions:

> We maintain that mental health counselors should look at all factors impacting a client's situation. Race may or may not be one of them. In general, race is not the real problem in the USA today. The significance that clients attach to it is the most important consideration. Individuals who perceive their race to be an impediment to achievement in life usually create for themselves a self-fulfilling prophecy…
>
> We agree that in the USA, the dominant racial group has defined historically minority groups, especially African Americans. For example, White Americans usually define Tiger Woods, the son of an Asian mother and an African American father, as Black, even though he does not define himself as such. He identifies with the cultural and racial heritages of both parents. His view of himself is healthy, because how people feel about themselves as human beings is more important to their well-being (sic) than how other people perceive or define them. (p. 76)

Putting aside the circularity of their statement that race is not the real problem and their blaming of victims for acting on their perceptions, Vontress and Jackson's (2004) position normalizes an expectation of heroic triumph by Blacks who are healthy enough to perceive a problem with racism and to attribute self-induced failure to those who do not expect miracles. Race is about how people see and treat each other differently as members of an advantaged or an oppressed ethnic group. Race is about the laws and practices that affect life chances and opportunities based on those differences. In the educational setting, Vontress and Jackson's argumentation would have us ignore racist teacher expectations, academic tracking, and limited access to social power (Rust et al. 2011). This is solipsistic reasoning about race and a complete disregard for the reality of racism under the guise of "cross-cultural" practice.

Vontress and Jackson continue:

> The Dimensions of Personal Identity Model is an impressive, creative, and useful contribution to the psychotherapeutic community. However, it is unfortunate that it and the competencies are restricted in application to four identifiable minority groups in the USA. People in our nation come from almost every country in the world. They, too, present themselves to mental health professionals as clients. (p. 78)

Vontress and Jackson (2004) also criticized the "exclusivity" of multicultural competencies that focus on US "minority" groups, arguing that the "majority of clients needing help in adjusting to American society" are those "countless immigrants from all over the world who require and should receive counseling too" (p. 75). These other immigrants, however, are not actually countless, nor are they a majority. Many were privileged in their homelands and had the resources to emigrate comfortably.

It is difficult to understand criticism of a framework to address the mental health needs of the people who suffer from racism. Vontress and Jackson's argument appears to be that competencies for each small immigrant ethnic minority group should have been foregrounded rather than multicultural competencies focusing on the people of color. But is the real issue when it comes to multicultural counseling and psychology in the current sociopolitical climate whether a dominant group should be served or whether people from disenfranchised groups should receive equitable service and attention?

Toward a More Critical Multicultural Counseling and Psychology

Virulently potent forms of racisms and apartheids use culture, ethnicity, religion, and other factors as coded signifiers. In this way, the true nature of racial oppression often is disguised. Hispanic people identified by others as Black do not escape double jeopardy as Black Hispanics because they identify themselves simply as Hispanics. Similarly, exclusionary practices against Haitians as potential carriers of HIV or discrimination against Muslims as potential terrorists or blood quantum laws meant to determine Nàtive American tribal membership can mask racism. A most grievous form of racism, for instance, is that directed against Dalit women in India and other countries in South Asia. Defenseless against the triple jeopardy of being poor, of being women, and of being Dalit, or "untouchable," and locked inexorably in a descent-based caste system over many centuries, Dalit women suffer violations traditionally reserved for them, such as extremely derogatory verbal abuse, naked parading, dismemberment, rape, ritualized prostitution, being forced to drink urine and eat feces, branding, pulling out of teeth tongue and nails, and accusations of witchcraft (which often are followed by violence, sometimes including murder). These intersectional forms of oppression call for multicultural counselors and psychologists who can think outside the Black/White binary.

Problematizing Race

A more contemporary line of thought problematizes race in terms of the emergence of transnational subjectivities in new forms of globalization (Conwill 2007). By problematize I mean that we examine understandings about race with questions like: *Who frames these understandings? For whom are the understandings framed? Why are they being framed in a particular way at this particular time? Who benefits from these framings? Who is harmed by them?*

Let us consider, for example, the essentialist historical notion of the "one-drop" rule: any amount of African ancestry, no matter how small, is enough to make a person "Black." When we problematize this belief, we do not simply swallow as fact the US racial paradigm that pathologizes Blackness and, say, the sexual intimacies between Black men and White women. Instead, we examine the international colonial division of racialized labor and the system of oppression it birthed and continues to propagate. Decolonizing begins with an acknowledgment rather than a denial of the hegemonic functions of racism. Counselors and psychologists who claim a "multicultural" view but look the other way, claiming they do not want to "get political" or talk about words like neoliberalism, allow White racism and White supremacy to "run the table." They colonize rather than decolonize. Problematizing allows us to step back from essentialist statements on race, re-evaluate their meanings, and complicate our thinking.

This acknowledgment can lead us toward the development of strategies for countering the colonizing, nationally and ethnically chauvinistic practices that often pass for "multiculturalism", toward decolonizing multicultural, counseling and psychology practice. By taking an intersectional view we can adopt one countermeasure against defensive posturing around racism, a step closer to authentically multicultural counseling and psychology practice.

The Treatment of Race in Intersectionality

In an intersectionality approach, race is one vector of advantage and disadvantage. Along with gender, sexual orientation, class, and other vectors, race is seen as a system of oppression rather than an essentialist component of individual personhood. As an outgrowth of critical studies, intersectionality directs inquiry into how these systems interact to produce differences in people's lived experiences, thereby privileging some and repressing others. This understanding is what Thomas et al. (2005) lacked when they complained that Sue did not explain what White people would need to do to earn their "privilege."

At the 2001 World Congress Against Racism (WCAR), Racial Discrimination, Xenophobia, and Related Intolerance in Durban, South Africa, many discussants addressed the issue of violence against women. They used the metaphor of intersecting streets to theorize intersectionality. A most clear and concise précis of intersectionality can be found in Section 119 (Gender) of the Declaration and Program of Action of the Non-Governmental Organizations (NGO) Forum at WCAR:

> An intersectional approach to discrimination acknowledges that every person be it man or woman exists in a framework of multiple identities, with factors such as race, class, ethnicity, religion, sexual orientation, gender identity, age, disability, citizenship, national identity, geo-political context, health, including HIV/AIDS status and any other status are all determinants in one's experiences of racism, racial discrimination, xenophobia and related intolerances. An intersectional approach highlights the way in which there is a simultaneous interaction of discrimination as a result of multiple identities.

In the following sections, I use the management of domestic violence in the lower-class Black community as a paradigmatic exemplar of the intersectionality of gender, race, and class, illustrating how essentialist notions of race that dominate much of what is called "multicultural" counseling and psychology falls short of the sorts of complex understandings required to achieve social justice practice. I use this example because domestic violence is a major cause of health problems among Black women.

Theorizing Intersectionality: Domestic Violence Among Poor Blacks

In order to explain intersectionality, many of the WCAR speakers used the analogy of a woman coming to an intersection and making a choice of which direction to take. This analogy engendered a restrictive perception of a forced choice, with two starkly contrasting options for many women of color in the US (Conwill 2007, 2010). Sokoloff and DuPont (2005) raised a similar objection to this model of intersectionality. The two frameworks are clarified in the following illustration.

One day, through a public service announcement, a domestically abused Black woman becomes aware of community resources to protect her from domestic violence. After her next experience being physically abused at home, she finds herself at an intersection. She can decide to go straight ahead, maintaining her identity as a woman who accepts beatings. She also has the option to proceed down a road marked "Black." This choice might mean staying within the confines of her Black community and talking to her girlfriends and religious advisor for support.

Her other alternative is to turn down the road marked "Woman." Emphasizing her gender oppression, she might seek police intervention or a restraining order. She could retreat to a shelter designed principally by and for White women and hire a feminist lawyer. She might feel, however, that choosing the "Woman" route would be acting "against the race." Depending on the type and level of support in her community, she might even expose herself to disapproval based on the community's principles of racial or ethnic solidarity.

The perceived forced-choice to follow either the "race route" or the "gender route" presents her with a dilemma that has implications for her identity and her acceptance in various communities, where the authenticity of her allegiances could be challenged. This two-dimensional "streets" model of intersectionality can be faulted for neglecting to recognize the simultaneity and mutuality among her gender, race, and class identities that were stressed at the WCAR Forum. It does not provide an option for which, for example, saying "yes" to gender does not mean saying "no" to race. Another metaphor, or model, for intersectionality—one that acknowledges this multiplicativity and indivisibility emphasized at WCAR was needed to move beyond the theoretical problems of the two-dimensional "intersecting streets" model of intersectionality.

Constructing a Metadisciplinary Ecological Model of Intersectionality

In order to lend itself to a more effective approach to understanding and responding to domestic violence theory, the model had to account for gender, race, and class variations, among variations related to other identities, as found in domestic violence studies (Bograd 1999; Sokoloff and DuPont 2005). It also had to represent the dynamic nature of these identities, recognizing how their related forms of oppression intersect with one another.

Many factors contribute to the phenomenon of domestic violence in lower-class Black communities. Hence, the management of domestic violence in lower-class Black communities should be informed by a *metadisciplinary* perspective that synthesizes what we know about domestic violence from a number of disciplines related to an analysis of the interaction of gender, race, class, and other systems of identity and oppression. The metadisciplinary perspective is characterized by a change in order (meta) from a counselor or psychologist's disciplinary knowledge base to an integrated perspective that subsumes the lived experience and shared knowledge bases of the client, the abuser, the provider, the implicated societal systems (health, legal, economic, religious), and so forth. These include the epistemological, formal, methodological, and functional aspects of the management of domestic violence among poor Blacks (Conwill 2001; West-Olatunji and Conwill 2010).

On one hand, the metadisciplinary perspective incorporates an overarching paradigm that can be differentiated from over-determined single-factor, essentializing paradigms. Resorting primarily to the discipline of criminal justice to address domestic violence among poor Blacks typifies the latter approach. On the other hand, the metadisciplinary perspective of intersectionality can be differentiated from a multidisciplinary collage, with the abuser's assignment to jail, anger management classes, Alcoholics Anonymous, court-ordered domestic violence groups, and counseling—all without addressing those societal structures that are deeply implicated in domestic violence in lower-class Black communities. This, I would argue, is a critical move from a colonizing practice that simplifies conditions through narrow "multicultural" views toward a decolonizing practice that respects complexity.

Poor Black communities function as an internal colony in the USA. In regard to race, metadisciplinary intersectionality does not allow us to spotlight the dramatic differences between White and Black rates of domestic violence and attribute them simplistically to race or culture. Instead, it focuses on how systems of inequity such as sexism, racism, and economic injustice interact with each other to produce complex realities. It challenges hegemonic functions of knowledge production in relation to domestic violence among poor Blacks by exploring status, power, influence, and wealth as it relates to the interpersonal, political, social, and economic order, including provider-client relations. For example, in the management of domestic violence among poor Black couples, a metadisciplinary ecological model of intersectionality can direct inquiry into how family assistance or enforcement of mandated incarceration policies for offenders can affect rates of domestic violence among lower-class Blacks (Conwill 2010).

Summary

Race as an essentialist construct has a colonizing function that helps maintain White supremacy, even in many of the most popular paradigms often described as "multicultural" counseling and psychology. This colonizing function must be acknowledged if multicultural counseling and psychology is to evolve toward an authentic social justice paradigm. Intersectionality is a corrective to essentialist notions of race and can help us progress toward such a decolonized paradigm for multicultural counseling and psychology.

References

Arredondo, P., Toporek, R., Brown, S. P., Jones, J., Locke, D. C., Sanchez, J., et al. (1996). Operationalization of the multicultural counseling competencies. *Journal of Multicultural Counseling and Development, 24,* 42–78.

Bograd, M. (1999). Strengthening domestic violence theories: Intersections of race, class, sexual orientation, and gender. *Journal of Marital and Family Therapy, 25,* 275–289.

Conwill, W. L. (2001). Millennial mandates for mental health. In T. McClam & M. Woodside (Eds.), *Human services challenges in the 21st century* (pp. 175–191). Reading: Council for Standards in Human Service Education.

Conwill, W. L. (2007). Neoliberal policy as structural violence: Its links to domestic violence in US Black communities. In N. Gunewardena & A. Kingsolver (Eds.), *The gender of globalization: Women navigating cultural and economic marginalities* (pp. 127–146). Santa Fe: School for Advanced Research.

Conwill, W. L. (2010). Domestic violence among the Black poor: Intersectionality and social justice. *International Journal for the Advancement of Counselling, 32*(1), 31–45.

Gupta, T. D., James, C. A., Maaka, R. C., Galabuzi, G., & Andersen, C. (2007). *Race and racialization: Essential readings*. Toronto: Canadian Scholars Press, Inc.

Kilson, M. (1975). Blacks and neo-ethnicity in American political life. In N. Glazer & D. Moynihan (Eds.), *Ethnicity: Theory and experience* (pp. 236–266). Cambridge: Harvard University Press.

Liu, W. M., Pickett, T., & Ivey, A. E. (2007). White middle-class privilege: Social class bias and implications for training and practice. *Journal of Multicultural Counseling and Development, 35*(4), 194–206. doi:10.1002/j.2161-1912.2007.tb00060.x.

McIntosh, P. (2002). White privilege: Unpacking the invisible knapsack. In P. S. Rothenberg (Ed.), *White privilege: Essential readings on the other side of racism* (pp. 92–102) New York: Worth.

Moynihan, D. P. (1965). *The Negro family: The case for national action*. Washington, DC: Office of Policy Planning and Research United States Department of Labor.

Pitman, F. (1926). Slavery on British West Indies plantations in the eighteenth century. *Journal of Negro History, 11*(4), 584–668.

Rust, J. P., Jackson, M. A., Ponterotto, J. G., & Blumberg, F. C. (2011). Biculturalism and academic achievement of African American high school students. *Journal of Multicultural Counseling and Development, 39*(3), 130–140.

Sokoloff, N. J., & DuPont, I. (2005). Domestic violence at the intersections of race, class and gender: Challenges and contributions to understanding violence against marginalized women in diverse communities. *Violence Against Women, 11*(1), 38–64.

Sue, D. W. (2004). Whiteness and ethnocentric monoculturalism: Making the 'invisible' visible. *American Psychologist, 59*(November), 761–769.

Thomas, K. R., Wubbolding, R. E., & Jackson, M. L. (2005). Psychologically correct race baiting? *Academic Questions, 18*(4), 49–53.

Vontress, C. E., & Jackson, M. L. (2004). Reactions to the Multicultural Counseling Competencies Debate. *Journal of Mental Health Counseling, 26*(1), 74–80.

West-Olatunji, C. A., & Conwill, W. L. (2010). *Counseling African Americans*. San Francisco: Houghton Mifflin Company/Cengage.

Chapter 10
(De)colonizing Culture in Community Psychology: Reflections from Critical Social Science

Mariolga Reyes Cruz and Christopher C. Sonn

Community psychology has an expressed commitment to engage culture as a key dimension of community research and action. Several developments reflect the increasing attention that the notion of culture is gaining in community psychology (O'Donnell 2006). However, calls for fully integrating culture in community psychology are still founded on an implicit premise that should be subjected to critical reflection; that is, "culture" is something "out there," external to the field and its practitioners, which can be integrated into community psychology work. On the contrary, we argue that community psychology is a cultural practice and a product. The field is an institutionalized endeavor molded by Western ways of being, knowing, and doing (Gridley and Breen 2007). Most important, as a social science, community psychology is shaped by Western academic traditions, discourses, and structures that reproduce historical power hierarchies intertwined with the legacy of colonialism (see Martín-Baró 1998; Parker 2007). As the field engages cultural matters more explicitly, particularly in diverse settings, what is required is a critical approach that accounts for the relationship between culture and power.

In this chapter, we bring to bear theorizing from critical social science to propose a *decolonizing standpoint* for understanding culture that we think is vital for deepening emancipatory practices in community psychology. Broadly speaking, critical social science is a normative, practical, ethical, and political endeavor. It

This chapter was originally published in the *American Journal of Community Psychology* in 2011 (volume 47, numbers 1–2, pp. 203–214) and is reprinted here with minor revisions with permission from Springer Science+Business Media. *The American Journal of Community Psychology* is a Springer journal.

M. Reyes Cruz (✉)
Footscray, Australia
e-mail: mreyescruz@gmail.com

C. C. Sonn
College of Arts, Psychology Discipline, Victoria University, Ballarat Road,
Footscray 3011, Victoria, Australia
e-mail: Christopher.sonn@vu.edu.au

R. D. Goodman, P. C. Gorski (eds.), *Decolonizing "Multicultural" Counseling through Social Justice,* International and Cultural Psychology, DOI 10.1007/978-1-4939-1283-4_10

aims to develop theory and practice that reveals distortions in individual and public discourse and action that serve to maintain systems of oppression. Critical social science engages in "inquiry that fosters enlightened self-knowledge and effective social–political action.... It rejects the idea of disinterested social science and emphasizes attending to the cultural and historical conditions on which the theorist's own intellectual activity depends" (Schwandt 2001, p. 46). Thus, critical social science is also a self-reflexive endeavor (Schwandt 2001; see also Kincheloe and McLaren 2000, 2005).

As critical community psychologists, we are particularly interested in a decolonizing standpoint to culture that can disrupt essentialist understandings of cultural matters that have served historically to marginalize others. This standpoint brings into clearer view ways in which power/privilege/oppression are reproduced and contested through racialized and ethnicized practices and discourses; that is, how social inequality is maintained and challenged through culture. Working from this perspective should lead us to question: What about culture are we trying to understand, to what end, from whose perspective? How does our current understanding of cultural matters in a particular setting help us foreground dynamics of social oppression and liberation?

To lay the groundwork for a critical approach to culture, we first consider how community psychology and other fields have explored cultural matters. We then locate the decolonizing standpoint within critical social science, particularly writings on the coloniality of power and knowledge from Latin American and Indigenous perspectives. Next, we present some of our work in diverse settings to show how we integrate critical social theories and methodologies to examine ways in which culture is implicated in the (re)production and contestation of inequality. First, we present critical ethnographic work in a racially and ethnically diverse school district where a colonial mentality permeates discourses about cultural difference and inclusion, masking ethnic and class exclusion. Then we turn to autoethnographic writing to show how a commitment to decolonizing practices is integrated with teaching psychology to mostly White students in ways that challenge the enduring legacy of colonialism at the level of social identities. We conclude by reflecting on the challenges and possibilities a decolonizing standpoint brings to community psychology. We hope such an endeavor would contribute to a community psychology that is critical, transdisciplinary, and intercultural from where we can engage in emancipatory theory, research, and action.

Culture in Community Psychology

Community psychologists have been increasingly aware of the role culture plays in community phenomena. The field has adopted cultural relativity and social diversity as values to uphold (Rappaport 1977; Sarason 1974; Trickett et al. 1994). Several publications in the *American Journal of Community Psychology* (AJCP) and related journals (e.g., *Journal of Community Psychology*) have been dedicated to different topics regarding culture. Some authors have argued for incorporating notions of culture into community psychology understandings of diverse settings (e.g., Trickett 1996). Others have explored ways in which research and practice in communities can be culturally anchored (Hughes et al. 1993). Harrell and Bond (2007) proposed an articulation of a diversity principle that fosters awareness of culture, power, and "self-in-community." Additionally, some theorists have pushed for interdisciplinary work that deepens community psychology understandings of the complexity of community life including its sociocultural dimensions (Christens and Perkins 2008; Maton et al. 2006; Reich and Reich 2006). Notwithstanding the increasing number of articles addressing culture directly, these are exceptions rather than the rule. Methodologically speaking, while the field has embraced alternative research methods such as qualitative interviews and community-based participatory research, studies for the most part continue to be anchored in positivist epistemologies. One is hard pressed to find in AJCP articles that address or use interpretive research methods. For instance, we found only 13 articles that engage ethnographic research and none that use discourse analysis. Thus, as reflected in the published literature, the field still struggles theoretically and methodologically to see culture in its full complexity.

Culture is not an easy concept to define, and there is no (inter)disciplinary agreement on a single meaning. Although historically the study of culture has been the domain of anthropology, such a disciplinary border has been blurred; the study of culture is now of interest to a variety of disciplines and fields including cross-cultural and cultural psychology, cultural studies, postcolonial studies, and community psychology (Jahoda and Krewer 1997; Ribeiro 2005; Shweder 1990; for recent examples in community psychology see Kral et al. 2011, and accompanying articles in the edited special issue of the journal; Guerra and Knox 2008; Lavee and Ben-Ari 2008; Gonzales et al. 2008; Roosa et al. 2009). Broadly speaking, culture is often used to refer to shared values, beliefs, practices, products, and norms of social groups (e.g., nation-states, ethnic groups). Other forms and levels of social organization and stratification have also been recognized as "having" a culture. For instance, families, people with disabilities, institutions, and corporations are said to have their own cultures. Griffin (2000; see also Greenfield 1997) notes that in psychology, culture is often seen as the backdrop for engaging with and understanding social practices. Yet, in other instances, culture is simply used as an euphemism, a proxy signaling dimensions of social inequality and oppression by way of race, ethnicity, and/or class.

Rappaport (2000) asserts that "the language chosen inevitably leads to the nature of interventions developed in exactly the same way that in science and problem solving the way the question is framed predetermines the answers obtained" (p. 109). It is evident that some community psychological understandings of culture seem to draw mainly upon conceptualizations developed by mainstream anthropology and cross-cultural psychology (e.g., Dinh et al. 2008; Lavee and Ben-Ari 2008; O'Donnell 2006). These inter- and intra-disciplinary conversations are important for expanding the ways in which we understand and engage with human diversity. However, as some have observed (e.g., Harrell and Bond 2007; Trickett 1994; Watts 1992), there remains a tendency in the field to present culture as "some-thing," as static, an essence that exists outside of the observer (i.e., researchers and practitioners).

A rudimentary review of publications in 2008–2013 issues of the AJCP reveals few studies (e.g., Berg et al. 2009; Gone 2011) that have engaged interpretive approaches to understanding people in context. Yet, most studies still rely on positivist models of knowledge production that position researchers as neutral expert knowers outside the phenomena of study (Dinh et al. 2008; Guerra and Knox 2008; Lavee and Ben-Ari 2008; for constructivist perspectives see Ibáñez 2001, Gergen 1996). From our perspective, advances in postcolonial and cultural studies and critical psychology can reposition community psychology's engagement with culture. Such understandings highlight the ways in which social categories emerge, are negotiated, and are sustained within relations of domination. In this sense, critiques leveled against mainstream approaches to culture in other disciplines also apply to community psychology. If we are to extend theorizing in community psychology to develop deeper understandings of cultural matters, the field must attend to contemporary debates that problematize how culture has been approached by different disciplines.

Bhatia and Ram (2001; Bhatia 2007; also Espiritu 2003; Gemignani and Peña 2007; Griffin 2000), for instance, have questioned the assumptions that underlie cross-cultural work using the notion of acculturation to illustrate the issues. The acculturation work developed by Berry (1997), among others, presents an ecological model for understanding the cultural and psychological changes that follow ongoing firsthand contact between different groups. Bhatia and Ram argued that the model assumes a kind of psychic unity of "mankind," that is, acculturation will take place in the same way for everyone. Little attention is given to how the distinct histories of colonialism and the ongoing dynamics of oppression and liberation in different (post)colonial contexts shape adaptation to a new society. In some of our own work, we have argued that memories of home and experiences of racialized exclusion turn acculturation and identity making into an ongoing process of negotiating power relations within broader social, cultural, and economic structures (Reyes Cruz 2002, 2006; Sonn 2002). To take Bhatia's and Ram's argument further, the standard against which successful acculturation is assessed is often determined by the dominant group, silencing diversity and dissent within the host society.

Okazaki et al. (2008) extended these discussions to argue for a critical consideration of colonialism in the psychology of culture that goes beyond the East–West dichotomy to also consider the histories of colonial relations between and within countries (see also Okazaki and Saw 2011). They draw on the work in the area of colonialism to show the role of social, political, and historical forces in shaping lives. The authors' point to similar critiques as those highlighted above to suggest that cross-cultural and cultural psychological models and, in our view, community psychological approaches need to be expanded to consider how major geopolitical and historical factors shape everyday lives.

For the purposes of this chapter, culture is understood as a process, an ongoing social construction that speaks of the ways in which we learn to live and make sense of life always in relationship to others within specific social/economic/political/historical contexts (see Geertz 1973; Jessen 2007). Also,

> …culture is a historically situated, collective product constituted by the values, beliefs, perceptions, symbols, and other humanly created artifacts which are transmitted across generations through language and other mediums…. Culture is simultaneously a product of human action as well as a determinant of future action, a composite of meanings and associated traditions, which define, inform, and constitute the range of our understandings and investments. (Misra and Gergen 1993, p. 226)

In sum, culture refers to a historical product, a process, and a means for action.

To the extent that community psychologists are interested in addressing issues of power and social justice, understandings of culture need to be placed within critical frameworks that examine the dynamics of the social reproduction and contestation of inequality. This is not to say that matters of diversity, translation, sensitivity, and knowledge of different groups are irrelevant to community psychology. However, taking concrete steps to becoming increasingly aware of cultural issues in research and practice without a critical standpoint runs the risk of perpetuating the ills of colonial relations (e.g., Gone 2007).

Coloniality of Power, Culture, and Knowledge: Crafting a Decolonizing Standpoint

Part of the difficulty the field experiences in seeing culture in its complexity stems from the continuing legacy of coloniality in the social sciences (psychology included). Western thought has been characterized by a longstanding tendency to partition reality and build knowledge on such multiple separations (e.g., "human beings/nature," "mind/body," "self/other," "object/subject;" Lander 2005; Ladson-Billings 2003; Smith 2012/1999). This worldview would have been just one among many if it had not been central to the globalization of the European colonial project launched with the conquest of Abya Yala (name some indigenous movements give to what is otherwise known as the American continent). The convergence of Western thought and ways of knowing with Eurocentric colonialism resulted in the imposition of a hierarchical articulation of difference (e.g., "civilized/uncivilized," "modern/primitive," "expert knowledge/general knowledge," "development/underdevelopment," "saved/condemn," "European/Other," "White/Other") to the benefit of the ruling classes.[1] Western/Modern social science was built upon this conceptualization of the world and has served to justify and naturalize this world order as "the way things are" (Cole 2003; Lander 2005; Smith 2012/1999), rather than a result of the history of power (Quijano 2000). The convergence among these forces and its continuing legacy is known as coloniality of power, culture, and knowledge (see the edited volume by Lander 2005; Quijano 2000, 2007; Santos 2010). Thus, to challenge coloniality, we must recognize that "all social and historical phenomena are part of or

[1] This particular form of Eurocentric power is intricately linked with the emergence of capitalism as the dominant economic and values system. Its establishment came about at the cost of vanquishing other ways of being and knowing that existed in what came to be known as Europe (see Lander 2005).

express a social relation or a web of social relationships. As such, social-historical phenomena cannot be understood outside the relational field it belongs to, its socio-historical totality" (Quijano 2000, p. 352).

There is a body of work that shows how coloniality shapes understandings of culture, and subsequently identity, to position the West as the standard in relation to the other cultural groups and justify their oppression and marginalization (e.g., Bulhan 1985; Hermans and Kempen 1998; Holdstock 2000; Said 1979; Sinha and Kao 1997; Smith 2012/1999). In Australia, some have argued that the Cartesian model of knowing that is dominant in social science research underpins much of the knowledge constructed about Aboriginal and Torres Strait Islander, people representing them as an inferior other and universalizing "whiteness" (Dodson 2003; Dudgeon and Fielder 2006; Martin 2003; Moreton-Robinson 2004). Similarly, Smith (2012/1999) argued that Western knowledge production processes have privileged Western ways of doing and being while it has dehumanized the Maori or Maori people knowledge, practices, and language. In Puerto Rico, school children learn about the history of slavery from the perspective of the White slave owners and White abolitionists while the dominant public discourse emphasizes an interracial national identity that silences everyday experiences of racism (Godreau et al. 2008).

These debates signal that ethnicity and race are not static, neutral, or objective markers but rather subjective, flexible, and politicized processes. Social group memberships based on ethnicity, race, and gender afford people differential access to power and privilege in different contexts. Power is (re)produced in and through cultural means, and this is manifested in everyday interactions. Seeing culture through the lens of coloniality unveils the masks of neutrality and objectivity that are part of this legacy (Quijano 2000; Santos 2011/2012). Decolonizing culture requires actively deconstructing notions of the other based on the enduring legacy of colonial relations, beginning to understand the meaning of difference and its micro-politics as well as its sociological/historical/economic/political context, and examining "the dialectic between the local and the global" (Rizvi 2007, p. 262).

Hall (1996) suggests that "questions of culture and ideology" are given "a formative, not merely expressive, place in the constitution of social and political life" (p. 443). From this perspective, culture is seen as a "system of continually contested meanings in which 'societies' and 'individuals' are (re)produced and transformed, but within a nexus of social relations around domination and subordination" (Griffin 2000, p. 20). Such a complex conceptualization of culture can lead us to deeper understandings of the interconnectedness between culture and power.

Approaching Culture from a Decolonizing Standpoint: Notes from the Field

This chapter is part of a broader effort concerned with developing a critical and transformative community psychology committed to decolonization, collective empowerment, and liberation (e.g., Glover et al. 2005; Huygens 2006; Moane 2003; Montero 2007, 2009; Nelson and Prilleltensky 2005; Watts and Serrano-Garcia

2003). Although, still far from mainstream, some social and community psychology work examines the intersections between culture, coloniality, and empowerment (e.g., Borg 2006; Gone 2007; Moane 2003; Reyes Cruz 2008a, b; Riggs and Augoustinos 2005; Serrano-Garcia 1994; Sonn 2004a, b). We wish to contribute to this broader project by articulating a decolonizing standpoint from where to understand culture within an awareness of a broader set of social/political/historical/economic arrangements.

A decolonizing standpoint is a transdisciplinary and political stance grounded in critical social theories and methodologies to understand and expose the continuing legacy of coloniality. Our decolonizing standpoint is informed by writings in critical feminism (Anzaldúa 1999; Hooks 1990); critical race theory (Ladson-Billings 2003; Ladson-Billings and Donnor 2005); Whiteness studies (Fine et al. 1997; Green et al. 2007); liberation and critical psychology (Freire 1972; Martín-Baró 1994; Montero 1997/2001, 2007; Parker 2005); coloniality of power and knowledge (Quijano 2000, 2007); the study of social reproduction of inequality (Bourdieu and Passeron 1977/2000; Lareau and Horvat 1999; Lareau and Weininger 2003); and the move toward foregrounding what Boaventura de Sousa Santos has termed the epistemologies of the South (Pascal and Leyva 2011; Santos 2011, 2011–2012). These different theoretical lenses are consonant with community psychology's general commitment to developing ways of being, knowing, and doing that contribute to decolonization and liberation. Shared within these theoretical lenses is a focus on the workings of power, where power is seen as produced in and through symbolic means within the broader context of social relations. Therefore, a key element of a decolonizing standpoint is to de-ideologize (Martín-Baró 1994), to deconstruct ideologies and discourses that obscure the workings of power. As Smith (2012/1999) has indicated, this requires researchers and practitioners to examine the motivations and the basic assumptions that inform knowledge production within contexts of intergroup relations (see also Santos 2010). The deconstruction opens the way to transformation as we recognize different ways of knowing and value the lived experiences and voices of the marginalized.

Our aim here is to show how we attempt to engage different settings from a decolonizing standpoint. First, we present material from Mariolga's critical ethnographic work with Mexican immigrant parents that revealed colonial ways of approaching the ethnic-other in an ethnically and racially diverse school district in the Midwest of the USA. Next, we offer autoethnographic writing by Chris that shows the ways in which Indigenous theorizing and Whiteness studies are translated to a diversity class with mainly White students in Australia. In both these sets of notes from the field, the intersections between power, culture, and knowledge are made evident to unmask coloniality in everyday discourse and action.

Notes from the Field Part I: Culture, Politics, and Capital in a Diverse School District

Public schools galvanize multiple stakeholders toward actions that reflect common, collective, and conflictive interests. Thus, schools cannot be understood without grappling with politics and power. For several years, I have been developing strategies to integrate critical ethnography with education organizing, working as a witness/actor in ground-up mobilization efforts (Reyes Cruz 2008a, 2012). Critical ethnography is ethnographic work framed within critical theory traditions. Just as in traditional ethnography, the ethnographer engages in prolonged participant-observation, writing field notes, conducting informal and formal interviews and analyzing public documents and artifacts. However, critical ethnographers aim to develop situated, self-reflexive work that connects everyday life experiences of people and communities with the workings of power in ways that amplify the voices of the oppressed and contribute to their struggle for liberation (Carspecken 1996; Kincheloe and McLaren 2000; Trueba and McLaren 2000).

After working in social services and academic research in New York City for several years, I moved to the US Midwest to pursue a doctorate in community psychology. The town, mostly White and of European descent, had experienced a substantial increase in monolingual Latino American immigrants in recent years. The challenges of ethnic diversity were becoming apparent as I began to engage in community work for education equity. I was no stranger to cultural dislocation: a racialized (post)colonial subject, a brown immigrant woman from the US territory of Puerto Rico, growing up between Puerto Rico, Spain, and the USA. While I could recognize significant differences between other immigrants from south of the border and myself (e.g., immigration status, formal education), I thought at least my experiences as a bilingual/bicultural immigrant could be useful to new immigrants facing the challenges of being a racialized and ethnicized minority.

At first, I became a volunteer at an after-school program serving working-poor Latin American children and their families. Soon, I was asked to be the program liaison to a public elementary school. This work led me to engage with school and school district staff in different efforts to address the needs of the new immigrant population. In the process, I also became an ally to a group of Mexican immigrant parents organizing to advocate for their children's educational rights. In the course of four years, I took on the thorny role of becoming a cultural broker for immigrants and others, translating language and cultural meaning in different settings and facilitating and negotiating communication across cultural and experiential divides (Reyes Cruz 2008a).

Initially, I entered the field in response to a community identified need for multicultural/bilingual professionals who could work with the new ethnic minority. But as the work developed, it became apparent that—beyond ethnic-based cultural differences—the main problems that marginalized immigrants faced had to do with power inequities in their relationships with institutionalized structures embodied by men and women, White, Black, Latino/a, and Mexican. The ways in which power was organized in school settings were entrenched in a culture that kept the poor and marginalized in a subordinate place. An understanding of the coloniality of power moved this work from focusing on issues of ethnic-based cultural rights (e.g., access to materials in Spanish) toward the social reproduction of inequality, particularly how cultural and political capital were enacted to maintain ethnicized working-poor immigrants at the margins of school decision-making.

The concept of cultural capital, as articulated by the late French sociologist Pierre Bourdieu, links macro- and micro-levels of analysis to account for the intersections between culture and power in everyday life. Cultural capital speaks about the ways of knowing, knowledge and practices of the ruling classes *and* their capacity to establish their norms as the main criteria for evaluating what is good, valid, and worthwhile (Lareau and Weininger 2003). The norms are not fixed or inherently "good" but rather serve the interest of the dominant classes and, thus, can and do continuously change.

One of the main sources of contention between Latin American immigrants and the school system was bilingual education. It was the first time the school district was mandated to offer services in Spanish. With limited resources and expertise, the school district implemented a bilingual program that was far from what many Latino American parents had hoped:

> The district indicated they wanted parent input on what types of programs would be implemented in the upcoming years and the coordinator wanted to make sure parents made informed decisions.... For several [public] meetings district staff described different models and their effectiveness.... Lucero [a Mexican moyher], wanted the program that would facilitate the students' bilingualism, support parent-child relationships by strengthening the children's knowledge of the home language, and equalize the academic-racial hierarchy of the schools.

Hasta ahorita el programa que más me ha convencido es el de dual immersion.... *O sea, ahora sí, no sé quién me dijo, "Estamos en Estados Unidos, tenemos que aprender inglés." Entonces, pero uno también como madre no quiere que sus hijos sólo agarren inglés. Imagínate al rato ¿qué comunicación voy a tener con ellos?...A lo mejor si se llega a hacer lo del* dual immersion *sean equitativas las cosas porque tanto como los americanos se van a tener que esforzar para aprender la materia.*	So far the program that has convinced me the most is dual immersion. Now, I don't know who said, "We are in the United States, we have to learn English." But as a mother I don't want our children to learn only English. Imagine then, what kind of communication am I going to have with them? And maybe if they end up having the dual immersion program things will be more equitable because Americans would also have to make an effort to learn the subjects [in a second language].

> When parents and staff finally met to decide what program they wanted implemented... district staff presented [choices] that had not been discussed before.... A mother asked... "What do you know about the effectiveness of these program options?" The district staff replied those were the options other districts were implementing; although they did not know how effective the programs were they believed it would be better than what the schools currently had. (Reyes Cruz 2008a, pp. 138–139)

While the school district engaged Latino American immigrant parents in symbolic participation, Mexican parents mobilized to demand authentic participation in school decision-making (Reyes Cruz 2008a; see also Anderson 1998). The parents were adopting the cultural norms valued by the schools (e.g., attending meetings, volunteering, working with their children at home) and raising the stakes for public accountability. However, their efforts were rebuffed and the Mexican parents did not have the necessary political capital to have a say. That is, at that time, they did not have the needed capacity and strength to influence decisions about public matters to their benefit (Mediratta 1995). The group was fraught with their own internal conflicts. And they were struggling against a fundamentally antidemocratic school culture. Despite the prevalent discourse on advancing parent participation in decision-making, building school–community collaboration, embracing diversity, and multiculturalism,

> certain cultural practices promoted individual over collective interventions couched in a colonial discourse that emphasized the deficits of marginalized families and their debt to those helping them. Most of the people involved, regardless of their position in the power hierarchy, would at times adopt the colonial discourse. This discourse served to squelch dissent with dominant school practices. (Reyes Cruz 2008a, p. 153)

The colonial discourse reflects what Memmi (1957/1983) describes as a "colonial mentality:" "the psychological consequences of oppression for both dominant and oppressed groups" (Reyes Cruz 2008a, p. 173).

Laura, a light-skinned Mexican immigrant mother, had summoned the principal, her daughter's teacher (both White US Americans), the bilingual teacher (a light-skinned woman of Mexican descent), and myself (the brown Puerto Rican ally-translator) to discuss some of her concerns regarding her child's schooling. The school was located in a predominately poor and African American neighborhood. Its students were mostly African Americans and immigrants from Latin America:

> [Laura] expressed her concern with what she described as "lack of respect in the school"…. She had seen staff mistreating children, particularly African American students. Her child was also being mistreated by other children and the adults were not intervening…. The principal explained that not all parents had the same vision as Laura, they were not interested in getting involved in the school or what their children do, they didn't teach their children respect, and that was what the school had to deal with…. Laura insisted the issue was a school-wide problem. She suggested that the staff work on the staff end and she could work with other parents…. The principal broke the silence, "You should encourage your daughter to come to the staff when others are bothering her and we will deal with the situation"…. On our way out…Laura said to me, *"No pueden ver más allá* (They can't see beyond their noses)…they want to make it about my child." (Reyes Cruz 2008a, pp. 153–154)

Coloniality worked at different levels: from the racialized/ethnicized ways in which staff enacted their cultural capital deciding what counted as valid knowledge, to the ways in which they promoted child-focused individualistic parent participation, separating the personal from the communal/public and quieting potential claims of collective discontent. By actively engaging in critical conversations about public education with different social actors, the Mexican parents opened spaces for challenging colonial relations. The parents showed they were critically watching, seeing what was being done to the children and communicating they were not going to stand for it.

Notes from the Field Part II: Autoethnographic[2] Reflections toward Decolonizing Interventions into Race Relations

I was a "colored" South African moving to Australia when, before I knew it, I was committed to the decolonization agendas of Indigenous Australians. I grew up during the Apartheid era in South Africa. My family immigrated to Australia in the mid 1980s, partly to find better economic opportunities and partly to find a way out of Apartheid. As I got immersed in Australian society, it became apparent that racism here was of a different kind. It was not a legal system; racism was more subtle, emerging through discursive networks and the micro-politics of power. In South Africa, I was labeled colored and positioned in-between Black and White. The membership afforded me privileges while being discriminated against by the same people imposing marginality on me. In Australia, there was no such explicit hierarchy, yet, I was constructed as a racialized outsider in relation to an ostensibly White majority.

For the past 14 years, I've worked in a predominantly White academic context as a researcher and educator in community psychology teaching mostly non-Indigenous students. I was already sensitive to how community psychology uses notions like race, ethnicity, and culture to categorize groups, often misrepresenting people like me. But that became further complicated as I engaged with the writings of Indigenous scholars in Australia and Aotearoa (often known as New Zealand; Martin 2003; Oxenham 2000; Smith 2012/1999). They were writing back, writing about decolonization and anti-colonialism, to assert Indigenous ways of knowing, doing, and being in the world. As I engaged in this work, nagging questions emerged. What are the implications of these writings for my research and teaching? How would I engage in empowerment praxis when the dominant ways of being, knowing, and doing of the discipline are named as problematic? I began to explore possible answers through collaborating in projects led by Indigenous Australians, raising the stakes for our White colleagues and students in research and teaching settings.

Part of my work as an ally to Indigenous Australians has been to work with the Centre for Aboriginal Studies at Curtin University in Western Australia to incorporate issues of diversity into psychology courses and to research individual and community responses to oppression. I was learning about the history and continuing oppression of Indigenous people and wanted to be involved in responding without imposing my agenda. The writing and activities of the Centre, particularly those focused on Indigenous Australians' rights to self-determination, made even more salient how some of the assumptions and theoretical tools that underpin psychology actually worked to silence and undermine Indigenous voices (e.g., being trained as "expert" and "objective knower" of others, developing models privileging Western ways of being and knowing, building theory based on core values such as individualism).

---

[2] Autoethnography is "an autobiographical genre of writing that displays multiple layers of consciousness, connecting the personal to the cultural" (Ellis and Bochner 2000, p. 739).

The exchanges with Indigenous Australian colleagues and our shared experiences led me to turn the gaze away from a superficial understanding of the cultures of others onto examining one's own culture in relation to other cultural groups. My discomfort recognizing the disempowering effects of the knowledge production practices of my discipline and from being othered in different contexts moved me to problematize normativity. I began deconstructing dominance through research and teaching while affirming the cultural identities and aspirations of those silenced in Australia's Eurocentric psychology. And then I discovered the critical writings in Whiteness studies and privilege.

Critical Whiteness writers argue that Whiteness signals "…the production and reproduction of dominance rather than subordination, normativity rather than marginality, and privilege rather than disadvantage" (Frankenberg 1993, p. 236). Those who belong to this group are typically not asked to reflect on their cultural identities because their culture is the norm. Thus, Whiteness is often invisible; members are blind to the privileges that they have by virtue of their group membership. The invisibility of Whiteness is what makes it so powerful; people are rendered blind to the ways in which culturally sanctioned practices can work in an exclusionary and often colonizing manner. These writings resonated deeply within me. After all, I feel the brunt of it.

I am outside Whiteness because I am a Black person, an immigrant in Australia, keenly aware of how racism is significant in the lives of people of color. And yet, I belong to a White institution and have been trained in a historically Eurocentric academic discipline. I am inside Whiteness. My colleagues and the majority of the students in psychology programs in Australia are ostensibly "White." I had seen White colleagues "being helpful" without necessarily considering or understanding the different discourses that position non-Indigenous people as helpers and Indigenous people as requiring help and the implications of these for empowerment work. Every day, we see how mainstream institutionalized systems in Australia privilege the knowledge and tools of Eurocentric psychology while looking suspiciously at Indigenous ways of being, knowing, and doing (Dudgeon and Oxenham 1990). Indigenous colleagues and I witness the ways in which non-Indigenous allies end up taking over spaces created for Indigenous people, often becoming recognized as experts on Indigenous matters.

As a response, a diverse group of colleagues—including Indigenous scholars—and I began to integrate as a key part of the Race Relations and Psychology course the history of race relations in Australia focusing on Indigenous writers. Students were challenged to explore key concepts (race, ethnicity, and culture) used in psychological research to examine difference to then turn to the Whiteness literature shifting the focus from the "other" to their own group memberships. This turn exposes taken for granted social positions and the privileges afforded because of those positionings. Problematizing how the cultures of "others" are typically treated as static and antiquated was central; this served to reveal how understandings of self and others are produced through historically situated discourses, taken for granted knowledge, and everyday practices within social and political contexts. Ultimately, the challenge is to grasp the implications of those understandings for everyday interactions.

Teaching about Whiteness to ostensibly White students has proven to be quite challenging. The notion of whiteness is contested by most students, and so it should be. Typically, the students' initial response is to resist or reject the notion. The initial rejection, more often than not, is about equating Whiteness with racism and they do not want to be seen as racist. The response is to disconnect from the history of race relations and engage in us/them constructions without considering the societal arrangements that Whiteness speaks to.

John, an older student, who identified his Irish ancestry, wrote in his journal for the class:

> I honestly believe that I had a head start though. I honestly think that I've been a person that's always been fairly sensitive to these issues. The fact that I had an Indian brother in-law from the age of 7, and grew up amongst lots of Italians and Greeks has probably helped—but I don't want to sell my own personality short either. Some people's hearts are in the right place.

Stewart, another older student, who identified as third or fourth generation Australian, wrote,

> A final thought occurred regarding privilege. Previously although I have stated that I recognize the privileges afforded to me due to my ancestry/identity, one sentence uttered by a fellow student; "Privilege is not something earned or deserved" has really caused me to question my ontology.

Their responses also get more complicated. Students fragment Whiteness, turning to hyphenated identities (Italian-Australian, Greek-Australian, or Macedonian-Australian) in an attempt to ethnicize their Australian-ness. However, a hierarchy within Whiteness is created with Australian (meaning Anglo-Celtic) remaining undisturbed at the top. I had to breathe deeply and find ways to empathize with the students' struggle. Luckily, I was not alone in this.

The experience with students of color has been the opposite. The topic of Whiteness is exciting; they want to hear about it, engage with it. For them it is obvious; they live and experience Whiteness. They know how they are positioned as "perpetual strangers" in a country that imagines itself as "White" (Hage 2000). These students', the Indigenous, the refugee, the immigrant, and the children of immigrants, senses of belonging are regulated by Whiteness in different ways in everyday settings and often through seemingly innocuous micro-practices including questions such as, Where are you from? and statements such as, "you are just like us."

This work creates contact zones, spaces where separated people come together, feel vulnerable and at risk (Somerville and Perkins 2003). The powerful ways in which we are positioned as "other" by and through discourses begin to be questioned. These contact zones represent opportunities for unmasking coloniality and engaging identity politics to examine the dynamics of oppression and possibilities for liberation (Sonn, Quayle, Mackenzie and Law, 2014). The work requires going beyond static and fixed understandings of self and other to engage conceptualizations of culture that are concerned with lived experiences. This is the work that called me into community psychology in the first place.

Summary and Concluding Remarks

Community psychology aims to address collective distress as a product of social dynamics of inequality, taking into account the multiple dimensions of diversity. The field has made important strides in developing an awareness and practice consistent with its positioning in favor of diversity in its multiple dimensions, recognizing deeper cultural processes that impact the problems we attend. However, community psychology still has work to do to understand the ways in which culture is intertwined with power/oppression/exploitation and locate those processes within historical/social/political contexts.

In this chapter, we have engaged in critical reflection of the ways in which the field's view of culture and those thought of as "other" is shaped by the continuing legacy of colonial relations. We contend that culture should be central to the field to the extent that community psychologists are committed to abandoning colonizing approaches to the marginalized other. Analyses of diversity and culture devoid of a critical understanding of the politics of context can easily fall into essentializing social inequality as issues of poor/rich, black/white, immigrant/non-immigrant, or "cultural" (to mean racialized and ethnicized) differences without challenging the roots of oppression/exploitation. Cultural matters, we argue, need to be approached from a decolonizing standpoint to understand how power, privilege, and oppression have historically been and continue to be intwined within "the cultural" in the multiple facets of community psychology work.

This chapter goes further in current community psychology theorizing by locating culture within coloniality and power, and showing alternative methodologies to engage culture from a decolonizing standpoint at the level of teaching, writing, and community research and action. Without a decolonizing standpoint for understanding cultural matters, the struggles of recent immigrant working-poor families in a school district would have been left at the level of, for instance, differences in cultural practices and understandings or lack of translation and quality of bilingual services. What would remain hidden is how cultural capital is enacted in everyday practices to maintain marginalized minorities subordinate to the ways of being, understanding, and doing of the dominant school culture (in our exemplar, White-middle class). Without a decolonizing standpoint, teaching diversity to a predominantly White student body in a racialized society would end up reproducing the marginalized "other" (e.g., focusing on understanding the culture of the ethnicized and racialized groups) rather than revealing the ways in which the colonial legacy has shaped the dominant culture positioning whiteness as a norm in academic and other practices.

While it continues to be vital for psychologists to develop their conceptual, intellectual, and personal capacities to work with diversity issues, this should not be an aim in itself but a road to an intercultural and critical praxis within community psychology. By interculturality, we mean a stance of recognition of the cultural rights of different groups and the imperative to learn from each other from a place of ontological, epistemological, and methodological parity (see Bonilla 2004; Dávalos 2005; Quijano 2007). That is, working toward interculturality is working to eliminate cultural capital in its normative function, chipping away at institutional processes that marginalize historically oppressed ways of being, knowing, and doing, including knowledge itself.

In our work, we have come to realize the importance of critically reflecting on our discipline and our own multiple positionings—those that afford us power within broader social/political/historical contexts and those that keep us at the margins. *Critical reflexivity* is more than individual-level self awareness. It also requires that we constantly evaluate ways in which we contribute to both liberation and oppression. To this end, we agree with others that *transdisciplinarity* focused on critical social theory is central to the development of an emancipatory community psychology, one devoted to transformative research and action. This is as much an academic as an ethical and political stance.

As we craft our decolonizing standpoint, we have found extremely valuable writings in critical race theory, Whiteness studies, feminist critique, Indigenous research, and coloniality. These literatures are concerned with decolonization by identifying deeper process of exclusion and oppression, de-centering the dominance of Western ways of knowing and doing, and bringing to the foreground Indigenous and other marginalized knowledges. With this come new opportunities to engage innovative methodologies to achieve socially just and transformative research and action. This includes going beyond the dominant modes of knowledge production (such as logical positivism) to include different practices that will affirm the knowledges of marginalized communities and thereby also contribute to social transformation. The next step in building a deeply decolonizing standpoint would be to outright anchor our praxis with the marginalized and the oppressed within the epistemologies of the South (Santos 2011; for interdisciplinary examples see the edited volumes by Pascal and Leyva 2011).

We believe community psychology can and should make important contributions to the study of cultural matters by revealing and addressing the experiential intersections between culture, power, and empowerment in everyday contexts. As a field, we recognize, as did Dewey (1938), that “in actual experience, there is never any such isolated singular object or event; an object or event is always a special part, phase, or aspect, of an environing experienced world” (p. 67 as cited by Cole 2003, p. 132). We believe the field must reinvent its institutional practices to develop and support intercultural, critical, and transdisciplinary praxis. To this end, we would like to see increasing concerted efforts to (a) develop intercultural competencies such as multicultural and multilingual skills (e.g., requiring students to take a second language and work in diverse settings where their social positions are de-centered); (b) examine the social and political history of the communities we work with as these are intwined with issues of health, equity, and self-determination; (c) expand community psychology’s theoretical and methodological horizons for understanding the micro-politics of culture, power, and knowledge in specific settings; and (d) create spaces and opportunities for critical reflexivity to explore and challenge our positions in power hierarchies. Ultimately, we hope that understanding cultural matters from a decolonizing standpoint will move us closer toward realizing the emancipatory values of community psychology.

References

Anderson, G. L. (1998). Toward authentic participation: Deconstructing the discourses of participatory reforms in education. *American Educational Research Journal, 35*(4), 571–603.

Anzaldúa, G. (1999). *Borderlands, la frontera: The new mestiza* (2nd ed.). San Francisco: Aunt Lute Books.

Berg, M., Coman, E., & Schensul, J. J. (2009). Youth action research for prevention: A multi-level intervention designed to increase efficacy and empowerment among urban youth. *American Journal of Community Psychology, 43,* 345–359.

Berry, J. W. (1997). Immigration, acculturation, and adaptation. *Applied Psychology: An International Review, 46,* 5–34.

Bhatia, S. (2007). Rethinking culture and identity in psychology: Towards a transnational cultural psychology. *Journal of Theoretical and Philosophical Psychology, 27–28*(2-1), 301–321.

Bhatia, S., & Ram, A. (2001). Rethinking "acculturation" in relation to diasporic cultures and postcolonial identities. *Human Development, 44*(1), 1–18.

Bonilla, A. (2004). La II Cumbre Continental de los Pueblos y Nacionalidades Indígenas de Abya Yala (Quito, 2004) [The II Continental Summit of the Indigenous Pueblos and Nationalities of Abya Yala (Quito, 2004)]. *Observatorio Social de América Latina, 15,* 257–266. (http://bibliotecavirtual.clacso.org.ar/ar/libros/osal/osal15/bonilla15.pdf. Accessed 21 Aug 2008).

Borg, M. B. (2006). Engaging diversity's underbelly: A story from an immigrant parish community. *American Journal of Community Psychology, 37*(3/4), 191–201.

Bourdieu, P., & Passeron, J-C. (1977/2000). *Reproduction in education, society and culture*. London: Sage.

Bulhan, H. A. (1985). *Frantz Fanon and the psychology of oppression*. New York: Plenum.

Carspecken, P. F. (1996). *Critical ethnography in educational research*. New York: Routledge.

Christens, B., & Perkins, D. D. (2008). Transdisciplinary, multilevel action research to enhance ecological and psychopolitical validity. *Journal of Community Psychology, 36*(2), 214–231.

Cole, M. (2003). *Cultural psychology: A once and future discipline*. Cambridge: The Belknap Press of Harvard University Press.

Dávalos, P. (2005). Movimiento indígena ecuatoriano: Construcción política y epistémica [Ecuadorian Indigenous movement: Political and epistemic construction]. In D. Mato (Ed.), *Cultura, política y sociedad: Perspectivas latinoamericanas [Culture, politics and society: Latin American perspectives]* (pp. 337–357). Buenos Aires: Consejo Latinoamericano de Ciencias Sociales.

Dinh, K. T., Weinstein, T. L., Nemon, M., & Rondeau, S. (2008). The effects of contact with Asians and Asian Americans on White American college students: Attitudes, Awareness of racial discrimination, and psychological adjustment. *American Journal of Community Psychology, 42,* 298–308.

Dodson, M. (2003). The end in the beginning: Re(de)fining Aboriginality. In M. Grossman (Ed.), *Blacklines: Contemporary critical writing by Indigenous Australians* (pp. 25–41). Carlton: Melbourne University Press.

Dudgeon, P., & Fielder, J. (2006). Third spaces within tertiary places: Indigenous Australian Studies. *Journal of Community and Applied Social Psychology, 16,* 396–409.

Dudgeon, P., & Oxenham, D. (1990). *The complexity of Aboriginal diversity: Identity and kindredness*. St. Lucia: University of Queensland.

Ellis, C., & Bochner, A. P. (2000). Autoethnography, personal narrative, reflexivity: Researcher as subject. In N. K. Denzin & Y. Lincoln (Eds.), *The handbook of qualitative research* (2nd ed., pp. 733–768). Thousand Oaks: Sage

Espiritu, Y. L. (2003). *Home bound: Filipino lives across cultures, communities and countries*. Ewing: University of California Press.

Fine, M., Weis, L., Powell, L. C., & Mun Wong, L. (Eds.). (1997). *Off white: Readings on race, power, and society*. New York: Routledge.

Frankenberg, R. (1993). *White women, race matters: The social construction of White women.* London: Routledge.

Freire, P. (1972). *Pedagogy of the oppressed.* Ringwood: Penguin.

Geertz, C. (1973). *The interpretation of cultures.* New York: Boston Books.

Gemignani, M., & Peña, E. (2007). Postmodern conceptualizations of culture in social constructionism and cultural studies. *Journal of Theoretical and Philosophical Psychology, 27*(2-1), 276.

Gergen, K. (1996). *Realidades y relaciones: Aproximación a la construcción social [Realities and relationships: Soundings in social construction].* Madrid: Ediciones Paidos S.A.

Glover, M., Dudgeon, P., & Huygens, I. (2005). Colonization and racism. In G. Nelson & I. Prilleltensky (Eds.), *Community psychology: In pursuit of liberation and wellbeing* (pp. 330–347). New York: Palgrave.

Godreau, I. P., Reyes Cruz, M., Franco Ortiz, M., & Cuadrado, S. (2008). The lessons of slavery: Discourses of slavery, mestizaje, and blanqueamiento in an elementary school in Puerto Rico. *American Ethnologist, 35*(1), 115–135.

Gone, J. P. (2007). "We never was happy living like a Whiteman": Mental health disparities and the postcolonial predicament in American Indian communities. *American Journal of Community Psychology, 40,* 290–300.

Gone, J. P. (2011). The Red road to wellness: Cultural reclamation in a Native First Nations community treatment center. *American Journal of Community Psychology, 47*(1–2), 187–202.

Gonzales, N. A., Germán, M., Kim, S. Y., George, P., Fabrett, F. C., Millsap, R., et al. (2008). Mexican American asolescents' cultural orientation, externalizing behavior and academic engagement: The role of traditional cultural values. *American Journal of Community Psychology, 41,* 151–164.

Green, M. J., Sonn, C. C., & Matsebula, J. (2007). Reviewing Whiteness: Theory, research and possibilities. *South African Journal of Psychology, 37*(3), 389–419.

Greenfield, P. M. (1997). Culture as process: Empirical methods for cultural psychology. In J. W. Berry, Y. H. Poortinga, & J. Pandey (Eds.), *Handbook of cross-cultural psychology* (2nd ed., pp. 301–346). Needham Heights: Allyn & Bacon.

Gridley, H., & Breen, L. (2007). So far and yet so near? In S.M. Reich, M. Reimer, I. Prilleltensky, & M. Montero (Eds.), *International community psychology: History and theories* (pp. 119–139). New York: Springer.

Griffin, C. (2000). More than simply talk and text: Psychologist as cultural ethnographers. In C. Squire (Ed.), *Reconfiguring psychology and culture* (pp. 17–30). London: Routledge.

Guerra, N. G., & Knox, L. (2008). How culture impacts the dissemination and implementation of innovation: A case study of the families and schools together program (FAST) for preventing violence with immigrant Latino youth. *American Journal of Community Psychology, 41,* 304–313.

Hage, G. (2000). *White nation: Fantasies of white supremacy in a multicultural society.* Australia: Routledge.

Hall S. (1996). New ethnicities. In D. Morley & K. Chen (Eds.), *Critical dialogues in cultural studies* (pp. 441–450). London: Routledge.

Harrell, S. P., & Bond, M. A. (2007). Listening to diversity stories: Principles for practice in community research and action. *American Journal of Community Psychology, 37,* 357–364.

Hermans, H. J. M., & Kempen, H. J. G. (1998). Moving cultures: The perilous problem of cultural dichotomies in a globalizing society. *American Psychologist, 53,* 1111–1120.

Holdstock, L. T. (2000). *Re-examining psychology: Critical perspectives and african insights.* London: Routledge.

Hooks, B. (1990). *Yearning: Race, gender, and cultural politics.* Boston: South End Press.

Hughes, D., Seidman, E., & Williams, N. (1993). Cultural phenomena and the research enterprise: Toward a culturally anchored methodology. *American Journal of Community Psychology, 21,* 687–703.

Huygens, I. (2006). Discourses for decolonization: Affirming maori authority in new zealand workplaces. *Journal of Community and Applied Social Psychology, 16,* 363–378.

Ibáñez, T. (2001). *Psicología social construccionista [Constructionist social psychology]*. México: Universidad de Guadalajara.

Jahoda, G., & Krewer, B. (1997). History of cross-cultural and cultural psychology. In J. W. Berry, Y. H. Poortinga, & J. Pandey (Eds.), *Handbook of cross-cultural psychology* (2nd ed., pp. 1–42). Needham Heights: Allyn & Bacon.

Jessen, R. A. (Speaker). (2007). The shift of land, Part 8: The global perspective (Radio Documentary). http://www.prx.org/. Accessed 21 Aug 2008.

Kincheloe, J. L., & McLaren, P. (2000). Rethinking critical theory and qualitative research. In N. K. Denzin & Y. S. Lincoln (Eds.), *Handbook of qualitative research* (2nd ed., pp. 279–313). Thousand Oaks: Sage.

Kincheloe, J. L., & McLaren, P. (2005). Rethinking critical theory and qualitative research. In N. K. Denzin & Y. S. Lincoln (Eds.), *The Sage handbook of qualitative research* (3rd ed., pp. 303–342). Thousand Oaks: Sage.

Kral, M. J., Ramírez, J. I., Aber, M., Masood, N., Dutta, U., & Todd, N. R. (2011). Culture and Community Psychology: Toward a renewed and reimagined vision. *American Journal of Community Psychology, 47*(1–2), 46–57.

Ladson-Billings, G. (2003). It's your world, I'm just trying to explain it. Understanding our epistemological and methodological challenges. *Qualitative Inquiry, 1,* 5–12.

Ladson-Billings, G., & Donnor, J. (2005). The moral activist role of critical race theory scholarship. In N. K. Denzin & Y. S. Lincoln (Eds.), *The Sage handbook of qualitative research* (3rd ed., pp. 279–302). Thousand Oaks: Sage.

Lander, E. (2005). Ciencias sociales: Saberes coloniales y eurocéntricos [Social sciences: Colonial and Eurocentric knowledge]. In E. Lander (Ed.), *La colonialidad del saber: Eurocentrismo y ciencias sociales. Perspectivas latinoamericanas [Coloniality of knowledge: Eurocentrism and social sciences, Latin American perspectives]* (pp 11–40). Buenos Aires: Consejo Latinoamericano de Ciencias Sociales.

Lareau, A., & Horvat, E.M. (1999). Moments of social inclusion and exclusion: Race, class, and cultural capital in family-school relationships. *Sociology of Education, 72*(Jan), 37–53.

Lareau, A., & Weininger, E. B. (2003). Cultural capital in educational research: A critical assessment. *Theory and Society, 32,* 567–606.

Lavee, Y., & Ben-Ari, A. (2008). The association of daily hassles and uplifts with family and life satisfaction: Does cultural orientation make a difference? *American Journal of Community Psychology, 41,* 89–98.

Martin, K. B. M. (2003). Ways of knowing, being and doing: A theoretical framework and methods for Indigenous and Indigenist research. *Australian Studies, Voicing Dissent. New Talents 21C: Next Generation Australian Studies, 76,* 203–214.

Martín-Baró, I. (1994). Towards a liberation psychology (A. Aron, Trans.). In A. Aron & S. Corne (Eds.), *Writings for a liberation psychology: Ignacio Martín-Baró* (pp. 17–32). Cambridge: Harvard University Press.

Martín-Baró, I. (1998). *Psicología de la liberación [Liberation Psychology]. Editado por A. Blanco*. Madrid: Editorial Trotta.

Maton, K. I., Perkins, D. D., & Saegert, S. (2006). Community psychology at the crossroads: Prospects for interdisciplinary research. *American Journal of Community Psychology, 38,* 9–21.

Mediratta, K. (1995). *Community-building approaches: A survey of strategies and an agenda for future work*. Unpublished manuscript.

Memmi, A. (1957/1983). *Retrato del colonizado [The colonizer and the colonized]* (5th ed.). Buenos Aires: Ediciones de la Flor.

Misra, G., & Gergen, K. J. (1993). On the place of culture in the psychological sciences. *International Journal of Psychology, 28,* 225–243.

Moane, G. (2003). Bridging the personal and the political: Practices for a liberation psychology. *American Journal of Community Psychology, 31,* 91–101.

Montero, M. (1997/2001). Political psychology: A critical perspective. In D. Fox & I. Prilleltensky (Eds.), *Critical psychology: An introduction* (pp. 233–244). London: Sage.

Montero, M. (2007). The political psychology of liberation: From politics to ethics and back. *Political Psychology, 28,* 517–533.

Montero, M. (2009). Community action and research as citizen construction *American Journal of Community Psychology, 43,* 149–161.

Moreton-Robinson A. (2004). Whiteness, epistemology and Indigenous representation. In A. Moreton-Robinson (Ed.), *Whitening race: Essays in social and cultural criticism*. Canberra: Aboriginal Studies Press.

Nelson, G., & Prilleltensky, I. (Eds.). (2005). *Community psychology: In pursuit of liberation and wellbeing*. London: Palgrace Macmillan.

O'Donnell, C. R. (2006). Beyond diversity: Toward a cultural community psychology. *American Journal of Community Psychology, 37,* 1–8.

Okazaki, S., & Saw, A. (2011). Culture in Asian American community psychology: Beyond the East-West binary. *American Journal of Community Psychology, 47*(1–2), 144–156.

Okazaki, S., David, E. J. R., & Abelman, N. (2008). Colonialism and psychology of culture. *Social and Personality Psychology Compass, 2/1,* 90–106.

Oxenham, D. (2000). Aboriginal terms of reference. In P. Dudgeon, D. Garvey, & H. Pickett (Eds.), *Working with indigenous Australians: A handbook for psychologists* (pp. 109–125). Perth: Gunada Press.

Parker, I. (2005). *Qualitative psychology: Introducing radical psychology*. Maidenhead: Open University Press.

Parker, I. (2007). *Revolution in psychology: Alienation to emancipation*. London: Pluto Press.

Pascal, C., & Leyva, X. (2011). *Reflexiones desde nuestras prácticas políticas y de conocimiento situado, Tomo I-II [Reflections from our political and situated practices, Vol. I & II]*. México: Las Otras Ediciones.

Quijano, A. (2000). Colonialidad del poder y clasificación social [Coloniality of power and social classification]. *Journal of World-Systems Research, VI*(2), 342–386.

Quijano, A. (2007). Coloniality and modernity/rationality. *Cultural Studies, 21*(2–3), 168–178.

Rappaport, J. (1977). *Community psychology: Values, research, and action*. Fort Worth: Holt, Rinehart, and Traveling Thunder.

Rappaport, J. (2000). Social responsibility and psychological language: Is anyone else up there? Commentaries on Prilleltensky and Nelson. *Journal of Community and Applied Social Psychology, 10,* 107–122.

Reich, S., & Reich, J. A. (2006). Cultural competence in interdisciplinary collaborations: A method for respecting diversity in research partnerships. *American Journal of Community Psychology, 38,* 51–62.

Reyes Cruz, M. (2002). *Multiple contexts, multiple identities: Puerto Rican women's perspectives on race, ethnicity, discrimination and identity*. Unpublished masters' thesis. University of Illinois, Urbana-Champaign.

Reyes Cruz, M. (2006). Mis muertos están conmigo [My dead are with me]: An autoethnographic text on racialization, identity and memory. *Qualitative Inquiry, 12*(3), 589–595.

Reyes Cruz, M. (2008a). *Mexican immigrant parents advocating for school reform*. New York: LFB Scholarly.

Reyes Cruz, M. (2008b). What if I just cite Graciela? Working toward decolonizing knowledge through a critical ethnography. *Qualitative Inquiry, 14*(4), 651–658.

Reyes Cruz, M. (2012). Standing against the coloniality of power: Claiming the right to democratic participation in the globalized neoliberal state. *Global Journal of Psychology Practice, 3*(4), 172–180. http://www.gjcpp.org/pdfs/2012-Lisboa-019-Standing%20against%20the%20coloniality%20of%20power.pdf. Accessed 1 April 2014.

Ribeiro, G. L. (2005). Post-imperialismo: Para una discusión después del post-colonialismo y del multiculturalismo [Post-imperialism: For a discussion after post-colonialism and multiculturalism]. In D. Mato (Ed.), *Cultura, política y sociedad: Perspectivas latinoamericanas [Culture, politics and society: Latin American perspectives]*. Buenos Aires: Consejo Latinoamericano de Ciencias Sociales.

Riggs, D. W., & Augoustinos, M. (2005). The psychic life of colonial power: Racialised subjectivities, bodies and methods. *Journal of Community & Applied Social Psychology, 15,* 461–477.

Rizvi, F. (2007). Postcolonialism and globalization in education. *Cultural Studies-Critical Methodologies, 7*(3), 256–263.

Roosa, M. W., Weaver, S. R., White, R. M. B., Tein, J., Knight, G. P., Gonzales, N., et al. (2009). Family and neighborhood fit or misfit and the adaptation of Mexican Americans. *American Journal of Community Psychology, 44,* 15–27.

Said, E. W. (1979). *Orientalism*. New York: Vintage Books

Santos, B. de S. (2010). *Descolonizar el saber, reinventar el poder [Decolonizing knowledge, reinventing power]*. Montevideo: Ediciones Trilce.

Santos, B. de S. (2011). Prólogo [Prologue]. In C. Pascal & X. Leyva (Eds.), *Reflexiones desde nuestras prácticas políticas y de conocimiento situado, Tomo I [Reflections from our political and situated practices, Vol. I]* (pp. 10–24). México: Las Otras Ediciones.

Santos, B. de S. (2011–2012). Introducción: Las epistemologías del sur [Introduction: Epistemologies from the South]. In CIDOB (org.) (Ed.), *Formas-Otras. Saber, nombrar, narrar, hacer [Other-Ways. Knowing, naming, narrating, doing]* (pp. 9–22). Barcelona: CIDOB Ediciones. (http://www.boaventuradesousasantos.pt/media/INTRODUCCION_BSS.pdf).

Sarason, S. (1974). *Psychological sense of community: Prospects for a community psychology*. San Francisco: Jossey Bass.

Schwandt, T. A. (2001). *Dictionary of qualitative inquiry* (2nd ed.). Thousand Oaks: Sage.

Serrano-Garcia I. (1994). The ethics of the powerful and the power of ethics. *American Journal of Community Psychology, 22,* 1–20.

Shweder, R. A. (1990). Cultural psychology-what is it? In J. W. Stigler, R. A. Shweder, & G. Herdt (Eds.), *Cultural psychology: Essays on comparative human development* (pp. 1–43). Cambridge: Cambridge University Press.

Sinha, D., & Kao, H. S. R. (1997). The journey to the east: An introduction. In H. S. R. Kao & D. Sinha (Eds.), *Asian perspectives on psychology* (pp. 9–22). New Delhi: Sage.

Smith, L. T. (2012/1999). *Decolonizing methodologies: Research and indigenous peoples*. London: Zed Books.

Somerville, M., & Perkins, T. (2003). Border work in the contact zone: Thinking Indigenous/non-Indigenous collaboration spatially. *Journal of Intercultural Studies, 24*(3), 253–266.

Sonn, C. C. (2002). Immigrant adaptation: Exploring the process through sense of community. In A. T. Fisher, C. C. Sonn, & B. J. Bishop (Eds.), *Psychological sense of community: Research, applications and implications* (pp. 205–222). New York: Kluwer/Plenum.

Sonn, C. C. (2004a). Negotiating identities across cultural boundaries: Complicating cultural competence with power and privilege. *Critical Psychology: International Journal of Critical Psychology, 11,* 134–149.

Sonn, C. C. (2004b). Reflecting on practice: Negotiating challenges to ways of working. *Journal of Community and Applied Social Psychology, 14,* 305–313.

Sonn, C. C., Quayle, A. F., Mackenzie, C., & Law, S. F. (2014). Negotiating belonging in Australia through storytelling and encounter. Identities: Global Studies in Culture and Power. http://dx.doi.org/10.1080/1070289X.2014.902376. Accessed 17 April 2014.

Trickett, E. J. (1996). A future for community psychology: The contexts of diversity and the diversity of contexts. *American Journal of Community Psychology, 24,* 209–229.

Trickett, E. J., Watts, R. J., & Birman, D. (Eds.). (1994). *Human diversity: Perspectives on people in context*. San Francisco: Jossey-Bass.

Trueba, E. T., & McLaren, P. (2000). Critical ethnography for the study of immigrants. In E. T. Trueba & L. I. Bartolomé (Eds.), *Immigrant voices: In search of educational equity* (pp. 37–73). New York: Rowman & Littlefield.

Watts, R. J. (1992). Elements of a psychology of human diversity. *Journal of Community Psychology, 20,* 116–131.

Watts, R. J., & Serrano-Garcia, I. (2003). The quest for a liberating community psychology: An overview. *American Journal of Community Psychology, 31,* 73–78.

Chapter 11
Decolonizing Traditional Pedagogies and Practices in Counseling and Psychology Education: A Move Towards Social Justice and Action

Rachael D. Goodman, Joseph M. Williams, Rita Chi-Ying Chung, Regine M. Talleyrand, Adrienne M. Douglass, H. George McMahon and Fred Bemak

Numerous scholars in the fields of counseling and psychology have called for the implementation of social justice counselor education and training (e.g., Bemak et al. 2011; Chang et al. 2010; Chung and Bemak 2012; Talleyrand et al. 2006; Toporek and McNally 2006). Despite the amount of scholarship on the subject, there remains

R. D. Goodman (✉)
Counseling and Development Program, College of Education and Human Development, George Mason University, Krug Hall 201C, MS 1H1, 4400 University Drive, Fairfax, VA 22030, USA
e-mail: rgoodma2@gmu.edu

J. M. Williams
Counseling and Development Program, College of Education and Human Development, George Mason University, Krug Hall 202C, MS 1H1, 4400 University Drive, Fairfax, VA 22030, USA
e-mail: jwilli32@gmu.edu

R. C.-Y. Chung
Counseling and Development Program, College of Education and Human Development, George Mason University, Krug Hall 202B, MS 1H1, 4400 University Drive, Fairfax, VA 22030, USA
e-mail: rchung@gmu.edu

R. M. Talleyrand
Counseling and Development Program, College of Education and Human Development, George Mason University, Krug Hall 201A, MS 1H1, 4400 University Drive, Fairfax, VA 22030, USA
e-mail: rtalleyr@gmu.edu

A. M. Douglass
Counseling and Development Program, College of Education and Human Development, George Mason University, Krug Hall 201D, MS 1H1, 4400 University Drive, Fairfax, VA 22030, USA
e-mail: adougla5@gmu.edu

H. G. McMahon
Department of Counseling and Human Development Services, College of Education, University of Georgia, 402 Aderhold Hall Athens, GA 30602
e-mail: gmcmahon@uga.edu

F. Bemak
Counseling and Development Program, College of Education and Human Development, George Mason University, Krug Hall 201E, MS 1H1, 4400 University Drive, Fairfax, VA 22030, USA
e-mail: fbemak@gmu.edu

R. D. Goodman, P. C. Gorski (eds.), *Decolonizing "Multicultural" Counseling through Social Justice,* International and Cultural Psychology, DOI 10.1007/978-1-4939-1283-4_11

concern that both multiculturalism and social justice are only embraced superficially, but may not truly be enacted in counseling and psychology training programs (Bemak et al. 2011). Indeed, programs including multiculturalism and diversity in their mission statements and developing courses on multiculturalism may give a superficial appearance of embracing multiculturalism whether or not they are committed to these principles throughout the program or across faculty members in a meaningful way. Additionally—despite calls to increase diversity in our profession—there remains a lack of diversity among both counseling and psychology students and counseling and psychology faculty members. While diversity alone does not create socially just counselors, the lack of diversity is evidence of a larger systemic bias and limits the inclusion of divergent perspectives on healing, wellbeing, and lived experiences. Included in these largely absent perspectives are lived experiences of encountering discrimination and bias, which may prevent the emergence of critical thinking and may lead to collusion with the status quo (Bemak 2008).

In this chapter, we explore how counseling and psychology training programs may unintentionally perpetuate colonizing practices through the very pedagogies and practices used to address multiculturalism and social justice. For the purposes of this chapter, we define colonizing practices in counseling and psychology training as educational practices that reproduce the existing conditions of oppression by failing to challenge the hegemonic views that marginalize groups of people, perpetuate deficit-based ideologies, and continue to disenfranchise the diverse clients and communities with whom our students will work. Further, we envision cultural competence as counseling that is congruent with a client's cultural values and norms, and consistent with the meaning of well-being and healing from their cultural perspective—not as superficial knowledge about a particular population. We define social justice as having shared basic values in a democratic context that promotes fair and equal access and opportunity without limitations that are based on race, ethnicity, culture, socioeconomic status, gender, sexual orientation, physical abilities, education, or language (Chung and Bemak 2012). In the counseling program in which all the authors are faculty members, we have worked to infuse a multicultural-social justice framework throughout the program over the past 13 years. While we continue to grow and face challenges, in this chapter we will describe some of the practices that we have found to be successful and provide recommendations for how our profession can revision and decolonize our educational practices. The chapter will focus on five areas that we see as critical in decolonizing the practice of counseling and psychology education: banking education versus education for critical consciousness, "othering" multiculturalism and social justice versus infusing multiculturalism and social justice throughout the curriculum, voyeurism versus voice, community as an afterthought versus community as integral, and political neutrality versus political engagement. We provide examples from our own practice as educators that we hope others can expand on and continue to improve in order to better develop future social justice-oriented counselors.

"Banking" Education Versus Education for Critical Consciousness

As the psychology and counseling fields continue to discuss the implementation of multicultural social justice in graduate training programs, attention focuses on the effectiveness and types of teaching pedagogies that will produce multicultural-social justice psychologists and counselors. To effectively educate psychologists and counselors to become culturally competent, social justice advocacy requires a paradigm shift from traditional teaching methodologies to creative teaching techniques (Chung and Bemak 2012). Paradoxically, many traditional teaching strategies are contradictory to the aims and goals of multicultural-social justice training. A teaching methodology that is widely utilized and prevalent in educational systems is the banking concept of education (Freire 1972), in which educators simply deposit information into their students with the implicit assumption that students are ignorant, and will willingly accept the information.

The banking concept of education is in direct contrast with the goals of multiculturalism and social justice in that it promotes disempowerment rather than empowerment, and reinforces the idea that educators/teachers have all the knowledge and students are simply empty vessels and subsequently passive recipients of information (Freire 1972). In the banking approach to education, students are not expected, nor are they given permission, to question, critique, analyze, discuss, assess, or evaluate information. Rather, students are expected to submissively take in and then regurgitate the information that has been given to them by their teachers. The banking approach to education promotes conformity, resulting in an unhealthy dependent relationship in which students are reliant on their teachers. This colonial mentality of education creates an unequal balance of power and crushes any form of independent thinking and inquiry, aiming to produce conventional and conforming individuals who simply accept rather than question information deposited into them (Chung and Bemak 2012).

Some may argue that banking is an effective strategy for disseminating knowledge, but it is our belief that this hierarchical model is an imperialist form of censorship and control that cultivates and ensures obedience, deference, reverence, submissiveness, and compliance—and that produces limited growth in students. In other words, a banking system of education perpetuates the status quo in terms of both knowledge and power. In our opinion, counseling and psychology training programs should utilize an educational philosophy built on the belief that students have the right to seek and attain critical consciousness and educators must provide the support, opportunities, and resources necessary for this educational process. The process of attaining critical consciousness involves genuine questioning, having healthy dialogues and discourse, opportunities for independent and divergent thinking, and the freedom to arrive at one's own decisions regardless of the status quo. The desired outcomes of this type of education are authentic empowerment, feelings of emancipation, and liberation (Chung and Bemak 2012).

To effectively train multicultural-social justice psychologists and counselors to proactively address injustices, it is imperative that educators adopt creative approaches to teaching. This requires educators to demonstrate the courage to develop creative and innovative teaching techniques, in spite of the fact that these approaches may result in criticism by colleagues or a lack of support by educational institutions, and initially may not be well received by students (Chung and Bemak 2012). To achieve this, the first step is to provide a learning environment that is supportive, in which students are encouraged and have the opportunity to develop critical consciousness about social justice issues. This can be achieved by decolonizing traditional teaching pedagogy and employing innovative teaching techniques. We encourage educators who are serious about multicultural-social justice training to explore various creative techniques that move towards decolonizing the banking concept of education.

An example of this can be seen in Chung and Bemak's (2013) utilization of ethnographic fiction wherein students have an opportunity to "walk in the shoes"of a client who is undergoing an unjust situation. Employing this technique broke new ground since ethnographic fiction is not known in the field of psychology or counseling, so there was little information about the efficacy of ethnographic fiction. However, students reported that ethnographic fiction proved to be a transformative experience. Exemplifying the overwhelming positive response by students is the comment from one student as follows: "This is one of the most unique projects in the counseling program, but I would venture to say that this project impacted me more than any other project and was one of the most challenging at the same time.... Not only did I learn a tremendous amount … but I had an opportunity to step into my client's shoe. I don't think that there was a better way to really tap into my client's experience than though this assignment" (Chung and Bemak 2013, p. 65). As a result of ethnographic fiction, students not only achieved critical consciousness, but the technique also propelled them to take action and move from critical consciousness to action that was rooted in an ecological perspective. Thus, as an outcome of the ethnographic fiction assignment, students not only advocated and educated family members and colleagues about the injustices faced by their client but also advocated on a broader systemic basis. The next sections will provide in-depth examples of innovative techniques that have proven to be effective in training multicultural-social justice psychologists and counselors.

"Othering" Multiculturalism Versus Infusing Multiculturalism and Social Justice

As noted, scholars have called for a transformation in counseling and psychology educators' approach to teaching multiculturalism and social justice in which these perspectives become internalized and are inherent parts of the nature of educators and students (e.g., Chang et al. 2010; Chung and Bemak 2012; Toporek and McNally 2006). In spite of the call for the infusion of multiculturalism and social justice throughout counseling and psychology curricula, use of a single course for multicultural counselor training continues to be a prevalent format in counseling and psychology education (Alvarez and Miville 2003). In our counseling program, we find it is important that all faculty members share the philosophy that multiculturalism and social justice are key components to being effective and ethical professional counselors, and not merely a professional specialty. Towards this end, program faculty members have grounded faculty hiring, teaching, and even the admissions process in this guiding belief.

First, it is our contention that counseling and psychology training programs that hire one or two faculty members who specialize in multicultural/social justice issues actually perpetuate the perspective that valuing multiculturalism and social justice is optional and limited. Therefore, we recruit and hire only faculty members who are committed to developing a faculty team that is unanimously committed to teaching from a social justice perspective. Faculty members join the faculty knowing that our multicultural-social justice orientation is core to our program; they then receive mentoring and further assistance from their colleagues to help them develop their abilities as multicultural-social justice educators and scholars. This mentoring and support helps to solidify a commitment to these issues in their teaching and also serves as a model for students to see that faculty research, writing, presentations, and professional service all are rooted in multiculturalism and social justice, which are themes that are central to the counseling and psychology profession and embedded in one's professional identity.

Many counselor education and psychology training programs responded to the need for multicultural training by adding a course on multicultural counseling while continuing to ignore these issues in the other courses. While adding a course on multicultural counseling may appear responsive, it can actually perpetuate the dominant perspective as the standard for training that forces multicultural issues to the periphery. One way that we have addressed this is to ensure that all courses in the curriculum are taught from a multicultural and social justice framework—something that is made possible in part by our faculty hiring and mentoring process. Infusing these issues throughout all the courses shifts the students' perspectives to view these issues as central to all facets of their professional functioning.

Implementing the suggestion to infuse multicultural issues throughout each course can also be a challenge. Many counseling and psychology textbooks continue to address multicultural considerations only in one chapter. This too perpetuates multicultural competence as an additional skill as opposed to central in all functioning as a professional counselor. In our program, we intentionally use course materials that infuse multicultural and social justice issues throughout. When appropriate materials are not available, we supplement more traditional course materials with readings and other media that present a critique of traditional materials or a counternarrative to the dominant perspective that portrays the multicultural-social justice perspective. For instance, in a diagnosis course, the *Diagnostic and Statistical Manual of Mental Disorders* (*DSM*) might be a traditional text for students. The instructor would also include materials that critique aspects of the *DSM,* such as resources on gender bias within borderline personality disorder (BPD) or the culturally bound nature of mental health symptoms. Classroom examples and case vignettes should be developed and presented in a manner that prompts students to think about multicultural and social justice issues—not just within some cases, but within all cases. This suggestion also pertains to graded assignments. The faculty members construct assignments that require students to attend to multicultural and social justice issues, such as case conceptualizations that include an assessment of the sociopolitical context and cultural views on well-being and healing. The students are then evaluated on their ability to infuse knowledge and awareness of these issues into their work.

Another important aspect to consider is how students' admissions to counseling and psychology programs can reflect and reinforce the commitment to multiculturalism and social justice. Graduate programs may unintentionally reflect bias and exclude students of color in their admissions process. For instance, the Graduate Record Examination (GRE) was normed on White, English-speaking, middle-class subjects (Baumgartner and Johnson-Bailey 2010), and analyses have revealed that students of color, nonnative English speakers, and individuals from lower socioeconomic backgrounds score lower on the GRE than middle-class, White individuals (Baumgartner and Johnson-Bailey 2010). Subsequently, programs that rely on GRE scores as central admissions criteria place people of color, immigrants, and individuals from lower socioeconomic backgrounds at a disadvantage. To remove this aspect of bias, our program does not utilize the GRE as part of the admission process.

Rather than using GRE scores as determinants of intelligence and admissions, our program conducts a comprehensive evaluation of student applicants to determine their committment to multiculturalism and social justice, their willingness to engage in tough issues related to social equity and change, their professional and personal experience related to multiculturalism and social justice, and their values. Towards this end, applicants to the program complete a written goal statement and participate in an intensive group interview in which their experience with, interest in, and openness to cultural diversity and social justice issues are discussed and assessed. This practice not only helps identify students particularly committed to and enthusiastic about multiculturalism and social justice but also sets the norm for future students regarding the central role multiculturalism and social justice will play in their educational experience. All admitted students know that multiculturalism and social justice are core values of the counseling program, and that their ability to be successful in their training depends on their willingness to view these issues as central to their education and future practice. In sum, our efforts to make multicultural and social justice perspectives central to the curriculum, faculty hiring, and admissions decisions challenge that status quo of higher education and engenders an educational environment in which students see multiculturalism and social justice as necessary and central to their future careers—not an optional (and thereby second class) specialty area.

Voyeurism Versus Voice

As we have noted, counseling and psychology programs are expected to promote critical consciousness and social justice agency among their students (Bemak et al. 2011; Toporek and McNally 2006). These expectations acknowledge the adverse impact of various forms of oppression (e.g., racism, sexism, heterosexism, poverty) on mental health outcomes (e.g., anxiety, posttraumatic stress disorder, depression, loss of sense of control, hopelessness, internalized oppression) particularly among society's most vulnerable populations. Faculty in counseling and psychology preparation programs must critically reflect on our practice as educators committed to social justice, and constantly be on the alert for pedagogies and practices that unintentionally reinforce and perpetuate a voyeuristic curiosity of the lives of the oppressed (i.e., people of color, the poor, women), instead of promoting individual and social responsibility for taking action with and on behalf of the oppressed. Collins (1993) defines voyeurs "as passive onlookers who do not relate to the less powerful, but who are interested in seeing how the 'different' live" (p. 37). Similarly, Kleinman et al. (1997) describe voyeurism as "…construing suffering at a safe distance, without the [individual or] social responsibility of real engagement" (p. xix). In this section, we explore how counseling and psychology education in multiculturalism may unintentionally encourage voyeurism, and provide teaching strategies that dislodge voyeurism and promote meaningful engagement and self-reflection.

Pedagogies and Practices that Potentially Encourage Voyeurism

Multimedia-Based Instruction

Faculty of counseling and psychology training programs often incorporate multimedia in their instruction to capture students' attention, explain difficult concepts, or emphasize the main point of the day. Multimedia instructional tools such as documentary video clips can help make the material come alive for students by potentially stimulating thoughts and eliciting (superficial or deep-seated) feelings and emotions (Berk 2009). These stimulated thoughts and emotions are often triggered and heightened by an inside look into the lives of the oppressed via multimedia. According to Adams et al. (2007), individuals are more likely to engage in social action when they feel emotionally connected to the issues at hand. Despite the seeming benefits of using multimedia-based instructional tools, it can potentially lead to voyeurism if done incorrectly. The following is a case example of how using video clips and other media outlets to teach about social justice and multicultural issues in counseling and psychology can be detrimental to the social justice orientation and praxis of students.

Case Study 1: Michael Michael is an assistant professor at a Mid-Atlantic region university. He currently teaches an advanced human growth and development course for preservice counselors. Michael teaches the course from an ecological perspective, which encourages an appreciation and understanding of social, cultural, environmental, and policy factors on human development. Michael decided to teach his class about the impact of poverty on the physical, cognitive, social, and emotional development of children and adolescents. Michael provided handouts and diagrams to students that explained the deleterious impact of poverty on human growth and development. In addition to the handouts, Michael showed a video clip of *The Line,* a documentary on poverty in the USA, which highlights stories of children and adolescents across the country living at or below the poverty line. His primary goal of showing the documentary was to encourage students to critically think about the following questions: What is poverty? What is it like to live at or below the poverty line? How does it shape your life? Why is it a problem that has to be solved? The students left the class that evening with a better understanding of poverty, how poverty shapes one's life, and even the importance of eradicating or at least reducing poverty.

While few would argue the importance of these insights, such an approach to teaching about poverty ignores the systemic, structural, and institutional inequalities that create, maintain, and perpetuate poverty. It also fails to examine the intersectionality of poverty, race, gender, class, ability, and ethnicity (to name a few), thereby excusing students from critically examining their own privilege and considering their privilege as part of the oppression of people who live in poverty and the potential to alleviate that oppression. Consequently, instead of promoting critical consciousness and praxis among students, Michael is potentially helping students to develop *passive empathy,* where students momentarily feel badly for a particular individual, family, or group experiencing poverty, but their larger worldview and understanding of their role in the larger system of oppression is not challenged (i.e., voyeurism) (Boler 1999; Kumashiro 2000).

To have a more meaningful experience, Michael could have supplemented the video with basic information regarding the various causes of poverty and the challenges people face in attempting to break through the cycle of poverty. Next, students could break into small groups and reflect on the following questions:

1. How has your perspective changed about what you think makes people poor in the USA?
2. What structural changes are needed to help a hardworking individual or family overcome poverty?
3. What outside obstacles might someone who is trying to overcome poverty face?
4. Who is responsible for bringing about such changes?
5. What could your role as a counselor or psychologist be to help address the issue of poverty?

In addition, Michael could challenge students to examine their own social class privileges and attitudes, biases, and stereotypes about people who live at or below the poverty line by completing materials and checklists for social class privilege of upper and lower social classes and discussing the results (Barratt 2005). Michael might have also considered supplementing his lesson by introducing models that are useful in conceptualizing effective counseling strategies for people living in poverty, such as the CARE model (Foss et al. 2011), which highlights the need to *C*ultivate relationships, *A*cknowledge realities, *R*emove barriers, and *E*xpand the strengths of poor clients. A unique aspect of this model is that it addresses the impact that multiple systems have on poor clients' lived experiences. This model emerges from a humanistic perspective that encourages the growth and the development of clients.

Cultural Immersion Assignment

Oftentimes, educators in counseling and psychology programs employ cultural immersion projects or assignments in their classes as a means of raising the self-awareness and cultural sensitivity of students. Simply put, cultural immersion projects (a) expose students to people who are different in culture or identities (e.g., language, religion, socioeconomic status, race, ethnicity, and sexual orientation) to represent that cultures' turf; (b) help students gain insight into the circumstances and characteristics of others; (c) allow students to experience what it is to be from a different group; and (d) help students gain insight into their own biases, values, identity, beliefs, assumptions, and behaviors (Hyland and Noffke 2005; Nieto 2006). Such an experience may help to facilitate the development of multiculturally competent and social justice-orientated counselors and psychologists. Nonetheless, these cultural immersion projects or assignments can potentially lead to voyeurism if handled incorrectly. The following is a case example that demonstrates how using a cultural immersion assignment can be detrimental to the multicultural competence of preservice counselors and psychologists.

Case Study 2: Alisa Alisa is an adjunct instructor at a small, predominately White, liberal arts college in the northeast of the USA. Alisa adheres to a multicultural-social justice perspective in her professional practice both as a practitioner and as an educator, thus she was excited about the opportunity to teach the multicultural counseling/psychology course. In an effort to help students increase their self-awareness and cultural sensitivity, Alisa decided to assign a cultural immersion activity wherein students immerse themselves for one hour in a setting in which they are a minority. Through this short assignment and subsequent discussions, many students expressed personal growth and new realizations as evident in their required three-page reaction paper. As a result, Alisa is determined to use the assignment again next semester.

Based on student feedback, the cultural immersion assignment was effective in exposing students to identities different from their own; however, Alisa failed to gather other data points to confirm the effectiveness of the intervention in terms of multicultural-social justice development. What Alisa neglected to learn is that most of her students began the semester believing that because they did not harbor overt feelings of prejudice, they were exempt from interrogating their own identity in relationship to others, or thinking critically about their own privilege (i.e., male, White, heterosexual, Christian, middle to upper class, able-bodied) and considering privilege as part of the oppression of others. Most students felt that the cultural immersion assignment was nothing more than an opportunity to learn about another culture. These attitudes, beliefs, and preconceived notions about the assignment and experience negatively impacted the students' ability to fully learn from their experiences.

Alisa should understand that simply placing students in spaces where they are the minority does not necessarily create opportunities for students to identify and challenge assumptions and to create new perceptions about traditionally marginalized groups (Hyland and Noffke 2005; Wiest 1998). According to Haberman and Post (1992), cultural immersion assignments may inadvertently result in reinforcing students' existing biases, stereotypes, and deficit views of the focus group. Moreover, Alisa must wrestle with the idea that these cultural immersions "reify White (male, heterosexual, Christian) privilege by signaling that privileged people have the right of voyeurism, the ability to observe and interpret without engagement" (Hyland and Noffke 2005, p. 380). Alisa should seek ways to more fully incorporate sustained and interactive contact between her students and people in the communities in which she sends her students.

Similarly, Alisa might set additional boundaries on the assignment to increase its effectiveness as recommended by Hyland and Noffke (2005). First, students should meet people from disenfranchised groups (e.g., ethnic/racial minorities, low-income people, persons with disabilities) in the environments in which the people from that group are born, live, learn, work, play, or worship. Cultural immersion assignments are most meaningful when students choose to interact in new places and with new people with whom they are uncomfortable at the time. Second, students should examine the lived experience, cultural heritage, and political and historical background of the focus group. Information (e.g., assigned readings or other assigned homework) about the focus group gives students a framework or perspective outside of their existing framework (often White or Eurocentric) in which to interpret the experience. Third, students should debrief the experience(s) with small group and large class discussions. Debriefing gives students an opportunity to reflect on the experience and make it meaningful by identifying what they learned about themselves and others, and make connections to the experiences of other groups.

Community as an Afterthought Versus Community as Integral

One of the ways in which we address the limitations of one-time assignments about marginalized communities is by increasing the opportunities for students to engage with communities meaningfully throughout the program. As previously stated, the counseling field's paradigm shift towards a social justice framework has prompted the need for change in counseling and psychology education practices and counselors' roles (Chung and Bemak 2012; Talleyrand et al. 2006). Although progress has been made in this area (i.e., development of social justice competencies), few counseling and psychology education programs provide opportunities for students to put social justice theory into practice beyond gaining exposure to "diverse populations" during their practicum and internship experiences (Baggerly 2006). Limiting discussion of diversity to only a multicultural counseling course or limiting the practice of community engagement to practicum and internship can be viewed as colonizing, since students' ability to experience diversity and social action is potentially a one-time event rather than something embedded within their training program. Furthermore, traditional models of practicum and internship training emphasize students' counseling skill competencies and client needs versus students' understandings of, experiences with, and creation of social change in the community (Baggerly 2006; Jett and Delgado-Romero 2009).

One strategy that can increase students' understanding, application, and commitment to social justice issues is the use of pre-practicum service learning activities that expose students to the real social concerns of clients in the community. Service learning can be defined as experiential learning that occurs outside of the classroom and allows students to integrate community service into their academic experiences (Barbee et al. 2003; Kenny and Gallagher 2000). We purposely include multiple field-based experiences and activities that stimulate critical thinking about social justice issues throughout the curriculum in order to give students a more complex and sustained experience related to social justice and multicultural issues. When "exposure to diversity" is contained only in one semester, this can generate a superficial and short-lived field experience. Counseling literature exists documenting the benefits of service learning for student counselors including increasing their counseling self-efficacy, increasing their awareness of social issues in the community, and increasing their multicultural and social justice competencies (Bemak et al. 2011; Jett and Delgado-Romero 2009; Vera and Speight 2003). Although service-learning initiatives have often been found to be beneficial for many students, counselor training models focused on pre-practicum service learning are greatly lacking (Malott and Knoper 2012). By integrating community outreach throughout the program in both required and optional forms, we insist that students view community outreach to marginalized populations as central to their learning and their role as a future counseling professional.

Case Example: Service Learning in Career Counseling

In alignment with our mission of embedding multiculturalism and social justice throughout the curriculum, the faculty has developed service learning projects for several classes and additional opportunities to volunteer under faculty supervision. One example of a service learning project is in the career counseling course. Given that the vocational counseling field emerged from Frank Parson's efforts to provide employment services to underrepresented and underserved populations during the early 1900s, it seems logical that including community based service experiences in a career counseling course would extend the advocacy work that Parsons initiated over 100 years ago. Additionally, the rapidly changing demographics in the USA, the widening gap between the upper and lower socioeconomic classes, and our current global economy underscores the contextual challenges faced by clients and their differing needs. As such, there is a need to return to the career counseling field's roots, including understanding how all clients make meaning of work based on their contextual experiences rather than solely on individual talents and personality expression (Blustein 2006; Flores and Heppner 2002).

To that end, the faculty conduct outreach to local community-based organizations that service disenfranchised populations (e.g., homeless shelters, community service boards) to collaboratively identify the career counseling needs. During the first six weeks of the semester, counseling students enrolled in the career counseling course are taught traditional (e.g., standardized tests, resume building) and nontraditional (e.g., conflict resolution, assertiveness skills) career counseling activities to prepare them for their work in the community. In addition, students engage in numerous class discussions focused on examining their biases towards underserved populations as well as processing their anxiety related to engaging in community-based work. Groups of three to four students are assigned to a community site during this period and are expected to conduct their own site visits to learn about the site culture and needs. They are also tasked to work with their site supervisor to design career interventions that are site appropriate. The emphasis of these interventions is on expanding beyond traditional career interventions and identifying the specific needs and strengths of the population, as well as what systemic barriers may impact their career success. During the second half of the semester, students conduct their interventions at their sites and receive supervision by the site supervisor and course instructor. Students are also responsible for getting feedback (i.e., written evaluations) from clients and site supervisors regarding the counseling experiences they have provided. This ensures that clients are part of the students' learning process and that career interventions attend to the multicultural-social justice considerations of the clients. Finally, students examine their experiences and write a reflection paper documenting their personal and professional growth experiences in order to integrate what they have learned with their identity as a social justice focused counselor.

In addition to service learning with marginalized populations (e.g., alternative high school students, substance-abusing mothers) who might not receive services or benefit from traditional (i.e., not culturally competent or social justice-focused) interventions, we work with students to avoid further marginalizing the populations with whom they're working. The faculty instructor closely supervises the counseling students' work at the site and focuses on systemic issues impacting the clients, such as bias in the job interview process or racism at the workplace. In their reflection papers, students noted that engaging in a service learning project has opened their eyes to the biases they possess and the real life experiences of clients in the community and has made them feel more confident in their counseling abilities. Additionally, clients evaluate the program so that their voices and opinions are seen as a measure of whether the program is working. Career outreach program evaluations indicate that 100 % of our service learning project sites have found the career interventions provided by our students to be helpful to their clients. As such, students learn that their counseling interventions in all settings must be tailored to the specific needs and cultural values of the clients they are working with, and that these interventions must include thoughtful attention to social inequities that impact the career development of their clients. Using service learning, they are able to see the importance of these principles in action and receive immediate feedback from clients and supervisors about their effectiveness.

In addition to required class activities such as service learning, it is also critical that community engagement be infused throughout a training program in other ways so that community engagement is integral and not seen as a peripheral or exotic one-time experience. Our program has sought to do this in several ways. First, we developed a required social justice counseling course that extends the foundational knowledge students gain in core courses and in their multicultural counseling course to examine systemic and human rights issues as they relate to counseling. In this course, students are further challenged to examine social justice issues in local communities and they also engage in service learning under faculty supervision. Often students work with local underserved communities and gain a better understanding of how systemic issues impact mental health and how counselors can advocate for their clients' well-being. Second, the faculty has developed opportunities for students to work with diverse clientele beyond required coursework. Voluntary community outreach projects have been established, with faculty offering their time to provide supervision for students. Students have volunteered support and paraprofessional counseling services with culturally diverse groups of students who have been suspended from school, youth who are identified as "at-risk," and recent immigrants from a variety of different countries. In order to further our commitment to education that fully integrates community outreach, the faculty created an online Social Justice Project Clearinghouse where interested groups submit information requesting services in partnership with the counseling program, including engaging students in semester or yearlong community support and volunteer services under faculty supervision. This clearinghouse allows students and faculty to expand their work with local community agencies, schools, advocacy organizations, and other social service providers to address issues of marginalization and social and economic inequities that affect our local communities.

Political Neutrality Versus Political Engagement

Despite the overwhelming evidence that systemic issues directly impact the well-being and mental health of individuals and communities, there continue to be calls within the counseling and psychology professions that we should remain apolitical in our approach to counseling and in our roles as educators. It is clear, however, that a position of neutrality is not neutral and is, in fact, a tacit agreement to the existing structures or power and privilege. The South African human rights activist Archbishop Desmond Tutu reminds us that, "To be neutral in a situation of injustice is to have chosen sides already. It is to support the status quo." We believe that it is the ethical responsibility of faculty educating future counselors and psychologists to engage their students in learning and thinking deeply about the social, political, and public policy issues that impact our clients and our society.

There is now significant evidence on the real impact of social injustice on clients in a number of areas. A substantial body of research has shown how experiences of discrimination can have deleterious physical and mental health implications (e.g., Paradies 2006; Williams et al. 2003). Furthermore, racism and racism-related stress have been shown to result in traumatic stress for people of color, or race-based traumatic stress (Carter 2007). Public policies also impact the well-being of individuals and communities. For instance, Menjivar and Abrego (2012) documented how the existence and enforcement of laws targeting immigrant communities resulted in these communities experiencing forms of *legal violence,* and resulted in discrimination, stress, and a constant state of fear. Examples abound of the ways in which an unjust environment can create mental health problems (e.g., living in poverty, persecution for religion or ethnicity, violence against women), and we now have ample evidence that we must examine these factors in relation to intrapsychic concerns of individuals. Furthermore, unequal structures impact the provision of services to those in need. For example, low-income communities are often more vulnerable to disasters because of their location and limited resources (for disaster protection or evacuation), and they are often provided with fewer resources following a disaster, making it more difficult for them to recover (Halpern and Tramontin 2007). All of these examples demonstrate that counseling and psychological practice are not separate from political issues and social injustice, but are directly affected by the policies and practices, both explicit and implicit.

Despite the evidence of the impact that policy and systemic factors have on the mental health of clients and communities, there remains resistance to engaging in social justice and public policy discussions in the fields of counseling and psychology. Some in our profession express outright that our profession should not engage in issues of advocacy and social justice, leaving that for other professions (e.g., King 2011). Further, while there is some movement within professional organizations to engage in public policy debates, the actions highlighted by professional organizations often focus fairly narrowly on issues that relate to advocacy for the profession of counseling. For instance, the American Counseling Association (ACA) website highlighted public policy issues of funding for school counselors and hiring within the Veterans Administration. While these are important endeavors, they do not go far enough to address the systemic issues that impact the work of counselors. If we are truly engaged in promoting the well-being of the clients we serve, then we have an obligation to address policies that negatively affect their well-being and to act against injustice. For instance, if we are concerned about the mental health of school-aged children and veterans, we should be examining the systemic sources of distress and lobbying to address these problems as well.

Educators in counseling and psychology who are concerned with multiculturalism and social justice must replace political neutrality with political engagement as we educate future counselors and psychologists. Integrating opportunities for political engagement within counselor education can take various forms. At a basic level, just as readings, case examples, and assignments should address diverse clients, they should also address social justice issues including political and public policy considerations. One example of this is the use of current news stories that discuss mental health concerns and contextual factors influencing individuals or communities. In teaching about action research to our master's level counseling students in an introductory research course, groups of students are given a recent news article about something that is happening in a community that impacts community members well-being. Students are asked to come up with ideas about how they would investigate this problem as action researchers (e.g., what they would want to know, how they would gather this data, what contextual factors they would need to consider). For example, students investigating the problem of sexual assault on women in the military might want to talk to women who had been sexually assaulted in the military to find out when and where women were vulnerable to attacks and about the mental and physical health impacts of these assaults.

While this may seem to reflect a social justice focus since we are exploring violence against women, to stop here would actually perpetuate a colonial mindset in that there is no examination of why and how the perpetrators are engaging in sexual assault, or how the existing structures and policies impact the occurrence of sexual assault or women's experiences after they have been assaulted. Without these examinations, counselors and researchers end up with recommendations that have to do with teaching women self-defense and providing post-trauma counseling instead of recommendations that are actively decolonizing, such as working with men to prevent the act of sexual assault and putting into place structures and policies that protect women and other service members. For instance, discussions can also include the recent legislations proposed in the US Senate that would take reporting of felonies (including sexual assault) out of the chain of command, increasing the likelihood of survivors to report assault and decrease fears of retribution or lack of promotion that survivors report accompany reporting of such crimes (Steinhauer 2013). Students can be asked to discuss:

1. How are current policies impacting the community's well-being?
2. What are the merits of the proposed policy in terms of the impact on well-being?
3. Who is expected to change or take action based on these policies (i.e., who is considered responsible for the problem of sexual assault)?
4. What values or beliefs do these policies reflect (i.e., view of women, individual versus collective responsibility)?
5. What can counselors and psychologists do to address the current policies?

This exercise is designed to facilitate students thinking about the connections in their specific article between counseling and policy, and also considering what policies they need to learn more about as they move forward in their education and careers.

Because experiences of systemic oppression and marginalization have a detrimental effect on mental health and well-being, exercises that require an in-depth exploration of political issues as they relate to the role of counselors must be infused throughout counseling and psychology curricula. For instance, events such as the killing of Trayvon Martin might be used to teach about crisis response and post-trauma community-wide interventions. However, these also need to be accompanied by readings on Florida's Stand Your Ground law or handgun legislation, and how these impacted not only this particular case but also the sense of safety or fear that is present in the communities of color. Further, materials that inform students about the political process are also an important aspect of counselor training. Speakers from political action groups or the policy and lobbying staff within professional organizations, such as ACA or APA, can be called upon to inform students about political action and the legislative process. Another example used in our program is an exercise focused on understanding the community-wide impact of anti-immigrant legislation in a nearby county. In an introductory community counseling course, the instructor shows part of the documentary *9500 Liberty* (Park and Byler 2011), which depicts the process of a debate on a new county law that would legalize racial profiling and the impact of this on the immigrant community. The video and supplemental reading provide an understanding of the local legislative process, which in itself is important for counselors to understand. The discussion focuses as well on conceptualizing counseling broadly: individual counseling services, community counseling, and advocacy. Counselors are asked to consider not only what traditional counseling services they would provide to this community but also what else they would consider that might be beyond the traditional counselor role.

Conclusion

While the commitment to multiculturalism and social justice has increased, there remain many aspects of counseling and psychology education that fall short of truly enacting training that decolonizes the traditional tenets of our field. Without interrogating these practices, a well-meaning faculty inadvertently perpetuates the status quo and endemic colonial ideas that subjugate marginalized groups. The faculty must model this interrogation and exploration within the classroom so that students can engage in this process and learn how they can continue to do so as they enter the profession. In developing the counseling and development program at George Mason University, the faculty created an atmosphere in which the entire program (faculty and students) endorse a commitment to social justice and multiculturalism. With this unified vision, we have been able to enact a number of unique programs, and, perhaps most importantly, we have infused multiculturalism and social justice throughout all aspects of the program. Social justice is not something that is separate or optional. In our view, understanding of and action for social justice is *required* to be an ethical and effective counselor.

References

Adams, M., Bell, L. A., & Griffin, P. (2007). *Teaching for diversity and social justice*. New York: Routledge.

Alvarez, A. N., & Miville, M. L. (2003). Walking a tightrope. In D. B. Pope-Davis, H. L. K. Coleman, W. M. Liu, & R. L. Toporek (Eds.), *Handbook of multicultural competencies in counseling and psychology* (pp. 528–545). Thousand Oaks: Sage.

Baggerly, J. (2006). Service learning with children affected by poverty: Facilitating multicultural competence in counseling education students. *Journal of Multicultural Counseling & Development, 34,* 244–255.

Barbee, P. W., Scherer, D., & Combs, D. C. (2003). Prepracticum service-learning: Examining the relationship with counselor self-efficacy and anxiety. *Counselor Education and Supervision, 43,* 108–119.

Barratt, W. (2005). Social class: The inequitable campus. http://wbarratt.indstate.edu/socialclass/acpa2005/default.htm/Handout_ACPA_2005.pdf. Accessed 11 Nov 2009.

Baumgartner, L. M., & Johnson-Bailey, J. (2010). Racism and white privilege in adult education graduate programs: Admissions, retention, and curricula. *New Directions for Adult and Continuing Education, 125,* 27–40. doi:10.1002/ace.360.

Bemak, F. (2008). Cross-cultural counseling: Bias. In F. T. L. Leong (Ed.), *Encyclopedia of counseling, volume four*. Thousand Oaks: Sage.

Bemak, F., Chung, R. C.-Y., Talleyrand, R. M., Jones, H., & Daquin, J. (2011). Implementing multicultural social justice strategies in counselor education training programs. *Journal for Social Action in Counseling and Psychology, 3,* 1–43.

Berk, R. A. (2009). Multimedia teaching with video clips: TV, movies, YouTube, and mtvU in the college classroom. *International Journal of Technology in Teaching and Learning, 5,* 1–21.

Blustein, D. L. (2006). *The psychology of working: A new perspective for career development, counseling, and public policy*. Mahwah: Erlbaum.

Boler, M. (1999). *Feeling power: Emotions and education*. New York: Routledge.

Carter, R. T. (2007). Racism and psychological and emotional injury: Recognizing and assessing race-based traumatic stress. *The Counseling Psychologist, 35,* 13–105.

Chang, C. Y., Crethar, H. C., & Ratts, M. J. (2010). Social justice: A national imperative for counselor education and supervision. *Counselor Education & Supervision, 50,* 82–87.

Chung, R. C.-Y., & Bemak, F. (2012). *Social justice counseling: The next steps beyond multiculturalism*. Thousand Oaks: Sage.

Chung, R. C.-Y., & Bemak, F. (2013). Use of ethnographic fiction in social justice graduate counselor training. *Counselor Education & Supervision, 52,* 56–69.

Collins, P. H. (1993). Toward a new vision: Race, class, and gender as categories of analysis and connection. *Race, Sex & Class, 1,* 25–45.

Flores, L. Y., & Heppner, M. J. (2002). Multicultural career counseling: Ten essentials for training. *Journal of Career Development, 28,* 181–202. doi:10.1177/089484530202800304.

Foss, L. L., Generali, M. M., & Kress, V. E. (2011). Counseling people living in poverty: The care Model. *The Journal of Humanistic counseling, 50*(2), 161–171.

Freire, P. (1972). *Pedagogy of the oppressed*. Penguin Books, London, UK.

Haberman, M., & Post, L. (1992). Does direct experience change education students' perceptions of low-income minority children? *Mid-Western Educational Researcher, 5*(2), 29–31.

Halpern, J., & Tramontin, M. (2007). *Disaster mental health: Theory and practice*. Belmont: Thompson Brooks/Cole.

Hyland, N. E., & Noffke, S. E. (2005). Understanding diversity through social and community inquiry. *Journal of Teacher Education, 56,* 367–381.

Jett, S. T., & Delgado-Romero, E. A. (2009). Prepracticum service learning in counselor education: A qualitative case study. *Counselor Education & Supervision, 49,* 106–121.

Kenny, M. E., & Gallagher, L. A. (2000). Service-learning as a vehicle in training psychologists for revised professional roles. In F. T. Sherman & W. R. Torbert (Eds.), *Transforming social inquiry, transforming social action: New paradigms for crossing the theory/practice divide in universities and communities* (pp. 189–205). Boston: Kluwer Academic.

King, J. H. (2011). Three paradoxes of the counseling social justice movement. *Counseling Today, 54*(3), 46–47.

Kleinman, A., Das, V., & Lock, M. (Eds.). (1997). *Social suffering*. Berkeley: University of California Press.

Kumashiro, K. K. (2000). Teaching and learning through desire, crisis, and difference: Perverted reflections on anti-oppressive education. *The Radical Teacher, 58,* 6–11.

Malott, K. M., & Knoper, T. (2012). Social justice in application: Counselor training in a legal context. *Journal for Social Action in Counseling and Psychology, 4*(2), 23–39.

Menjivar, C., & Abrego, L. T. (2012). Legal violence: Immigration law and the lives of Central American immigrants. *American Journal of Sociology, 117,* 1380–1421.

Nieto, J. (2006). The cultural plunge: Cultural immersion as a means of promoting self-awareness and cultural sensitivity among student teachers. *Teacher Education Quarterly, 33,* 75–85.

Paradies, Y. (2006). A systematic review of empirical research on self-reported racism and health. *International Journal of Epidemiology, 35,* 888–901.

Park, A., & Byler, E. (2011). *9500 Liberty* [Motion picture]. USA: Interactive Democracy Alliance.

Steinhauer, J. (2013). Sexual assaults in military raise alarm in Washington. *The New York Times*. http://www.nytimes.com. Accessed 7 May 2013.

Talleyrand, R. M., Chung, R. C.-Y., & Bemak, F. (2006). Incorporating social justice in counselor training programs: A case study example. In R. L. Toporek, L. Gerstein, N. Fouad, G. Roysircar-Sodowsky, & T. Israel (Eds.), *Handbook for social justice in counseling psychology: Leadership, vision, and action* (pp. 44–58). Thousand Oaks: Sage.

Toporek, R. L., & McNally, C. J. (2006). Social justice training in counseling psychology: Needs and innovations. In R. L. Toporek, L. H. Gerstein, N. A. Fouad, G. Roysircar-Sodowsky, & T. Israel (Eds.), *Handbook for social justice in counseling psychology: Leadership, vision, and action* (pp. 37–44). Thousand Oaks: Sage.

Vera, E. M., & Speight, S. L. (2003). Multicultural competence, social justice, and counseling psychology: Expanding our roles. *The Counseling Psychologist, 31,* 253–272. doi:10.1177/0011000003031003001.

Wiest, L. R. (1998). Using immersion experiences to shake up preservice teachers' views about cultural differences. *Journal of Teacher Education, 49,* 358–365.

Williams, D. R., Neighbors, H. W., & Jackson, J. S. (2003). Racial/ethnic discrimination and health: Findings from community studies. *American Journal of Public Health, 93,* 200–208.

Afterword

Diversity and Homogenization

Rethinking Multicultural Counseling and Psychology in a Global Age: Twelve Assertions and Considerations

By Anthony J. Marsella

There can be no doubt that our global age requires a new proportional response from multicultural counseling and psychology. To a large extent, the issue of "multiculturalism" as an ideological foundation for the new interdependencies of our changing world must be understood and embraced, for it constitutes the very foundation for life itself. Understanding and supporting differences—especially "cultural" differences—have become a necessary value for individuals, societies, and nations. The variations, expressed as diversity, represent the very essence of expressions of life.

Cultural diversity, as a source of alternative ways of constructing reality, is as important as biological diversity in promoting and sustaining choices, options, and alternatives. The most critical problem facing our world today is the effort to homogenize individuals, societies, and nations, especially with regard to Western values and behavior patterns (e.g., consumerism, materialism, commodification, conformity, celebrity identification, fast-food dietary preferences, competition, force/violence).

The intentional and unrelenting insistence on exporting this popular culture across the world—at a time when the world is faced with the onset and continuation of major crises related to this cultural context for living—is being contested and rejected. The homogenization demanded from this effort seeks absolute acceptance and agreement, and is supported in this end by the mass surveillance, monitoring, archiving, and enforcement of this destructive way of life. The end result of this systematic and illegal effort to invade and dispel any privacy is moving our society and world toward a dystopian existence. This means centralized totalitarian control by those with wealth, power, and position. This is no longer disputable, even as it proceeds uninterrupted to exact its tolls upon us.

R. D. Goodman, P. C. Gorski (eds.), *Decolonizing "Multicultural" Counseling through Social Justice,* International and Cultural Psychology, DOI 10.1007/978-1-4939-1283-4

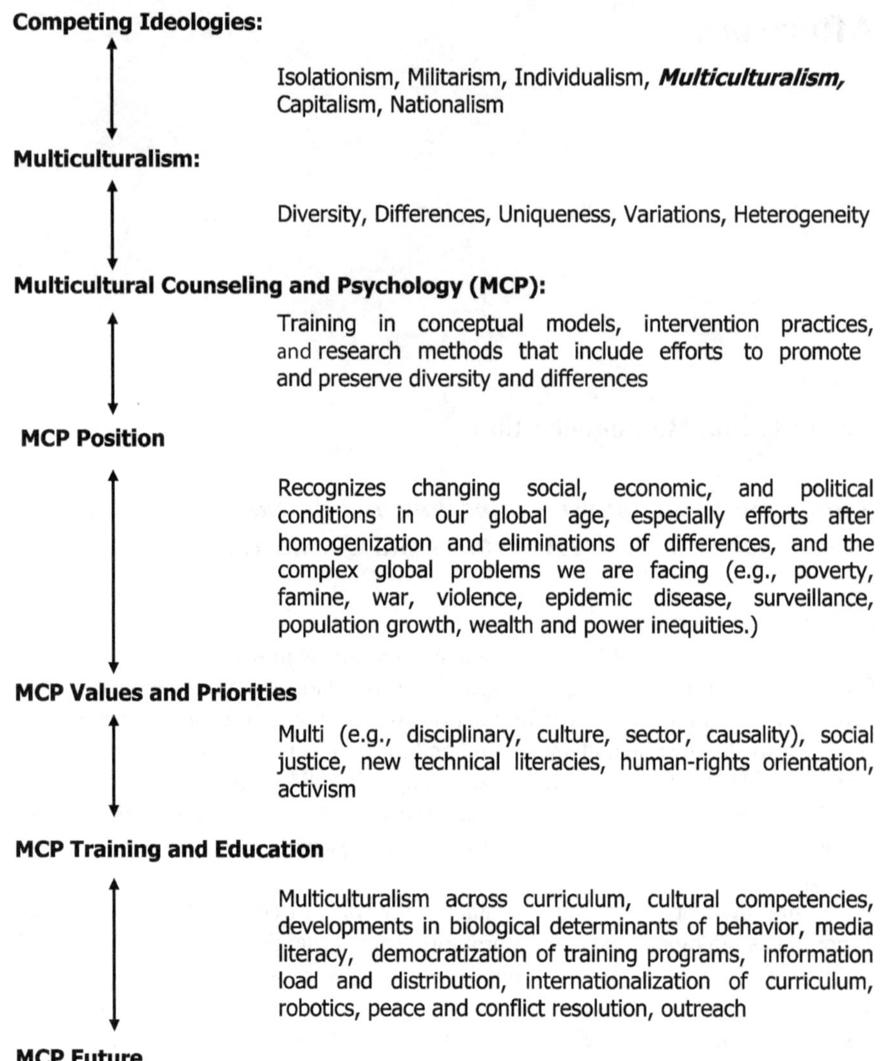

Fig. 1 Ecology of multiculturalism and its consequences

Figure 1 is a graphic representation of my concerns and my views on multiculturalism as an ideological foundation that best supports the nature of life itself. Figure 1 displays the ecology of pathways from ideology to practice for multicultural counseling and psychology.

Thus, my suggestions for rethinking multicultural counseling and psychology reside, above all, in the recognition and appreciation that "multiculturalism," as an ideology, represents an essential foundation for rethinking our global directions. I list some proposed changes below:

1. *Ideology*: Adopt "multiculturalism" as an ideological foundation for counseling and psychology. The struggle in our world today is to accommodate and assist diversity in life rather than promoting homogenization.
2. *Across the curriculum*: By itself, multiculturalism will be unable to stand, even if it is pursued in counseling and psychology. Encourage multiculturalism as a foundation across the university curriculum and across related training and education programs.
3. *Recruit students*: Identify and recruit students who grasp the essential value and importance of multiculturalism and continually monitor student progress and development in these areas, insisting on active learning and community-based experiences and training.
4. *Social justice*: The issue of social justice, with all of its implications revealed in widespread poverty, famine, disease, income disparities, crime, and other inequities, must be recognized as an essential arbiter of intervention and prevention efforts. Excessive reliance on reductionistic approaches to mental health related to locating life problems in brain and CNS conditions (e.g., neurochemical, neurotechnologies) must be seen, in part, as medical solutions to social problems. This does not deny their potential use, but acknowledges their potential abuse. Most scholars now accept the fact that the greatest contribution to addressing mental health problems does not reside in more health care workers and services, nor in greater use of medications, nor even in the typical replies of early identification of problems, but is addressing the massive social, economic, political, and moral problems we face (e.g., poverty, unemployment, malnutrition, substance abuse, crime, homelessness, violence/war, wealth inequities). These are the major sources of despair, hopelessness, anxiety, anger, and all patterns of disorder, disease, and deviance.
5. *Socioeconomic-political view of counseling and psychology*: In accordance with the thinking of pioneer figures such Paulo Friere, Ignacio Martín-Baró, and Isaac Prilleltensky, multicultural counseling and psychology must be conscious of the socio-political nature of the challenges we face because these challenges are ultimately issues of the distribution and abuse of power. This issue must be present, and must be explored in assessment, change, consultation, and in all healing efforts. This supports a social justice emphasis with all of its implications for restorative justice.
6. *New conceptual models*: The "best" conceptual models for driving training and practice in multicultural counseling and psychology are, in my opinion, those that acknowledge complexity, interactive, and multivariate relationships. These include general systems theory, ecology theory, and holistic theories. These systems recognize the connections across different levels of analysis. Within this framework, macro-social levels of analysis (i.e., wealth distribution) have implications for biological levels (i.e., neurosynaptic transmitters) via connected levels of knowledge.

7. *Multi-everything*: Given the existence of massive global problems, solutions must be considered within multidisciplinary, multisectoral, multicausal, and multicultural frameworks. This requires a reconsideration of current coursework, conceptual models, and intervention and preventions efforts. For example, in a multicausal model, formative causes lead to precipative causes, and these lead to exacerbative causes and maintenance causes. In this model, what may appear as a formative problem in fact resides in past efforts after solutions.
   In some ways, the best term to describe multicultural counselors and psychologists I vision is "multitalented healers;" this includes becoming counselors to the world. Obviously, multicultural counselors and psychologists cannot do everything, but they must be capable of knowing, understanding, and acting when and where they can, and be willing to refer to others when they cannot. Stasis is unacceptable. I was told there is an old Chinese curse: "May your children be born in interesting times." We are, unfortunately, living in interesting times.
8. *New skills and talents*: Reliance on traditional (conventional) training programs in counseling and psychology without recognizing the massive social and technical changes occurring can result in extinction. While the impulse to help and to make a difference should remain, it should be augmented by new skills and talents. Examples include: conflict resolution, community network building, increased ethnocultural and racial competencies, disaster management skills, and collaborative opportunities with other sectors (i.e., police, churches, charity groups, ethnic associations, and consultation models and skills).
9. *Merging roles, functions, and identities*: To a large extent, the multicultural counselor and psychologist must be able to merge personal (existential, social), citizen (activism, participation), and professional roles rather than thinking of these as separate roles with separate responsibilities, obligations, and duties.
10. *Universal Declaration of Human Rights*: Although professional ethics and guidelines for behavior exist across many fields, I believe it might be useful to provide all entering students with a copy of the Universal Declaration of Human Rights (UDHR) as a guide for belief and action. There can be no escape or denial of the global context of our lives and the many challenges this presents. Because of this, multicultural counselors and psychologists recognize that they must keep aware of social, economic, political, and moral events and forces shaping individual and collective behavior. Because of their crucial role and function, the task and role of "wisdom keepers" needs to be considered part of their identity. Professional ethics codes are too often subject to abuse and interpretation. The UDHR is an explicit statement, written in a clear language, that is hard to ignore or contend with as human beings.
11. *Continuing education*: "Too much to do, too little time, no adequate preparation!" This is often the reply of counselors and psychologists. Continuing education offers an opportunity to earn certificate-level knowledge and skills and can assist in addressing "burnout" and stasis in work locations and responsibilities. More opportunities must be developed.

12. *The calling*: Amidst their demanding daily rounds and heavy schedules, multicultural counselors and psychologists must keep reminding themselves of their calling. Their work is not that of a technician, although technical skills are required; their work is not that of a professional with finely honed talents and refined training, although these are required; and their work is not that of solving all problems brought before them, although they cannot desist from doing their part. Their life is that of a fully functioning person. They are motivated by acknowledging the importance of promoting and preserving diversity as an ideological foundation for life. Homogenization is the goal of those imposing control; diversity is the goal of those seeking growth, development, opportunity, and choice—personal and collective liberty.

None of what I have said is new to most multicultural counselors and psychologists, nor is what I have said original to me. Scores of others have come before me to speak of these issues and concerns. The issues and concerns are well known. The solutions are widely recognized to be complex and to be limited by funding, under-staffing, unexpected work expectations and professional conflicts and disagreements—many which reside within and across different ethnocultural and racial groups.

There are so many things that need to be said—words of inspiration, words of comfort, and words of consolation. Life is becoming more difficult each day for all of us. All I can do at this point is to join others who offer multicultural counselors and psychologists the challenge and the opportunity to live a life connected to our world, and, in the process, to help advance life by their presence and actions. That is the big inspiration, comfort, and consolation!

Index

R. D. Goodman, P. C. Gorski (eds.), *Decolonizing "Multicultural" Counseling through Social Justice,* International and Cultural Psychology, DOI 10.1007/978-1-4939-1283-4

W

Z

CPSIA information can be obtained
at www.ICGtesting.com
Printed in the USA
LVHW080330300822
727169LV00010B/194